THE HISTORY
OF THE
SUFFOLK REGIMENT
1946–1959

THE HISTORY
OF THE SUFFOLK
REGIMENT
1946–1959

by

Major F. A. GODFREY, MC, BA

LEO COOPER
LONDON

First published 1988 by Leo Cooper Ltd

Leo Cooper is an independent imprint of the
Heinemann Group of Publishers,
10 Upper Grosvenor Street, London WIX 9PA

LONDON   MELBOURNE   JOHANNESBURG   AUCKLAND

ISBN: 0–85052–2536

Photoset by Deltatype Ltd, Ellesmere Port
Printed in Great Britain by
Redwood Burn Ltd, Trowbridge
and bound by WBC Ltd, Maesteg

CONTENTS

FOREWORD   ix
PREFACE   xi
INTRODUCTION   1

CHAPTER I: The 1st Battalion – Egypt and
                  Palestine 1945–1948   3
CHAPTER II: The 2nd Battalion – India and
                  Home 1946–1947   24
CHAPTER III: The 1st Battalion – Grecian
                  Interlude 1948–1949   34
CHAPTER IV: The 1st Battalion – Malaya
                  1949–1953   42
CHAPTER V: The 1st Battalion – Home and
                  Trieste 1953–1954   96
CHAPTER VI: The 1st Battalion – BAOR
                  1954–1956   115
CHAPTER VII: The 1st Battalion – Home and
                  Cyprus 1956–1959   137
CHAPTER VIII: The Depot 1946–1959   170
CHAPTER IX: The Territorial Army in Suffolk
                  and Cambridgeshire 1947–1961   198
CHAPTER X: Amalgamation 1959   228
APPENDIX I: Roll of Honour 1946–1959   235
APPENDIX II: Honours and Awards 1946–1959   236
APPENDIX III: The appointment of Colonel-in-
                  Chief   240
APPENDIX IV: Colonels of the Regiment, Honorary
                  Colonels of Battalions,
                  Commanding Officers, Adjutants,
                  Quartermasters and Regimental
                  Sergeant Majors 1946–1961   244

APPENDIX V: The Two Hundredth Anniversary
                  of the Battle of Minden 1959   249
APPENDIX VI: The Suffolk Regiment War
                  Memorial Homes   252
APPENDIX VII: Battle Honours of the Suffolk
                  Regiment   255
APPENDIX VIII: Battle Honours of the
                  Cambridgeshire Regiment   256
APPENDIX IX: The presentation of Colours to the
                  1st Battalion by Her Royal Highness
                  the Princess Margaret, CI, GCVO,
                  Colonel-in-Chief of the Suffolk
                  Regiment on the 23rd May 1955   257
APPENDIX X: Major Trophies won between 1946
                  and 1959   263
APPENDIX XI: Affiliated Regiments   265
INDEX   268

MAPS

Drawn by John Mitchell

1. Egypt and Palestine 1946   6
2. The Federation of Malaya and Singapore 1949   50
   and the State of Selangor
3. Trieste and Austria   98
4. BAOR 1954   116
5. Cyprus 1956   139

FOREWORD

by Brigadier W. C. Deller OBE
Chairman of The Council of The Suffolk Regiment

I commend to you this, the fourth volume of the history of The Suffolk Regiment.

The initiative for producing this history came from my predecessor, the late Lieutenant-General Sir Richard Goodwin. He, in common with many of us, felt most strongly that the last thirteen years in the story of the Regiment from the end of the Second World War to amalgamation with The Royal Norfolk Regiment on 29 August, 1959, had to be recorded so that future generations could know how those who served during those years carried out their duty and maintained the traditions and ideals of an English county regiment built up since 1685.

These thirteen years were difficult ones for the army as a whole and for the Infantry in particular. Post-war conditions, both at home and abroad, led to reductions in the size of the army and its budget. At the same time political turmoil and a withdrawal from Empire, frequently leading to a breakdown in law and order and sometimes open insurrection, placed a continual burden on a decreasing number of infantry battalions. It was in operations resulting from these conditions that the 1st Battalion, the Suffolk Regiment spent all but three of these thirteen years. The story is, therefore, worth telling.

The history has been written by Major Bob Godfrey who served in the Regiment during much of the period. On behalf of everyone who served at any time during the years under review I thank him for all the hard work he has put into it. He has spent months reading and researching the story and in the process has interviewed and talked with a wide spread of those who served in both the Regular and Territorial Battalions of the Regiment at some time during the period covered by the history. It has taken nearly four years from concept to printing but I am confident you will agree that it has been well worthwhile.

Finally, I would like to place on record the great pride and delight with which we who served in The Suffolk Regiment watch the way in which the standards and traditions of the old Regiment are being maintained by The Royal Anglian Regiment who proudly trace their ancestry back to 1685. May the motto, given to The Old Twelfth by its Colonel in 1745, Scipio Duroure, forever remain the guiding light of the present Regiment.

STABILIS.

The Keep,	W. C. Deller
Gibraltar Barracks,	Brigadier
Bury St Edmunds.	

PREFACE

It has been an honour and a privilege to write this the fourth and final volume of The History of The Suffolk Regiment.

During the time that I have been involved in the research for the book, I have been reminded forcefully again and again of the real nature of the Regiment. It has never been one which gained praise for fanciful deeds of extravagant valour, but, time and time again, it has been extolled for its steadiness and quiet, grim determination in the face of daunting odds and in extremely hostile conditions.

I believe that, in this brief chapter of its history, the Regiment has shown itself to be true to these traditions in a variety of situations which have taxed it to the utmost degree.

One tour of duty of the 1st Battalion particularly demonstrated the quality of the Regiment. I refer, of course, to the years 1949–1953 when it served in Malaya during the Emergency. A high standard of leadership, insistence on tough realistic training and constant alertness contributed to the outstanding name the Battalion earned in Malaya. But it was, above all, the dogged perseverance on the part of the men of the Battalion in the face of the most difficult physical conditions and confronted by an elusive enemy, extremely dangerous when tracked down and brought to battle, that won a reputation for the Regiment unequalled by any other British battalion throughout the twelve years of the Emergency.

The Regiment also saw active service in Palestine and Cyprus in the post-Second World War years, and confronted ugly internal-security situations in both India and Trieste. Wherever it went, it won praise for its devotion to duty and steadiness, and as a result frequently found itself coping with crises as senior commanders recognized the worth of a Suffolk Battalion.

No history of the Regiment would be complete without mentioning its Territorial Army component, nor indeed if reference were not made to the Cambridgeshire Regiment, always part of the Corps of the Suffolk Regiment.

The story of the 4th Battalion and the Cambridgeshires in the post-Second World War years demonstrates, if nothing else, the amazing perseverance of the volunteer spirit in the face of constant change, brought about by an admixture of economic crises combined with what might almost be termed political whimsy. That a small hard-core of 'Terriers', officers and men in both Counties, stayed the difficult course, gives much hope for the future.

In compiling this history I have attempted to kill two birds with one stone. Authors of such works frequently find themselves criticized, either because they have filled the pages of their history with too much repetitive detail, or because they have painted only a general picture of the passage of time.

To satisfy the military historian who demands accurate detail on the one hand, and the general reader who seeks an interesting story creating the atmosphere of a particular tour of duty on the other, I have divided each chapter into two distinct parts.

Part one attempts to explain why the particular unit of the Regiment was where it was and what it was like to be there, highlighting only certain significant events. Part two provides as nearly accurate an account as is possible with the source material available of the detailed experiences of the unit in chronological order.

Following this format has led to some repetition; I hope the different sorts of reader who delve into the history will understand the reason why.

My work has been greatly helped by many members of the Regiment and it is a great sadness that Lieutenant-General Sir Richard Goodwin, KCB, CBE, DSO, DL, who gave me total support and got the whole project under way in the first place, has not lived to see it published.

The Regimental History Sub-Committee under the Chairmanship of Colonel W. A. Heal, OBE, has been most helpful and ever ready with advice and assistance in the planning stages; for this my particular thanks.

My thanks too are due to many others of the Regiment, who have helped either by allowing me to interview them, by lending me documents and photographs or by taking the trouble to complete the elaborate questionnaire which I sent to them.

Lastly, I am indebted to Charmian, my wife, for actively assisting me in a variety of ways as the project has advanced, and for accepting my lengthy sojourns in the study over the last three years.

F. A. Godfrey

Strumpshaw
Norfolk

INTRODUCTION

The end of the Second World War saw Battalions of the Suffolk Regiment spread throughout the length and breadth of the world. The 1st Battalion was in Germany and the 2nd Battalion in Burma. The remnants of the 4th and 5th Battalions, together with their Territorial Army comrades of the 1st and 2nd Battalions of the Cambridgeshire Regiment were scattered in small groups in prisoner-of-war camps throughout the Far East. The 8th Battalion was in the Blakeney area of Norfolk and the 31st Battalion in Gibraltar.

With the cessation of hostilities, it was expected that the Army would be much reduced in size, leaving only the regular Battalions of the Regiment posted to peacetime garrisons, much as had been the case before 1939. But the world after 1945 was to prove to be very different in nature from what it had been before. New forces were at work which, added together, were to provide peacetime challenges of an unprecedented nature.

The developing cold war between the Soviet Union and the Western Democracies was radically to affect Great Britain and thus the British Army. The formation of the North Atlantic Treaty Organization in 1949 led to the creation of the British Army of the Rhine, turning the army of occupation overnight into a standing army on the continent – a totally new experience for the British soldier and one which effectively signposted the way to much closer unity with the continent of Europe.

At the same time a rising tide of nationalism and communism in the various constituent parts of the British Empire was to provide the backcloth to a succession of campaigns in different territories. The Army found itself constantly grappling with political and terrorist organizations which had little in common, save the one aim of bringing an end to British rule.

With the loss of India in 1947 and the withdrawal from Empire that this event heralded, there also began to make itself felt in the Army yet another force which was to have dramatic consequences. The end of Empire meant a reduced need for military garrisons and led, inevitably, to a reduction in the size of the Army.

All these developments were dramatically to affect the Suffolk Regiment. Between 1946 and 1959 it played its part in the defence of Western Europe and found itself engaged in a succession of campaigns, one after another, across the world's stage. Its 2nd Battalion was placed in suspended animation in 1948, and in 1959 it ceased to exist as a regular element of the British Army consequent upon amalgamation.

Colonel W. N. Nicholson, CMG, DSO, in his third volume of *The History of The Suffolk Regiment*, dealing with the years from 1928 to 1946, concluded by describing how the 1st Battalion moved from Germany to Egypt in 1945; how the 2nd Battalion withdrew from Burma back into India in the same year; how the Territorial Army Battalions of Suffolk and Cambridgeshire were repatriated to the United Kingdom in 1945 and 1946, and how the 8th and 31st Battalions returned to England to be disbanded.

Our story picks up the threads from this moment and carries it through to the point when the Regiment amalgamated with the Royal Norfolk Regiment in 1959, and thus brought to an end 274 years of loyal and steady service to The Crown.

CHAPTER I

THE FIRST BATTALION:

EGYPT AND PALESTINE 1945–1948

'Twixt the Devil and the Deep Blue Sea'

Part I

Scarcely had the dust of war settled in North-West Europe when the Battalion, together with the whole of the 3rd Infantry Division, was warned for a move from Germany to the Middle East. It was intended that the Division should bolster the forces at the disposal of the Commander-in-Chief, Middle East Land Forces, and it was to form a strategic reserve available for rapid deployment anywhere in the region.

These plans were, however, soon to be modified. The situation in Palestine was rapidly deteriorating and it became necessary to deploy more and more troops there in an attempt to stabilize matters. As a consequence of this, the Battalion was to spend the next two and a half years partly in Egypt, where it retained its original 'Fire-Brigade' role, and partly in Palestine where it struggled to maintain order in ever-worsening conditions.

A rising tide of nationalist feeling in Egypt at this time led to pressures for the Army to leave the main Egyptian towns, where it had been based during the war, to concentrate in the Canal Zone. When in Egypt, the Battalion never experienced the open hostility faced by units in Cairo and Alexandria, but rather, a sense of resentment among the few Egyptians with whom they came in contact. However, there were constant minor incidents and, worst of all, persistent attempts to steal anything that could be moved. Security of weapons, and indeed vehicles, proved a nightmare and such items as tent walls disappeared with staggering regularity.

In Palestine the situation was different. The Battalion was to spend two periods there, from December, 1945, to March, 1946, and from January, 1947, until the British Mandate ended in May, 1948. During the first brief tour conditions were reasonably stable, but by January, 1947, when the second deployment to Palestine began, it was found best to assume that every Arab and Jew was an enemy till he proved otherwise.

Throughout the 1939–1945 War the situation in Palestine had remained relatively calm. This was not to say that the fierce intercommunal strife between the Jews and Arabs which had escalated during the 20's and 30's had come to an end, but rather that both sides accepted the period of the War as an opportunity to build up their resources while waiting to see which side would win. Among the Jews there was an earnest hope, naturally enough, that the Allied Powers would defeat Nazi Germany and, for that reason alone, they desisted from major military action against the British Administration.

For the Arabs, however, it was altogether different. Many of them hoped for a Germany victory, seeing that as a possible body blow to the Jewish cause, and likely, at worst, to curtail further Jewish immigration into Palestine, and, at best, to eliminate the Jews from the country altogether.

The Allied Victory in Europe in 1945 came as a signal to both communities to prepare themselves for a renewed struggle. The Jews were hopeful that the Nazi atrocities, now revealed in their full horror, would swing World opinion in their favour and bring them support for the creation of a State of Israel. They also hoped, for the same reason, that the immigration of Jews escaping from their terrible experiences in Europe would no longer be impeded.

The Arabs understood the signal equally well and prepared themselves for a fight to the finish, hoping always for support in their struggle from neighbouring Arab States already striving to loosen their ties from the European powers.

Up to September, 1947, when the Government announced the decision to end the Mandate in Palestine, the Jews in particular were determined, using any means at their disposal, to pressure the British to leave. They were ruthless in their methods and used acts of terrorism, sabotage and even conventional warfare to achieve their aims. They were very highly organized. Their largest force was the Hagana which was sponsored by the World Zionist Federation and was formed on conventional military lines. It was, after the Mandate ended, to become the nucleus of the Israeli Defence Forces. Terrorist attacks directed against the British and the Palestinian Arabs were perpetrated by less conventional groupings, among whom Irgun Zvei Leumi and the Stern Gang were the most active.

Well versed in the use of weapons and explosives, the Jewish groups attacked the British ferociously when they caught them off their guard. Soldiers were gunned down in the streets, abducted, or blown up in their vehicles by landmines. Headquarters were bombed and camps attacked and weapons and vehicles were stolen.

The Arabs were never as effectively organized as the Jews during this period. Up to the announcement of the British withdrawal, they were seldom active against the British except in some isolated cases, being fearful of pushing the Mandate power towards a departure which would leave them at the mercy of their more efficient enemy. After the announcement, they directed their fiercest military and terrorist attacks against the Jews, only acting against the British in the pursuit of weapons to build up their military capability.

The sophisticated Jewish armoury was largely made up of weapons smuggled into the country and supplemented by others obtained from British and Arab sources. The Arabs were much less well armed and equipped, receiving little help from outside Palestine and being largely reliant on weapons stolen from the British or captured from the Jewish enemy.

The two tours of duty in Palestine put the Battalion on to a war footing and it was thrust into an ever deteriorating internal security situation. In general terms, the army in Palestine was required quite simply to maintain law and order, while protecting the Government and itself from enemy attack. During the first short Palestine tour the Battalion found it possible to achieve these aims and at the same time, on occasion, to relax – to play games and swim and evn go on visits to Jerusalem and other Holy Places. The final period of seventeen months was a different matter. There was little or no opportunity to lower its guard and, towards the end, when the pressures were increasing, there was no movement outside camp except on duty.

On a day-to-day basis the Battalion was given an extraordinary variety of tasks in Palestine, but the one continuous grinding necessity was the provision of guards. So heavy was the call for this duty that, on occasion, the Commanding Officer was hard-pressed to sustain the commitment, and the 'nights-in-bed' state of the Battalion caused grave anxiety. But morale was sustained even though, in the last notes for the *Regimental Gazette* sent home from Palestine, D Company's scribe lamented thus: 'We can supply well-

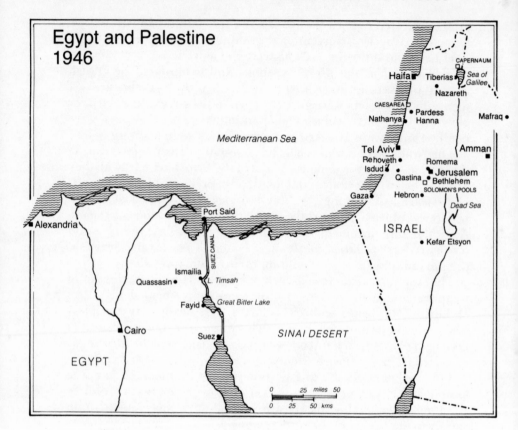

Egypt and Palestine
1946

trained Guards for any purpose. We can guard railways, dumps, prisoners, High Commissioners, camps and bakeries. We can stand guard and look for hours at a strip of country. We can guard cinemas and cook houses, vehicles and arms dumps. In fact, there is nothing we cannot guard. We have been travelling the Middle East doing our duty by guarding GHQ and the new Married Families Quarters in Fayid, to Cairo where we guarded the British Flag, to Qastina where we guarded over twenty thousand weapons, to Jerusalem where we guarded H.E. the High Commissioner for a month, then to Pardess Hanna where we have guarded railways and boats, bridges and cinemas.'

In common with the Army as a whole, the Battalion was also facing a period of what might be called post-war turbulence. Officers and men came and went on postings with bewildering regularity. By 1947 there was scarcely an officer or man left who had been with the

Battalion in Germany at the end of the War. Such instability created desperate problems, but somehow these were overcome and the Battalion continued to function effectively and with spirit.

Its many duties, in addition to guards, included the cordoning and searching of villages and towns, operations which required careful planning and infinite patience and almost invariably resulted in only limited success. Patrols, too, were frequent, both on foot and by vehicle, checking roads and the railway for any attempt at sabotage. Platoons or companies on stand-by were frequently rushed to the coast in search of ships and boats arriving on the beaches with illegal immigrants. Those who witnessed the arrival of such boats will never forget the extraordinary squalor and privation which had been suffered by the immigrants on their voyage, nor the euphoria which seized them when they reached their 'Promised Land'.

Indeed the plight of the immigrants on the one hand and the brutal ferocity of the terrorist gangs on the other typified the starkly contrasting experiences of the men of the Battalion as they struggled to do their job with compassion or determination, as the occasion warranted.

While in Egypt, between tours in Palestine, the Battalion resumed its Middle Eastern Reserve role and it was always ready to implement contingency plans to deploy to trouble spots. It was never actually despatched, but the uncertainties engendered by the numerous orders to move to a state of readiness for imminent departure militated severely against attempts to implement a full and comprehensive training programme which was sorely needed. The requirement to provide heavy guards for its own lines and frequently for Brigade and Divisional Headquarters also had its effect on training, and at one time the whole Battalion was ordered to Fayid to protect what was to be the new GHQ Middle East Land Forces which was under construction there.

Living conditions for the Battalion during this Middle Eastern tour varied hugely, according to where it was. In Palestine camps were usually tented with a few Nissen huts for armouries, stores and messes. The tents were modified, having breeze block or stone walls and were known from the days on the Indian North-West Frontier as 'wana' huts. The ingenious would construct doors to the tents to keep out the sand and the cold desert winds. Conditions in such camps were never pleasant. In the winter rain churned paths and tracks into a sea of mud and dripped relentlessly through the tent roofs, and in summer dust and sand crept everywhere.

Nelson Lines in Moascar Garrison in Egypt, where the Battalion found itself for most of the time between the Palestinian tours, provided the only respite from such conditions. This fine barracks, built at the turn of the century, was the first permanent accommodation occupied.for any length of time by the Battalion since it had left the U.K. in 1944 for the D-Day landings in Normandy. Everyone enjoyed a brief taste of luxury.

As the end of the Mandate in Palestine drew nearer, the situation there became increasingly tense, as both the Jews and Arabs built up their military strength. In the international political arena attempts were made to find a solution acceptable to both Jews and Arabs to the problem of what should happen after the British left. British and American proposals were met with open hostility from both sides and the United Nations plan fared scarcely better. Members of the Battalion in Palestine at the time could certainly see no easy resolution of the dispute and sensed that it would smoulder on.

March and April, 1948, saw the Battalion back-loading its heavy stores in preparation for the final move out of Palestine. At the end it was the last unit to leave Jerusalem, having covered the withdrawal of the remainder of the 2nd Infantry Brigade. The journey to Egypt was made by road and not one vehicle broke down on the way.

The move marked a tidy end to a very untidy tour of duty, from which the Battalion extricated itself with honour and dignity. Not surprisingly, the news of a posting to Greece which was announced on arrival in Egypt was greeted by everyone with relief and delight.

Part II

In October, 1945, the 3rd Infantry Division was ordered to the Middle East from North-West Europe. The Advance Party, of the 1st Battalion, comprising eight officers and thirty-two men, under the command of Major C.A. Boycott, flew from Brussels to Cairo in a converted bomber aircraft. There was no heating and it was bitterly cold and Major Boycott's dachshund, illegally smuggled aboard the plane in a holdall, was passed from man to man during the journey and used as a hot water bottle!

The main body of the Battalion travelled in a somewhat less speedy manner. It departed from St Peter's Station in Ghent at 0600 on 2 October. The Battalion Band, which had fortuitously arrived in Wetteren from England the day before on a tour of Belgium and Germany, gave the train a rousing send-off, playing Speed the Plough and Auld Lang Syne. There followed a two-day train journey through France to the port of Toulon, a sea journey from there to Alexandria aboard a very crowded converted French pleasure cruiser, the *Ville d'Oran*, and thence in railway cattle trucks a journey of 150 miles to Tahag, some distance from the Suez Canal, where the Advance Party, with help from German prisoners-of-war, had erected a tented camp.

Approximately fifty percent of the officers and men of the Battalion, who were due for early release, remained in Germany when it moved to Egypt. As a consequence it was considerably under-strength when it arrived in the Middle East.

Senior appointments within the Battalion soon after arriving in Egypt were:

CO: Lieutenant-Colonel F.A. Milnes
2ic: Major C.A. Boycott
Adjt: Captain R.M. Williams, MC
QM: Lieutenant F.H. Wyatt
RSM: RSM Tridini

Company Commanders included Major H. Crabtree, Major T.M. Stokoe, Major A.C.L. Sperling, MC, Captain H.G. Taylor, Captain A.C. Woodward, MC, and Captain C.J. Howell. Among the Warrant Officers were CSM Keeble, CSM Morgan, MM, CSM Boast and CSM Edis.

The Battalion was accommodated in a camp at Tahag, somewhat remote from other units of the 3rd Division, which were generally deployed in garrisons along the Suez Canal itself. The tented camp was a mixed blessing. Although extremely spartan, its very isolation did allow for a brief uninterrupted period to assimilate drafts arriving to make up the depleted numbers which travelled from Germany. It also afforded a chance to draw up and issue the necessary weapons and equipment to bring the Battalion to a state of readiness for action.

While in Tahag a West African R.A.S.C. Company in the adjacent camp mutinied and the C.O. was told to sort it out. The Duty Company was A Company, commanded by Major Crabtree, and it was given the task of quelling the trouble. The Company was turned out in full Battle Order and with bayonets fixed, doubled out of camp, along the road and into the R.A.S.C. lines. It must have made a formidable sight, as the mutineers instantly capitulated.

The stay in Tahag was to be very brief, as, early in December, 1945, 3rd Division was ordered to move north into Palestine. The Battalion moved by road through the Sinai Desert and the journey was broken by a night stop at a staging post in the desert, sleeping in two-man bivouac tents.

For two weeks after arrival in Palestine the Battalion was accommodated in a temporary tented camp at Nathanya, between Tel Aviv and Haifa. It then moved to a camp some twenty miles to the North where it remained until the middle of February, 1946. This period was to prove a good introduction for what was to come later in 1947 and 1948.

The Battalion was engaged on a variety of duties including patrolling harbours and the coastline, in an attempt to prevent illegal Jewish immigration and cordoning and searching of villages, looking for terrorists, weapons and supply caches. Cordon and search operations rarely achieved their purpose. Barking dogs always gave warning of the approach of troops and no terrorist was ever caught, though diligent searching sometimes led to finding weapons or useful documents. It did, however, keep the enemy on the move.

Maintaining the security of installations was the dominant task. Guards were supplied for Brigade Headquarters and Haifa Police Station throughout this period in Palestine and, of course, it was necessary to provide a strong guard over the Battalion Camp itself, as there were frequent terrorist attempts to gain access to the armouries of police and military installations.

There were occasional lulls in activity and Christmas was celebrated in reasonable style. The Battalion Padre, the Reverend H.G. Woodall, organized a large number of trips to visit the Holy Places at Palestine. Almost half the Battalion got the chance in this way to visit Nazareth, Cana, the Sea of Galilee and Capernaum, among other places.

In February the Battalion was withdrawn to Egypt. The fifteen-hour journey was by train and the new location was Nelson Lines at Moascar, a garrison suburb of the town of Ismailia which lies on the Suez Canal at the northern end of Lake Timsah close by the Sweetwater Canal. At about this time the Battalion notes supplied for the *Regimental Gazette* highlight a major problem – the constant changes of personnel. It was only some eight months since hostilities had ceased in North-West Europe and most of the officers and men had been with the Battalion since D-Day and, group by group, were sent back to the United Kingdom for demobilization. Drafts of new recruits arrived and were assimilated with little difficulty, if with scant opportunity for specialized training. The loss of experienced Officers, Warrant Officers and Senior NCOs was another matter, however, and the CO was hard-pressed to maintain the command structure within the Battalion at this time. In early 1946 a two-month period saw the departure of no less than five Company Commanders leaving a gap which it must have been difficult to fill.

For those returning to the UK preparatory to demobilization, to attend courses, or being lucky enough to get a spell of leave, the journey was made by the Mediterranean Lines of Communication (MEDLOC) route. A passenger ship plied from Egypt to the French port of Marseilles. The sea trip was pleasant enough, but then the journey was by rail to the Channel ports. The coaches had no windows and were bitterly cold in the winter months. There were no catering facilities on board the train and meals were supplied at stations on the way. Trains were frequently ten or twelve hours late departing and if you were scheduled to leave after breakfast at 0800 you would be quite likely to be served your next stone-cold meal of stew at 0300 the following morning!

Nelson Lines, Moascar, where the Battalion now found itself, was a permanent barracks and conditions were far more comfortable than in the tented camps in Palestine or at Tahag. Strong guards were needed still, but with the Battalion not on a permanent operational basis, it was possible to initiate training to up-grade both company and specialist personnel. An ambitious programme of a wide variety of sports was also organized. As the Egyptian weather warmed up a summer timetable was instituted whereby training ceased at lunchtime, leaving afternoons and evenings free for sports and recreational activities.

Minden Day was celebrated on 1 August in great style, commencing with a swimming gala at the Africa Beach on Lake Timsah. Besides a water-polo competition there was a freestyle relay and finally a boat race. All these competitions were won by B Company. In the afternoon the highlight of the day took the form of donkey races, organized by the 2ic. They were described in the *Regimental Journal* as no make-shift affair, and included a tote, a paddock, a good course, a starting gate, brightly dressed jockeys and most important of all, 'the cream of the local donkey world'! A German prisoner-of-war band played during the intervals between the races.

The evening was taken up with a concert in the NAAFI gardens, followed by an all-ranks dance in the Moascar Garrison gymnasium at which the Brigade Commander, Brigadier J.G. Bedford-Roberts, was the chief guest. Minden roses for all ranks were made by the Nuns of the Cairo English Convent.

The period July to September, 1946, saw an increase in training activity at platoon and company level and the whole Battalion fired its annual classification on the rifle and the LMG. Several cadres were run, including 'MT, 3" Mortar, Intelligence, Signals and, for Junior NCOs, Drill and Duties. The Brigade Commander visited the latter on 26 August. The Battalion also took its turn in providing patrols to protect a nearby supply depot to safeguard against looting.

Consistent with its fire-brigade role, on 11 August the Battalion was placed at forty-eight hours' notice to move to Khartoum for internal security duties. It remained at this state of readiness for a week but was then stood down. On 30 August the Battalion was ordered to prepare two companies for an air move, again to Khartoum, on 1 September, with the remainder of the Battalion to follow, less a rear party. Aircraft were loaded with jeeps, trailers and equipment, but the notice was extended to three days on 1 September and finally cancelled on 8 September.

Demobilization, group by group, led to dwindling numbers in the Battalion, despite some reinforcement. As a result A Company was temporarily disbanded in August.

The Commanding Officer, Lieutenant-Colonel F.A. Milnes, went on leave from 9 July until 18 October, and the Battalion was commanded in his absence by Major C.A. Boycott.

Throughout the autumn of 1946 the Battalion persevered in its attempts to train specialists to replace those due for demobilization. Platoon and company training also went ahead.

The knowledge that it was likely to find itself back in Palestine at any moment, as the situation there continued to deteriorate, added a sense of urgency to this uphill struggle. But there were problems nearer at hand.

Relationships between the UK and the Egyptian Government were tense, the latter pressing for the British Army to withdraw into the Canal Zone, and thus to evacuate the main Egyptian towns. The Headquarters Middle East Land Forces was in the process of moving from Cairo to Fayid on the western shore of the Great Bitter Lake. Troubles in Cairo during this period dictated the need for greater security and units in the Canal Zone were required to supply men to assist with guards and patrols in the city. D Company was sent in this role to the capital city from 20 October to 10 November, though there were no incidents to relieve the monotony.

On 30 October General Sir Miles Dempsey, KCB, KBE, DSO, MC, ADC, C-in-C Middle East Land Forces, presented decorations to officers and men of the 3rd Infantry Division. Major A.C.L.

Sperling, MC, and CSM W Morgan, MM, received their awards, won in the closing stages of the War, from the C-in-C at this ceremony.

The Chief of the Imperial General Staff, Field-Marshal Viscount Montgomery, inspected the 8th Infantry Brigade with other troops at Kitchener Lines in Moascar on 26 November. His extended tour of Palestine and Egypt at this time presaged a period of considerable activity, particularly with regard to a redeployment of Forces in Palestine. But the next move for the Battalion was not to be so far afield.

The Battalion left Nelson Lines in Moascar on 6 December, 1946, moved into tented camps 19 and 21 at Fayid and came temporarily under command of Canal Zone South District. The reason for the move was to provide a permanent guard for the new GHQ Middle East Land Forces installations and married families' quarters being built and occupied during this period.

Such a large guard duty commitment effectively prevented the Battalion from engaging in any proper training, beyond using local thirty yards ranges for Sten gun practice. The boring and persistent régime of such duties was thoroughly disliked by all and the news of a pending move in 1947 was greeted with pleasure; anything would be better.

On 11 December, 1946, Lieutenant-Colonel F.A. Milnes relinquished command on departure to the UK to take over command of No 12 PTC at Bury St Edmunds. This, his second tenure of command (his first was during the withdrawal to Dunkirk), had been a difficult one, encompassing the moves from North-West Europe to the Middle East, followed by others within the theatre. It had been an uphill struggle keeping the Battalion together throughout the period of post-war turmoil. Yet he had succeeded, and he left behind a Battalion which was to prove itself very effective in the next few years. His experience and calm determined manner were invaluable to the Battalion.

Major A.C.L. Sperling, MC, assumed command temporarily on his departure.

On 23 December, Lieutenant-Colonel G.H.M. Harper arrived to take over command of the Battalion. He hardly had time to settle down before the next move. This, on 16 January, 1947, was back into Palestine. The months of December, 1946, and January, 1947, saw the whole of the 3rd Division back in the Holy Land to bolster the forces prepared to support the final phase of British involvement there.

The Battalion found itself briefly stationed in dreadful tented camps at Qastina near Gaza in Southern Palestine, almost totally commited to guard duties. At first two companies were needed to guard Divisional Headquarters and one to guard installations at El Jira. When it is realized that forty men were needed each night to guard the Battalion camp as well, the problems become evident. It is not surprising that the *Battalion Quarterly Historical Report* covering the stay at Qastina stated bluntly that opportunities for training were limited.

A foretaste of future activities was experienced when the Battalion took part in a large operational cordon and search of the small town of Rehoveth, which lies between Tel Aviv and Jerusalem, on 7 March. Then, on 12 March, companies were deployed along the coast to round up illegal immigrants who got ashore when the SS *Susannah* ran on to the beach at Isdud.

On 19 March the Battalion moved to Jerusalem and was briefly based in Alamein Camp. Though the location was fresh, the duties undertaken were much as before. B and C Companies were deployed to guard Zone A of the City and D Company was needed to provide the guard at Government House, the residence of the High Commissioner. The Government House Guard was one of the more attractive duties which had to be undertaken. The Guard was housed in Nissen huts which were a great improvement on tents. The officers of the Company not actually on duty found themselves dining from time to time with His Excellency The High Commissioner. The remainder of the Battalion was fully employed in providing operational patrols and, needless to say, more guards to protect Alamein Camp itself.

Such a commitment could scarcely be sustained for long and it was with some relief that on 14 April the Battalion left Jerusalem for a tented camp, Camp 87E, at Pardess Hanna to the north-west of Jerusalem, not far from Nathanya where the Battalion had briefly found itself in December, 1945.

In Pardess Hanna the guard requirement was slightly less and each day one company was released for training, which was a great relief as well as an urgent necessity. This latest change of location also signified a sad change in the order of battle. The Battalion joined the 2nd Infantry Brigade of the 1st Infantry Division on 15 April. It thus left the 8th Infantry Brigade of the 3rd Infantry Division within which it had served since the beginning of the Second World War in September, 1939.

At Pardess Hanna there were also occasional operational duties of a more interesting nature. On 14 May Major R.M. Williams, MC, was in command of a training patrol from the Junior NCO's Cadre. The patrol was moving along the main railway line from Haifa south towards Egypt when it bumped into an armed group of Jewish terrorists, intent on blowing up the line. In the skirmish that followed two of the terrorists were captured with their weapons and explosives and brought back to the Battalion guard tent.

A few days later B Company, with two sections of carriers, carried out a search of Shuna Settlement. Twelve persons were detained and an arms cache located. On 19 May a large draft of 220 joined the Battalion, thus allowing A Company to be reformed after a period of nine months in suspended animation. Most of these officers and men came from the 2nd Battalion, the Bedfordshire and Hertfordshire Regiment, consequent on that Battalion going into suspended animation.

Although the situation in Palestine was rapidly reaching a climax which would lead to the withdrawal in May, 1948, the spring and summer months of 1947 were to provide some opportunities for what might be termed the normal peacetime military activities. It was a period of relative calm before the final storm began.

On 22 and 23 May the Battalion team came second in the 2nd Infantry Brigade Motorcycle Trials and on 30 May the Battalion won the Brigade Rifle Meeting. Of interest also is the note in the *Regimental Gazette* recording the reforming of the Corps of Drums under Drum Major Peatfield. The Drum Major started work on 27 May with a group of twenty-seven men of whom scarcely any had any formal musical training. The aim was to be able to parade on Minden Day. In fact they did better by taking part with the Band in a massed beating of retreat on 27 June. On 12 June Lieutenant-Colonel G.M.H. Harper left for the U.K. on leave and in his absence Major R.M. Marsh assumed command of the Battalion.

The departure on leave and demobilization of many officers, senior ranks and men at this time once more seriously weakened the command structure in the Battalion and reduced its numbers drastically. The constant inevitable inter-posting of officers between companies did little to stabilize the situation. In one set of notes for the *Regimental Gazette* one officer was welcomed both on assuming command of Support Company and of the Carrier Platoon!

July, 1947 saw an upsurge in operations. While the main activities continued to be patrolling railway lines and providing guards, a number of major cordon and search operations were also undertaken. On 15 and 16 July the Battalion was under the command of the 1st Guards Brigade on Operation Tiger, which involved cordoning and searching Nathanya. The Battalion took part in the search and screened approximately 900 men in two days. Several suspected terrorists were detained.

The Battalion took part in another Brigade operation to cordon and search Pardess Hanna itself on 21 July, and on 22 July D Company put a cordon round and searched Shuna Settlement. Finally, on 29 July, the coastline near Caesarea was combed with meticulous care but no result.

All these operations resulted from the kidnap of two sergeants in Field Security in Nathanya in mid-July by the terrorist group Irgun Zvei Leumi. They were seized in Nathanya as hostages for three Jews who were under sentence of death. The NCOs were not found and the death sentence was carried out on 29 July. On 31 July the bodies of the men were found hanging from a eucalyptus tree, and when they were cut down a booby-trap exploded seriously wounding an officer.

Following in rotation with other formations the 2nd Infantry Brigade spent some six weeks training in Transjordan in August and September. On 6 August the Battalion Advance Party, comprising A Company, went to Transjordan, followed on the 9th by the remainder of the Battalion as the Brigade Advance Party. The first task was to site and set up the Brigade Camp at Mafraq, not far from Amman, the capital of Transjordan.

During the period 25 August to 6 September companies were put through brigade exercises using live ammunition. The next week, from 8 to 13 September, was devoted to battalion-level exercises, in which all brigade units used live ammunition.

On 9 and 10 September the Battalion conducted a large-scale exercise with full supporting arms. The exercise was broken down into three phases: a forty-five mile move across open desert in transport, an advance to contact and, finally, a set-piece dawn attack. From 14 to 16 September a Brigade Group exercise with full supporting arms set by the Commander of the 1st Infantry Division was executed.

This brief spell in Transjordan provided a welcome respite from the often frustrating routine of guards and patrolling in Palestine. Before the exercises got under way there was an opportunity for some relaxation. A battalion sports meeting took place on 29 and 30 August, and on 30 August, also, the Band and Drums joined in a massed beating of retreat for King Abdullah I of Transjordan.

Major K. J. K. Pye joined the Battalion in Transjordan on 16

August and took over temporary command of the Battalion from Major Marsh.

18 September saw the Battalion temporarily returned to Camp 87E at Pardess Hanna and thence it moved to Alamein Camp in Jerusalem where it was to remain until the last days of the Mandate in Palestine.

On arrival in Jerusalem on 26 September the Battalion was immediately committed to operational duties with A Company under Major Williams, guarding Government House, B and C Companies manning the gates in Zone A of the old city and D Company providing an immediate action platoon at ten minutes' notice, as well as guards for the Headquarters, the 2nd Infantry Brigade, and the Battalion Lines and numerous other occasional tasks.

On 18 October Lieutenant-Colonel G.H.M. Harper returned from United Kingdom leave to resume command of the Battalion vice Major Pye.

Senior appointments held in the Battalion at this time included:

CO: Lieutenant-Colonel G.H.M. Harper
2ic: Major K.J.K. Pye
Adjt: Captain H.E.W. Wiggington
QM: Major F.W. Garrard
RSM: RSM Isaacson

Company Commanders included Major P.B. Forrest, MC, Major R.M. Marsh, Major R.M. Allen, OBE, (Royal Norfolk Regiment), Major D.P. Apthorp, MBE, (Royal Norfolk Regiment) and Major I.D. McDowell (Essex Regiment). Senior Warrant Officers included RQMS Warren, CSMs Gingell, Duffy, Ramplin, Randall, Bullen and Kingston.

This return to operations in Jerusalem coincided with the first official announcement that the British Government intended to relinquish its responsibilities in Palestine and withdraw. Later in November the deadline for withdrawal was announced as 15 May, 1948.

Within the Battalion, which would depart in May, an end to the continual round of guards could now be seen. Furthermore there was a slight easing of tension, because, with the announcement of the British departure, Jews and Arabs alike turned their attention more directly on each other. There was no point in putting pressure on the British now that they were definitely leaving. It made more sense for each to fight to secure the best advantage for its own cause after the British had gone.

The net result for the Battalion was that the main emphasis operationally switched from active attempts to destroy illegal Jewish and Arab organizations to one more in the nature of peace-keeping, hoping to minimize' conflict between the two communities.

In November elements of the Battalion participated in two major cordon and search operations in Jerusalem. On 14 November D Company took part in a Brigade operation in which it was required to search the area to the north of Bazalel Street. The operation lasted from 0600 until 0920 and several suspects were detained, though nothing of importance was found. On the 17th the CO commanded a mixed force drawn from all three Battalions in the Brigade in a cordon and search operation in the area south of Bazalel Street. The operation again lasted from 0600 until just after 0900. Of three hundred and sixty-seven people screened, fourteen were detained as suspect and were handed over to the police.

On 15 December the guard duties in Zone A were reduced and C Company returned to Alamein Camp to take over D Company's duties, leaving a reinforced B Company in the city with A Company at Government House.

The constant and high level of operational activities meant that Christmas, 1947, passed almost unnoticed and certainly without any major form of celebration. On 28 December a platoon was despatched at short notice to Romema in an attempt, through a show of force, to ease the tension which had developed between Jews and Arabs in that area. A degree of calm was restored and the platoon left the area on 3 January, 1948.

Throughout the previous six months the Battalion strength had remained roughly on the thousand mark. The losses from drafts departing for demobilization were roughly made up by the arrival of new recruits, as well as drafts from other battalions in the East Anglian Brigade. December saw a marked change in this pattern, however, and the movements in and out of the Battalion witnessed a net reduction of 164 men. As a result Divisional Headquarters authorized the reduction of the strength of Sp Company by fifty percent and the placing of D Company into suspended animation. No more drafts now arrived before the Battalion left Palestine and by the end of January, 1948, the remaining three rifle companies had been reduced to two platoons each. This meant that those remaining in the Battalion would be working to maximum effect throughout the last three months of the tour.

The New Year saw the arrival of Major I.L. Wight, OBE, to take over from Major Pye as second-in-command, the latter going on

promotion to take over command of the Divisional Training School
at Nathanya.

On 15 January, 1948, the Battalion was visited by Lieutenant-
General G.H.A. MacMillan, CB, CBE, DSO, MC, the GOC-in-C
Palestine.

One company continued to guard the High Commissioner's
residence, while the remainder of the Battalion provided guards and
an increasing commitment to escort convoys of various types. Such
convoys became a necessity following the permanent closure of the
railway as a result of terrorist activity. It was also necessary to
provide one immediate action platoon at ten minutes' readiness to
move. The platoon was frequently called out to respond to incidents
and when this happened a second platoon was placed at ten minutes'
notice.

The Battalion's area of responsibility from January, 1948, until
April, included the Talbiah and Katamon Quarters (Zone A) of
Jerusalem, Der Abu Tor, and the open country south of Jerusalem to
Bethlehem.

One interesting and somewhat unorthodox tactic was tried in an
attempt to curb the activities of the Jewish and Arab snipers in the
city. The newly arrived Commander of the 2nd Infantry Brigade,
Brigadier C.P. Jones, CBE, MC, authorized the deployment of two
6-pounder anti-tank guns on the flat roof of a house with an excellent
field of observation over the surrounding buildings, from which
sniper fire could be observed. The guns were man-handled piece by
piece up several flights of stairs and reassembled on the roof. An
attempt was made to reinforce the structure of the building as there
were fears that it might crumble from the violence of the recoil of the
guns when fired.

A target was finally located and one round of high explosive was
fired. The sniping came to an abrupt halt and the building did not
collapse, though fearful wailing developed below as a result of all the
windows in the house being shattered. The resident family was
mollified when reminded that broken glass was a small price to pay
for freedom from the constant threat of snipers' bullets.

The guns continued to play a very effective part in quietening
inter-communal violence in the Battalion area of responsibility.

There was one amusing sequel to the deployment of these guns,
which was to cause the RQMS a headache after the Battalion
arrived in Greece. At one stage the 1st Battalion, the Highland Light
Infantry, took over responsibility for the guns and their Detachment
Commander persuaded his Suffolk counterpart to take over his guns

rather than go through all the trouble of changing the guns over on the roof. As a result the wrong weapons went with the Battalion to Greece!

22 February witnessed a really vicious incident, somehow typical of the depressing conditions in which the Battalion strove to carry out its duties at the time. Craftsman Burke, REME attached, was driving a truck in Jerusalem with Private Bennington as his escort when it was blown up by a land mine laid by Jews. Both men were wounded and instantly taken to a nearby Jewish clinic to be cared for. As they lay on operating tables having their wounds dressed, a Jewish terrorist burst into the room, ordered the doctor to one side and fired at the two men with a machine gun. Craftsman Burke was killed outright and Bennington left also for dead, though he was to make a remarkable recovery after being rescued and evacuated to the British Military Hospital.

Road escort duties carried out by the Battalion were many and varied, including escorts for Jewish burial parties to the Mount of Olives, for Jewish food convoys into the old city and for the Palestine Potash Company lorries between Jerusalem and their works by the Dead Sea.

One particular incident on Easter Sunday, 28 March, provides an interesting insight into the tasks the Battalion was confronted with at this time. It did not involve any shooting, but was not without excitement for the Commanding Officer. A Jewish agricultural settlement was established at Kefar Etsyon, some fifty miles out of Jerusalem on the Bethlehem road. It was surrounded on all sides by Arab settlements and the Brigade was routinely required to provide escort vehicles for Jewish vehicles supplying the settlement, to protect them on their journey through Arab-held territory. The Jews were not allowed to carry weapons or change places with personnel at the settlement.

On one occasion the Jewish vehicles were searched and it was found that the rules had been broken. The Brigade Commander refused thereafter to provide escorts with the results that the Jews decided to run the gauntlet unescorted. They caught the Arabs unprepared and reached the settlement unscathed, but the return journey was a different story. The convoy was ambushed in hilly country just south of Solomon's Pools on Saturday, 27 March. It was brought to a halt and lay surrounded all that night.

Word reached Brigade HQ and the next afternoon, after discussions had been held with both Jewish and Arab represent-atives, a group comprising two companies from the Battalion with a detachment from the Life Guards, the 95th Battery, 48th Field Regiment, RA, and a Sapper detachment commanded by the Commanding Officer, moved to the ambush area.

It had been agreed by both sides that the ambush party should be withdrawn under escort by this group. But it was clear that the Jews in the ambush would not know what was happening and it could not be certain that the Arab ambushers had been briefed as to the plan. The troops were deployed overlooking the ambush area and the CO walked alone down the valley road, overlooked by the Arab ambush party, to the Jewish vehicles, to tell them that it was safe to move.

210 Jews, including forty-five who were wounded, left their vehicles and weapons and walked with the CO back to the Army vehicles and were evacuated. Not a single shot was fired but it was a tense moment for all, particularly the CO. The next day a party from C Company under Major McDowell returned to the ambush site and recovered eleven Jewish bodies.

As the date for withdrawal drew closer, life in Alamein Camp became less and less congenial. Conditions there had always been rather Spartan; it was a tented camp with a few Nissen huts for stores, armouries and canteens. The camp was very crowded, containing as it did two Batteries of Gunners and several other detachments of Brigade supporting arms and services.

By March, 1948, it was made even less comfortable, as all stores apart from those needed to maintain military efficiency were backloaded for transit out of Palestine; even beds and chairs eventually disappeared.

While such tribulations were accepted with fortitude and not a little grumbling, there was a more serious discomfort to be borne. The camp was surrounded on all sides by settlements – to the north and south Jewish and to the east and west Arab. In consequence the Battalion not infrequently found itself in a sort of no-man's-land; the stray shots between the warring factions tore through tents and huts. One such bullet killed an unlucky REME Senior NCO, AQMS J. Cole, as he sat writing a letter in his tent. WOII Cole was the Armourer attached to the Battalion.

The month of April saw a number of changes as the final stages of the withdrawal were implemented. On the 22nd Alamein Camp was evacuated and the Battalion was moved into the old city of Jerusalem. The withdrawal from the camp was carried out under difficult circumstances accompanied by much sniping as the Jews and Arabs sought to be the new occupants. Three men of the

Battalion were slightly wounded in the process and the battle which followed left the Arabs in possession.

The Battalion took over duties in the old city from the 1st Battalion, the Highland Light Infantry and deployed to cover Zone C, the Measherim Quarter and the Notre Dame and St Paul's areas. It was split up with Battalion HQ and A and C Companies in the Hospice of Notre Dame de France by the Jaffa Gate and B and Sp Companies in St Paul's, opposite the Damascus Gate of the old city.

The Nuns of the Hospice of Notre Dame de France undertook while the Battalion HQ was there to repair the Colours. They would not take any payment, but gratefully accepted a bag of flour and a bowl of sugar as a token of acknowledgement of their fine needle-work.

The Battalion deployed in this way until the final withdrawal from Palestine. In these last days no attacks were made on it, but patrols and guards in the old city were still a hazardous business, with the ever-present chance of being caught in the cross-fire between the feuding communities.

On 13 May the GOC-in-C, General MacMillan, paid a farewell visit to the Battalion HQ, accompanied by the Chief Secretary to the Government, Sir Henry Gurney (later High Commissioner in Malaya when the Battalion arrived there in 1949). That same day at 1800 A Company evacuated the old city and at 0500 the next day occupied the area of the Italian Hospice in order to cover the withdrawal of the 85th Field Battery, RA.

At 0800 B Company provided a Guard of Honour with Colours at the Damascus Gate in honour of the final departure of HE The High Commissioner, General Sir Alan Cunningham, CB, DSO, MC. Immediately after HE's departure the Battalion, complete, with-drew southwards through the city, passing through areas of the other two battalions of the Brigade: the 2nd Battalion the Royal Warwick-shire Regiment and the 1st Battalion the Highland Light Infantry.

Positions were taken up on the southern edge of the city astride the Bethlehem road to cover the withdrawal of the remainder of the Brigade. During this deployment three men of B Company suffered slight injury from Jewish trip mines, through which their platoon had inadvertently moved.

The Brigade passed through in a seemingly never-ending stream of vehicles (some seventeen miles long!) and in their turn the Battalion also withdrew without incident, A Company claiming the honour of being the last organized sub-unit of British troops to leave Jerusalem.

The Battalion, with the rest of the Brigade group, bivouacked on the night of 14 May on the stony hillsides overlooking Solomon's Pools and then crossed into Egypt the next day, 15 May. Egyptian armoured columns, driving into Palestine to support the Palestinian Arabs, passed the Battalion as it made its way towards the Egyptian frontier.

The whole move was made in Battalion transport and not one vehicle broke down. Orders had been issued that any vehicle that did break down was to be burnt and abandoned. It did not come to this though a number of burning vehicles from other units was passed during the long and desperately tiring journey. The route passed through a few scattered villages and towns and in Hebron serious attempts were made by the local population to steal from vehicles as they slowly moved through the very narrow streets.

The Battalion arrived at Quassasin in the Canal Zone on 17 May and was accommodated in the Polish Camp. It remained there until, a week before sailing, it was moved to 156 Transit Camp at Port Said prior to embarking for Greece, its new station. The few days respite in Egypt allowed all to have a well-earned rest. Most of the men took short leave at leave camps at Port Fuad and Lake Timsah.

Because of an establishment re-organization Support Company was disbanded in Egypt and D Company reformed, thus allowing the Battalion to arrive in Greece with a full complement of four rifle companies. The Battalion sailed from Port Said on 18 June aboard the Trooper *Samaria*, which, as one company note in the *Regimental Gazette* described it, 'was a malignant vessel of few virtues and lots of hammocks'.

Thus came to an end a tour of duty which none had enjoyed and all were thankful quickly to forget.

CHAPTER II

THE SECOND BATTALION:

INDIA AND HOME 1946–1947

'The Last Days of the Raj and of "The Battalion in the East" '

Part I

1946 found the 2nd Battalion in Napier Barracks in Lahore, whence it had moved from Burma in the closing stages of the war against Japan. In the early post-war months it seemed to those in the Battalion that life might be returning to the well-known happy routine of the pre-Second World War years, but it was not to be for two reasons.

In the first place, British rule in India was soon to come to an end. Indian political groups were demanding that independence, promised during the war, should be granted forthwith, and during 1946 political disturbance increased throughout the country. The Muslims could not agree with the Hindus over the way that independence should be determined and while the latter saw the whole country remaining as one Indian State, the former were adamant that a separate Islamic State of Pakistan should be created. The fears of ordinary Muslim and Hindu peoples in India mounted, and inter-communal strife broke out in areas where both lived side by side.

In the Punjab, where the Battalion was stationed, the Sikhs formed a large part of the population and they were even more fearful of the future than the Hindus and Muslims. The territory lay on the boundary between the bulk of the Hindus to the south and east and the majority of the Muslims to the north and west and was, after partition, divided between India and Pakistan.

Scarcely had the 2nd Battalion been drawn into the problem of policing this developing crisis than the second blow fell. In February, 1947, the Commanding Officer received a top secret letter from the C-in-C India, confirming that the Battalion was about to be placed in suspended animation consequent upon the decision to reduce the size of the Army by eliminating the 2nd Battalions of all Infantry Regiments of the Line.

Nonetheless, the period in Napier Barracks in Lahore did mark a return to pre-war peacetime soldiering, at least briefly, and for those few who remained there. The postings into and out of the Battalion at the time make up a bewildering catalogue and give an idea just how few this was.

The accommodation blocks of Napier Barracks had been built of stone in the late 19th century, with high ceilings and flagstone floors, ideal for living comfortably in the moderate winters and also as comfortably as possible in the desperately hot and humid conditions that prevailed as the summer months came to an end and everyone longed for the monsoon rains. At this time of the year barrack-room temperatures reached 100°F and it was impossible to be really at ease. Many blocks had plunge baths just outside so that soldiers could fall into them to cool off when conditions became intolerable.

At the height of summer in 1946, on one occasion, no less than forty men were in the care of the Medical Officer suffering from heat exhaustion, while tinea and other skin problems abounded.

The daily routine in barracks was geared, as it had been for generations in India, to the pattern of the weather. Reveille was sounded at 0600 when 'Char-Wallahs' would appear with hot tea and even egg 'banjos' for the hungry. Some men would shave themselves, but there were innumerable Indian bearers who would shave soldiers as they lay in bed, some still asleep, or so it was averred. First parade would be at 0630 when PT or drill would be normal before the heat became too oppressive. Breakfast was served at 0800, after which, until midday, lectures and weapon training would fill the programme. In the afternoon all fell into a restless, sweaty sleep and the organized part of the day would end with games from 1700 onwards.

Uniform in barracks comprised the pith helmet to which the Wolseley helmet gave way in 1946, shirt, shorts, boots, hose tops held in place by red and yellow Minden flashes, and short-length puttees. When engaged on training or, later on, operations out of barracks, the heat was ignored. The pith helmet gave way to the soft hat as worn in Burma during the war and shorts were replaced by long trousers.

In October, 1946, the Battalion moved to Ferozepore where it was accommodated in Gough Barracks, where conditions were very similar to those in Napier Barracks. But, as the political situation worsened, so did the peacetime routine of the Battalion begin to fragment.

Routine vehicle patrols were initiated in consultation with the police, to instil calm into the rural areas around Ferozepore and then, in February, 1947, the Battalion moved to Jhelum to participate in the long-awaited Brigade training.

On 5 March, however, a deteriorating internal security situation forced the cancellation of the Brigade Camp and by 7 March the Battalion was sent to Amritsar to restore order in that riot-torn city. Withdrawn from Amritsar on 10 March, it returned to Ferozepore where it was to remain until leaving India.

The end of British rule in India was already in sight. In the month that the Battalion broke up, it was agreed that the two states of Pakistan and India would be formed and in July, 1947, the date for the transfer of power was suddenly brought forward from 1948 to August, 1947, only some six weeks ahead, in a desperate bid to restore calm to the sub-continent.

But by then the 2nd Battalion had to all intents and purposes ceased to exist. Its demise was felt deeply by those who had been a part of it, perhaps for almost all their service, and yet the sense of corporate shock, which might have been expected, was scarcely apparent. Perhaps it was too soon after the experiences of Burma which inevitably led to a desire to enjoy life come what may, or was it that there were by then in the Battalion so many officers and men from other units and arms of the service that the family feeling had, to a degree, evaporated? There was too a reluctant acceptance that British rule in India was about to come to an end, and that would leave no role for the Battalion in any case.

The dispersal of the Battalion began in early June, 1947, with the bulk of the officers and men transferring to other Battalions in the Brigade Group still in India. The small cadre that remained sailed for England on 21 June and arrived in Bury St Edmunds on 12 July, 1947. After various parades, it dispersed for the last time, bringing to an end one hundred and five years of continuous service.

Part II

The end of the Second World War in the Far East found the

Battalion stationed in the Punjab in northern India, very much understrength after the deprivations of the Burma campaign. It was located in Napier Barracks in Lahore. Lieutenant-Colonel H.W. Dean had, in September, 1945, taken over command from Lieutenant-Colonel K.C. Meneer who had been in command during the latter stages of the War.

Notes from the Battalion appearing in the *Regimental Gazette* in 1946, told of the constant changes of personnel as demobilization went ahead. New drafts arrived to help compensate for the departures, but the Battalion remained very weak in numbers.

A limited amount of training was possible and there were constant requirements to provide men for internal security duties, and the winter of 1945–46 saw a company detached to Amritsar for this purpose.

A great deal of inter-platoon and company sport was played and, initially, with the euphoria that the end of the war had brought, morale was high.

Christmas Eve, 1945, witnessed an interesting occasion when the Battalion Colours were returned from Lahore Cathedral where they had been held in safe custody during the Burma campaign. The whole Battalion paraded and marched to the Cathedral, where the Bishop of Lahore handed back the Colours during the course of a service of dedication. Following the service, the Battalion formed up and the Colours were marched on parade. The General Salute was then taken by the District Commander, Major-General A.B. Blaxland, CB, OBE. The Area Commander, Brigadier A.W.W. Holdworthy, DSO, MC, was also present. The newly-formed Drums were on parade for the first time and performed extremely well.

1946 saw a gradual deterioration in the political scene in India and the Punjab was no exception. For the most part order was maintained by the police and the Battalion was not called on to play an active part in keeping the peace. It was, however, involved in precautionary deployment and companies were detached from time to time to potential trouble spots. In this way C Company spent several months in Amritsar and, although ostensibly for training, companies rotated on detachment to Dalhousie. A spell in Dalhousie, a hill station, was much enjoyed by those lucky enough to get there. The days were pleasantly warm and fires and a blanket were needed at night.

The Battalion Rifle Meeting for 1946 was held in March and RSM G.S. Jasper was the individual champion shot.

Throughout 1946 the haemorrhage of demobilization continued to take its toll and rifle companies were reduced to two platoons. There were some replacements and cross-postings from other Regiments and Arms. One batch of recruits for the Battalion even came as a result of inter-service transfers from the Royal Navy and the Royal Air Force.

The loss of officers and senior ranks returning either home to the U.K. or to their parent regiments was hard to overcome and the command structure of the Battalion was difficult to maintain. Company Commanders changed with bewildering rapidity as witnessed in the notes for the *Regimental Gazette* published in December, 1946, in which one field officer was welcomed to both D and HQ Company simultaneously as the new Officer Commanding!

On 19 October, 1946, the Battalion was transferred from Lahore to Ferozepore where it moved into Gough Barracks. The journey was made by road transport – a three- to four-hour dusty ride.

From the outset 1947 promised to be more eventful for the Battalion than the year just passed. The quickening pace of moves towards independence for India and the ever-increasing likelihood that two states, one Muslim and one Hindu, would emerge engendered ever more anxiety among the population, particularly in the regions where large numbers of each community lived in close proximity to the other.

Already in 1946 there had been major and bloody disturbances in other parts of the country, notably Calcutta, Bombay and Bengal. It could only be a matter of time before the Punjab too erupted. Some fifty-six percent of the population of the Punjab were Muslims, the rest was made up of Sikhs and Hindus. The huge state also lay in the area between the major concentration of Muslim and Hindu peoples and was home for the warlike Sikhs, who would support neither Muslim nor Hindu. If a Muslim Pakistan and a Hindu India were to be created, what would happen to the Punjab? This was the question on everyone's lips.

Initially, after arrival in Ferozepore, hopes in the Battalion ran high that the area would remain calm. Winter in the Punjab is a comparatively crisp and energetic time and a full training period was eagerly planned. Long marches and cross-country runs were instituted to improve fitness for all and a programme of rural motorized patrols, designed to calm the fears of the villagers, provided an attractive diversion for those who took part. The patrols would last for one or two days, and nights would be spent in the open country. The villagers generally welcomed the patrols for the sense of stability they brought with them.

Then preparations went ahead for a six-week training period, the first major exercises since the war, which were to be run by Brigade HQ, the 23rd British Independent Brigade Group, to which the Battalion belonged.

There were some anxieties that the political situation might cause the cancellation of this training, but preparations went ahead and the Advance Party departed for Jhelum in the foothills to the north of Lahore.

The main body of the Battalion arrived at Dina Camp near Jhelum on 11 February, 1947, and quickly settled in. The camp was shared by the 2nd Battalion, the Royal Norfolk Regiment, also in the Brigade Group, and it was pleasant to be located side by side with friends from East Anglia.

The Battalion remained in Dina Camp for a fortnight, during which it carried out exercises directed by Brigade HQ. Infantry co-operation with armour and engineers, as well as battalion-level exercises were conducted for a fortnight and then the Battalion moved further into the hills for a week to what was known as 'Salt Lake Camp'. There exercises with the Gunners, firing live ammunition, were carried out. On completion of this phase the Battalion returned to Dina Camp on 4 March to continue training.

The situation in the Punjab had been worsening during the past three weeks and there had been one occasion already during camp when the Battalion had been warned for internal security duties. Now, on return to Dina, camp training was finally cancelled and the CO was ordered to move the Battalion to Lahore by road immediately. The order to move was issued at 2030 on 5 March, and by 2300 the first convoy set off.

Driving through the night, the Battalion reached Lahore just as dawn was breaking on 6 March and started to settle down in Napier Barracks, expecting to be called out at any time in support of the civil power. Shortly after midday further orders were received to return by road to the home station, Gough Barracks in Ferozepore. On arrival there the same evening everyone unpacked and went to bed to catch up on lost sleep, but at midnight the Battalion was ordered to turn out for yet another move, this time a journey of some forty miles to Amritsar.

On 20 February Lord Mountbatten had been appointed Viceroy of India and the British Government had at the same time announced its intention to hand over power in India not later than

June, 1948. The announcement signalled the imminent departure of the British, but gave no hint of to whom they intended to hand over power. In the Punjab this led to an intensification of intercommunal fighting as all factions sought to secure their own futures. Serious trouble broke out, initially in Lahore on 5 March, to be followed a day or so later in the other towns of the province, where fire-raising, looting and killing became widespread.

These developments help explain the extraordinary moves of the Battalion during those critical days. When it finally reached Amritsar it was confronted with a very serious situation indeed. Rioting was widespread in the city and a forty-eight-hour curfew had been ordered in an attempt to stabilize the situation. Companies were detached and based at different police stations in the city, from where a heavy programme of patrolling was immediately instituted in order to enforce the curfew.

By 10 March order had been restored in Amritsar and the Battalion, less one company, handed over its duties there and returned to Ferozepore. C Company, under Major V. Hudson, remained behind in Amritsar for approximately a month and was then relieved by B Company under Major P.D.F. Thursby. The city remained generally calm while C Company was there, but one night after B Company took over it erupted in a further spate of bitter inter-communal fighting. It was, in such a large city, only possible with one company to protect key points, such as the wireless station, the railway station and the post office. An attempt was made to impose a curfew with little success and the situation was only restored to normality with the arrival during the night of a complete Gurkha brigade. Only in daylight the following morning was the full horror of the rioting revealed.

Meanwhile, back in Ferozepore, for the next month or so the remainder of the Battalion was heavily involved in an intensive rural patrolling operation, designed once more to quieten the anxieties of the villagers.

Senior appointments in the Battalion at the end of March, 1947, were held as follows:

CO: Lieutenant-Colonel H.W. Dean
2ic: Major K.M.J. Dewar
Adjt: Captain A.J. Boddington
QM: Lieutenant H.W. Goodliff
RSM: RSM G.S. Jasper

Company Commanders at the time included Major R.J. Hildesley, Major P.D.F. Thursby, Captain H.P. Lawrence, Captain

R.D. McLellen, Captain G.P. McIlwaine and Captain W.A. Theobald. Warrant Officers included CSM A. Antenbring, CSM Cunliffe, CSM L. Siggs and CSM S. Winter.

In October, 1946, the Secretary of State for War had made a statement in the House of Commons, outlining future cuts in the size of the Army. Everyone knew that, with the imminent loss of India, the Army there would be under threat and rumours had been alive in the Battalion for some time that it might be disbanded.

On 5 February, before the Brigade Camp and the riots in the Punjab which followed it, the CO had received a personal letter from the C-in-C in India warning of the possible placing of the Battalion in 'suspended animation'. This was followed in March by formal executive orders confirming that this would happen. The Battalion was given the sad news on returning to Barracks from Amritsar to Ferozepore.

An officer was flown back to the War Office in London to make plans for the dispersal of personnel from the Battalion. It was agreed that a small cadre would return to the Depot at Bury St Edmunds, with the Colours, the Officers' and Sergeants Messes' silver and other property. Eight other ranks would be posted to the 1st Battalion in the Middle East and the remaining officers and men to other units of the East Anglian Brigade in India. Seven officers and 225 other ranks would go the 1st Battalion, the Essex Regiment and five officers and 230 other ranks to the 2nd Battalion, the Royal Norfolk Regiment.

Throughout April and May, 1947, preparations were made for the dispersal of the Battalion. A final ceremonial parade was held with the Colours on 7 May, when the Inspecting Officer was the Brigade Commander, 23rd British Independent Brigade Group, Brigadier A. de L. Cazenove, CBE, DSO, MVO. The Colours were carried by Lieutenant P.S. Rich and Lieutenant P.F.A. Richards. In the evening the whole Battalion sat down together for a farewell dinner. It was a unique and sad occasion. Speeches were made by the Brigade Commander and the Commanding Officer.

Three days later a further sad event took place – a farewell dinner and dance at the Sergeants' Mess in Gough Barracks on 10 May, 1947.

The following officers of the Battalion and their wives were present: the Commanding Officer, Lieutenant-Colonel H.W. Dean, Major and Mrs K.M.J. Dewar, Major R.J. Hildesley, Major P.D.F. Thursby, Captain A.J. Boddington, Captain and Mrs W.A. Theobald, Captain H.P. Lawrence, Captain S.N. Hales, Captain

M.V. Skitmore, Captain W. Drake, Captain P.A.J. Keeble, Captain Heining (RMO), Lieutenant (QM) and Mrs H.W. Goodliff and son and daughter, Lieutenant A. Wain, Lieutenant J. Gurdan, Lieutenant P.F.A. Richards, Lieutenant K.A. Channon, Lieutenant P.S. Rich, Lieutenant F.M. Orange-Broomhead, 2nd Lieutenant R.W. Wiggington, Lieutenant C.A. Brown, 2nd Lieutenant J.S. Meyer, 2nd Lieutenant M.W. Bliss and 2nd Lieutenant F.S. Jepson.

Other guests, who were numerous, included the Ferozepore Station Commander, Lieutenant-Colonel E.L. Spencer and Lieutenant-Colonel (QM) J. Hill, a former Quartermaster of the 2nd Battalion.

Sergeants' Mess Members present included RSM and Mrs G.S. Jasper, RQMS V. French, CSM and Mrs S. Winter, CSMs B. Wicks, L. Siggs, G. Simpson, A. Antenbring and J. La-Frenais. CSgts J. O'Leary, J. Clegg, E. Wicker, J. Pickering, R. Athroll and R. French. Sgts J. Bracey, R. Chisholm, G. Stone, R. Thorpe, L. Norman, W. Vincent, L. Porter, R. Abrahams, J. Woodhead, R. Seaman, G. Elliott, N. Bonsor, P. Chamberlain, A. Thompson and J. Mitchell.

At the conclusion of the dinner, the RSM proposed the loyal toast and there followed a number of further toasts after which the whole party retired outside to the cool of the tennis courts where many other guests joined the gathering and dancing went on until the early hours of the morning.

By early June drafts for the other regiments had been posted and the Cadre to return to the U.K. prepared for the move. It included among its numbers the following officers and senior ranks:

CO: Lieutenant-Colonel H.W. Dean
2ic: Major K.M.J. Dewar
Adjt: Captain A.J. Boddington
Major R.J. Hildesley
Captain M.V. Skitmore
RSM G.S. Jasper
RQMS V. French
CSM S. Winter
CSM A. Antenbring

The Colours, silver and heavy baggage left Ferozepore for Bombay under escort on 15 and 16 June, and Battalion HQ and families followed on 18 June. All embarked and sailed on the S.S. *Mooltan* on 21 June. The ship docked at Southampton after a fairly comfortable voyage on 12 July.

The late Colonel of the Suffolk Regiment, Colonel W.N.

Nicholson, CMG, DSO, and Mrs Nicholson, were at Southampton to welcome the Cadre home. It then travelled by train to Bury St Edmunds. 'The Suffolk Regiment' engine drew the train on the final stage from Liverpool Street.

On arrival at Bury St Edmunds station the Cadre was welcomed by Lieutenant-Colonel Sir Edward Warner, Bart, DSO, MC, DL, representing the Lord-Lieutenant, Brigadier E.H.W. Backhouse, the Colonel of the Suffolk Regiment, Lieutenant-Colonel F.A. Milnes, commanding No 12 PTC and Major F.V.C. Pereira commanding the Depot, the Suffolk Regiment. Others present included Captain F.J. Lockett, Captain H.R. Cotton, RSM Chalk, MBE, MM and CSM K. Duffy. The station was decorated with bunting and the Cadre paraded and the Colours were marched on to the Regimental March played by the Band, the 2nd Battalion, the Northamptonshire Regiment.

The Deputy Lord-Lieutenant and the Colonel of the Regiment made brief speeches of welcome on behalf of the County and the Regiment, and then, headed by the Band, the Cadre marched to the Angel Hill to receive a Civic Welcome from the Mayor of Bury St Edmunds, Councillor G.L. Coates, together with members of the Corporation. In his speech of welcome, the Mayor drew attention to the proud history of the Battalion over the one hundred and five years of its existence and the CO responded by thanking the town for the warm welcome home.

Just over two weeks after the Cadre returned home, on Minden Day, 1947, the Colours of the Battalion were handed over to the Depot for safe-keeping during a ceremonial parade. It was a sad occasion because, although the Battalion was in theory going only into 'suspended animation', it took a wealth of optimism on the part of those present to believe that it could ever again come to life.

CHAPTER III

THE FIRST BATTALION:

GREECE 1948–1949

'A Brief Moment to Recover and Prepare'

Part I

The Battalion arrived in the port of Piraeus in Greece on 19 June, 1948, after a somewhat cramped and unpleasant journey. From there it travelled by road south along the coast some ten miles to its new home at Aliki Camp.

After the traumas of life in Palestine everyone hoped for a chance to settle down to retrain and, perhaps, to enjoy life. Greece seemed peaceful enough on first inspection, but it was, in fact, a country torn in two, as it had been since the closing stages of the Second World War. It was split by the ravages of civil war as Greek Government forces struggled against a formidable Greek communist guerrilla army. The communists controlled large tracts of territory in the mountainous north of the country and clung tenaciously to their possession.

By the time the Battalion arrived, however, British military units were not actively engaged on the side of the Government against the communist forces. The Greek National Army and Police Force, trained and equipped by the British, had proved themselves gradually more capable of controlling the situation and the British forces served only as a guarantee for the future of Greek democracy.

While contingency plans existed to support the Greek Government in its struggle, should it have become necessary, the need to intervene never actually arose while the Battalion was in the country, and for the first time since 1939 it found itself not to be under pressure. It was to be a brief but nonetheless welcome respite, an interlude between the rigours of Palestine and the challenges to come.

The opportunity was seized upon to engage in intensive and realistic training for war, while at the same time using the relaxed atmosphere to forge ahead in the field of games and recreation.

Guards had to be found and escort duties done, but at no stage did they prevent at least two companies from engaging in organized training. The highlight of the training activities occurred when two companies at a time went into camp on Mount Parnis, which lies some twenty miles north of Athens.

In the winter months of November and December, 1948, Battalion exercises were held. The exercises were very strenuous and were made tough by extremely bad weather. The sunny summer days had given way to rain and bitterly cold winds from the north.

Cold winds were blowing figuratively from the east also in the winter of 1948–1949. The threatening posture of the Soviet Union which led to the blockade of Berlin might scarcely have registered with the Battalion in its isolated garrison in Greece, had it not been for the three extra months of service imposed on the National Service soldiers as a result.

In April, 1949, the brief stay at Aliki came to an end, as the Battalion sailed on HMT *Empire Test* northwards through the Aegean Sea to Salonika. It had been warned for posting to Malaya, and the move to Salonika was made in order to facilitate the smooth transfer of a number of men between the Battalion and the 1st Battalion, the Bedfordshire and Hertfordshire Regiment, which was already in Salonika.

The last few weeks in Salonika before sailing to the Far East were spent in training for the type of operations that the Battalion would be engaged in on arrival in Malaya. As was said in the *Regimental Gazette* at the time, 'The main problem was to do jungle training in a country practically devoid of trees'!

Towards the end of the stay in Sobraon Barracks in Salonika the days raced by and on 10 June, 1949, the Battalion set sail for Malaya aboard HMT *Dilwara*.

Part II

19 June, 1948, saw the Battalion arrive at Piraeus, the port of Athens on board the SS *Samaria*. The camp which the Battalion was to

occupy was at Aliki, some ten miles south of Athens along the coast road past the airport.

Aliki Camp was composed of permanent single-story buildings which had previously been a Greek sanatorium for children suffering from tuberculosis. All the sides of the buildings opened up, and in the hot weather this proved extremely pleasant. But when winter arrived and with it biting winds, the huts were very draughty and cold. As a summertime location, the camp was first class, sited as it was on a promontory surrounded on three sides by the sea and beautiful sandy beaches.

Immediately it took over the camp, the Battalion set about improving the rundown conditions which they found. Work services to refurbish it were slowly put under way and after a few months life became much more pleasant.

On arrival in Greece the Battalion remained in the 2nd Infantry Brigade of the 1st Infantry Division. Units of the Division were scattered throughout the Mediterranean and the remainder of the 2nd Infantry Brigade, which comprised the 1st Battalion, the Bedfordshire and Hertfordshire Regiment and the 1st Battalion, the East Surrey Regiment, were located with Brigade HQ in the northern Greek town of Salonika.

The Battalion had no active internal security role after arrival in Greece, though there were contingency plans to provide protection for British lives and property in the event of civil disturbance. It did have the constant task of providing various guards, however, which normally required from one to two companies on duty at any one time. British installations in the Athens area needed protection, as did shipments of stores arriving at Piraeus. The whole routine was less stressful and rather more monotonous than the recent experiences in Palestine and it did at least allow quite a large proportion of the Battalion to be freed for the training programme which was quickly put in hand to make up for the lack of opportunity inevitably experienced over the last months on operations there.

Cadres were organized for NCOs, weapon training and specialist weapons and officers' study days were frequently held.

In August the Cadre of the 2nd Battalion joined the Battalion and in September the Band arrived from the depot.

On 3 September Lieutenant-Colonel G.H.M. Harper handed over command to Lieutenant-Colonel I.L. Wight, OBE, who had become 2ic of the Battalion towards the end of the Palestine tour.

Company Commanders with the Battalion at this time included Major O.K. Leach, Major W.W. Cook and Major A.F. Campbell.

The newly arrived Quartermaster was Captain Longstaff and included among the Warrant Officers were RQMS Warren and CSMs Winter, Gingell, Ramplin, Kingston and Smith.

The last four months of 1948 saw an increase in the tempo of training. A Brigade training directive required all battalions to spend a period of three weeks out of barracks, concluding with a twenty-mile march. As the Battalion guard commitments in the Athens area prevented the whole Battalion going into the field together, it was decided that the exercise would be carried out by two companies at a time.

Mount Parnis, some twenty miles north of Athens, was chosen as the area for this training and the base camp was established high on the beautiful wooded slopes of the mountain. On 11 September B and D Companies moved out of Aliki Camp to begin their spell in the field.

Training was done progressively, starting at the individual level, and advancing through section to platoon tactics. One day was devoted to the platoon in the attack. On the evening of 5 October, both companies set out on a night march down the slopes of Mount Parnis to rendezvous with Battalion HQ and the other two companies at the foot of the mountain.

With the rendezvous effected and all companies deployed, the Battalion mounted a major exercise: a deliberate dawn attack. The Brigade Commander watched the exercise and was evidently pleased with what he saw. After it A and C Companies moved to the base camp on Mount Parnis for their three-week traiing, while B and D Companies returned to barracks and guard duties.

A further full battalion exercise was conducted in November in the area of Mount Kitsi. The Mediterranean summer had broken and the scheme, which lasted for forty-eight hours, in which the tactics of a battalion withdrawal were practised, was carried out in a continuous heavy rainstorm, with the additional hazard of strong cold winds.

This weather pattern heralded a ferocious winter, with biting winds and rain, one of the worst on record in Greece. The improvements carried out to Aliki Camp during the summer were a help, but the children's hospital buildings were still very draughty, and portable oil stoves did little to warm them up.

1948 had been a good sporting year for the Battalion. On arrival in Greece it took over from the 2nd Battalion, the Duke of Cornwall's Light Infantry in the South of Greece Cricket League. The Battalion was required to field an A and a B Team. Starting mid-season from very low positions in the league both teams won most of their matches and finished second and sixth respectively.

As the only major unit entered, the Battalion easily won the Army in Southern Greece Athletic Meeting held during the summer.

Hockey also featured in the sporting programme. The Battalion played a number of games against units in the Athens area, but could not find a strong enough opponent to really put the team to test.

On 9 December an open boxing tournament was staged at Aliki Camp. Most of the boxers came from the Battalion, with Athens Area REME Workshops, the Royal Navy and the Royal Air Force providing additional contenders.

Early in January, 1949, CSM Randall took the Battalion Boxing Team to Salonika to compete in the Brigade Inter-Unit Championships. The team fared badly against the teams from the 1st Battalion, the East Surrey Regiment and the 1st Battalion, the Bedfordshire and Hertfordshire Regiment, but Private England brought the featherweight title back to Aliki Camp with him.

The Battalion Hockey Team made the same journey later in the month, and beat both Brigade HQ and the 1st Battalion, the Bedfordshire and Hertfordshire Regiment, losing only, to the 1st Battalion, the East Surrey Regiment.

Between 17 and 19 January, 1949, the First Cruiser Squadron of the Royal Navy visited Greece under command of Lord Louis Mountbatten. Various sporting and social activities took place and a number of officers and men from the Battalion visited the ships in Piraeus harbour.

Training at company level continued into the new year, as and when guard duties permitted. Specialist cadres also went ahead and in mid-February a 'skeleton' Battalion HQ together with Company HQs went to Salonika to participate in a Brigade signals exercise.

Towards the end of February B and D Companies combined to stage a demonstration of the company in the attack, for the benefit of a large group made up of commandos and officer cadets from a Greek training establishment in Athens.

The Brigade Commander, Brigadier C.P. Jones, CBE, MC, carried out his annual administrative inspection of the Battalion early in March and reported favourably on what he found. It was at this time that the Battalion was warned for a tour of duty in Malaya to start in the summer. It was also announced that, prior to leaving for the Far East, the Battalion would move briefly to Salonika where it would exchange men either too young to go on active service or with too little time before demobilization, with the 1st Battalion, the

Bedfordshire and Hertfordshire Regiment, in return for soldiers qualified by age and with sufficient service left to do to go to Malaya. This sensible move was made the more easy through the closer integration already coming into being, consequent on the forming of the East Anglian Brigade.

On 11 March the Battalion was honoured with a visit from the Chief of the Imperial General Staff, Field-Marshal Sir William Slim, who was carrying out a tour of Mediterranean garrisons. A and C Companies combined to form a guard of honour, under the command of Major O.K. Leach, at Athens airport, both for the arrival and departure of the C.I.G.S. Field-Marshal Slim also visited Aliki Camp, took the salute at a ceremonial parade and lunched at the Officers' Mess.

Following this visit, preparations were set in train for the move to Salonika. The opportunity was taken to say farewell to an important guest list headed by the British Ambassador to Greece, when the Band and Drums beat retreat on the parade ground at Aliki Camp.

On 3 April the Battalion embarked on board HMT *Empire Test* at Piraeus, for the two-day voyage northwards through the Aegean Sea to Salonika. On arrival there, it moved into Sobraon Barracks vacated by the 1st Battalion, the East Surrey Regiment, which was to replace the Battalion in Aliki Camp.

Immediately after arrival in Salonika 'Operation Sort-out' began, and a large group of officers and men were exchanged with the 1st Battalion, the Bedfordshire and Hertfordshire Regiment. This administrative move went smoothly and, immediately, with no external duties or distractions, the Battalion moved into a short period of intensive training in preparation for the active service tour in Malaya. The barren hills of Greece scarcely provided ideal conditions for an introduction to jungle warfare, but the best possible preparations were made for what lay ahead.

A light-hearted member of the Battalion at the time coined an expression to describe the preparatory training as a series of 'JEWTs', that is Jungle Exercises Without Trees!

The Battalion was very much under strength in the weeks before departure for Malaya and, to make matters worse, a large draft of recruits due to join from Colchester was delayed in order to be given additional training. They were already on board a troopship bound for Greece when they were disembarked at the last moment and returned to Colchester for an intensive period of simulated jungle training prior to joining the Battalion after arrival in the Far East.

On 6 May the Battalion Advance Party left for Singapore. It was commanded by Major W.A. Heal, OBE, who had recently arrived in Greece to take over as 2ic of the Battalion. It also included Major J.C. Devy, Major W.W. Cook, Lieutenants W.C. Deller and P. Thain and 2nd Lieutenants J.G. Starling, L.A. Palmer and J.N. Kelly. Captain W.J. Calder joined the party at Port Said.

One last public occasion remained before the Battalion also left Salonika. On 24 May, Empire Day, the beating of retreat by the Massed Bands and Drums of the 1st Battalion, the Suffolk Regiment and the 1st Battalion, the Bedfordshire and Hertfordshire Regiment took place in Aristotle Square in Salonika. Large crowds gathered to watch the display and among the official guests to be invited were His Excellency the Governor-General of Northern Greece and his wife, General Grigiropoulos, commanding the Greek C Corps, the British Consul General and the Archbishop of Salonika.

Bandmaster G. Stunnel, ARCM, and Drum Major Miller played major parts in this extremely successful military occasion.

Just before leaving Greece, the following letter was received from His Majesty's Lieutenant of Suffolk, addressed to the Commanding Officer:

> Kenton Hall,
> Debenham,
> Suffolk.

Suffolk is very proud of its County Regiment: indeed it has every reason to be so and we hope that the Regiment will always be aware wherever it may be, it is in our thoughts and has our good wishes.

Long separation from homes and families is a burden; but we at home will never forget that it is honourable service to our King and Country that keeps you often in trying conditions overseas.

I learn that you have had to postpone plans to celebrate the centenary of your old and valued Colours and the amalgamation of the 1st and 2nd Battalions. We would all have liked to have had that celebration at home, so that we could have paid public tribute to this great occasion in the Regiment's history.

However, duty takes you further afield to Malaya; there you will be on ground that holds memories for all of us; sad and bitter as those memories are, we know that throughout the war alike in the distress of prison camps as in valorous action, the good name of the Regiment was always supreme.

As it was in war, so it is and will be in your difficult task of establishing peace and order; you will add yet more distinction to the honour of the Regiment.

So, as you embark on yet another adventure, we in Suffolk and at home wish you God Speed and duty done, a safe and happy home coming.
Signed: Stradbroke, H.M. Lieutenant for Suffolk.

A special order of the day, addressed to the Battalion, was published by the Commander of the 2nd Infantry Brigade, Brigadier C.P. Jones, CBE, MC, on 8 June, 1949. The order ran as follows:

It is with great regret and an acute feeling of loss that I say goodbye to the 1st Battalion, the Suffolk Regiment, which I have had under my command for the past eighteen months.

The Battalion has now been in the 2nd Infantry Brigade for over two years and has had varied experiences during that time, from the disquiet of Palestine to the peacefulness of duties in Greece. The tasks it has been called upon to perform have been many, some exciting, some dull, but the Battalion has done all that has been asked of it in an admirable manner and without question. Its high quality has never varied, despite the rapid turnover of men; its steadiness and reliability have been an example to all.

The Battalion has always identified itself with the Brigade, and has shown a spirit of eager, friendly co-operation which has been a delight to me and to my staff. We are most grateful.

You now leave the Brigade for Malaya, where you will see active service. I wish you good fortune and success in the difficult task ahead of you and I hope that the Brigade may have the good fortune to collect the Battalion back into the fold some time in the future.

On 10 June, 1949, relieved by the 1st Battalion, the Oxfordshire and Buckinghamshire Light Infantry, the Battalion sailed from Salonika on board HMT *Dilwara* bound for Singapore.

CHAPTER IV

THE FIRST BATTALION:

MALAYA 1949–1953

'The Suffolks Do It Again'

Part I

From July, 1949, to January, 1953, the Battalion was, almost without respite, heavily committed in the fight against communist terrorism in Malaya. It found itself in Malaya at a time when the communist campaign was at its fiercest and, for the most part, in operational areas where terrorists were most active. In consequence it was under the heaviest possible pressure for three and a half years and experienced its most active operational tour of the post-Second World War period.

The Malayan Communist Party (MCP) was first formed in 1930. Before the Second World War it had established itself on a firm basis both in Singapore and the Malayan peninsula. Its strength was built out of the depressed economic state of the area, consequent upon the effects of the worldwide depression of the 1920s and 1930s. Until the war its activities were largely confined to fermenting unrest in Singapore and on the large European-owned and managed rubber estates in the peninsula.

When war came in 1939 the MCP was the only effective local political organization in Malaya and Singapore. Its following came almost exclusively from among the Chinese. The Malays and Indians were little interested in communism then or later during the Emergency and, in any case, were not effectively organized nationally in a political sense.

When the Japanese threat to Malaya and Singapore became apparent in 1941 the British Authorities provided training and weapons to the MCP in the hope of building up a local force to offer resistance to them. The MCP created the Malayan People's Anti-Japanese Army (MPAJA) which remained in being throughout the war. It was active on a limited scale against the Japanese and also provided a convenient organization to receive support in the closing stages of the war when small British army groups, collectively known as Force 136, together with supplies of arms and equipment, were introduced into the country.

With peace restored, the MPAJA was disbanded and most of its weapons were handed over to the British Authorities. However, some weapons were carefully hidden away and, more important, the nucleus of the organization remained in being.

Initially, after the war, the MCP reverted to the policy of stirring up industrial unrest, but following the call to worldwide insurrection initiated by the Moscow-dominated Communist Information Bureau and believing that what Mao Tse-tung was achieving in China it could aspire to in Malaya, the MCP began to prepare organized, armed insurrection. In order to achieve their aim, they re-established the old military organization of the MPAJA, re-naming it the Malayan Races Liberation Army (MRLA).

The insurrection started in June, 1948, when the MRLA attempted to establish itself in remote areas which it hoped to be able to dominate and from which, ultimately, to extend its influence.

The MRLA was generally organized into regiments, companies and platoons, though the strength and effectiveness of these units scarcely made a uniform pattern. Early in the Emergency there was a tendency to operate in large groups with anything from fifty to 200 men, who would all live in the same camp, located within easy reach of the jungle edge. This was a necessity in order that the unit could obtain food and gain intelligence from isolated peasant communities 'squatting' illegally and remote from population centres and Government supervision.

Followng the example of Mao Tse-tung, the MRLA at first sought completely to dominate one or two remote areas of the country. Isolated police posts were overrun and the local population was won over to the communists' side. It was soon realized, however, that conditions in the Federation of Malaya were rather different from China. The country covers an area roughly the size of England and Wales and, though four-fifths is covered in dense jungle, communications to even the remotest inhabited parts were not too difficult. Despite initial problems the Security Forces (SF) were able to counter such activities with comparative ease and the attempt to 'liberate' selected areas was abandoned.

In consequence the MRLA turned to less ambitious activities and attempted to achieve their aim by concentrating on three particular areas. Firstly, through a variety of means they tried to weaken the resolve of the Government and the morale of the SF. Police posts were attacked; police and army vehicles were ambushed on the roads and SF patrols into the jungle were also trapped in ambushes. Secondly, they turned their attention to the European managers of rubber estates and tin mines. Through murder and ambush, they hoped so to intimidate these men and their families, living as they often did on distant plantations remote from the protection of the SF, that they would be forced to flee. In this way they tried to slow down and eventually stop the production of tin and rubber – the lifeblood of the Malayan economy. Lastly, they tried to win the Chinese element of the population to their side, either by persuasion or intimidation. The Chinese 'squatters' were often easily persuaded by MRLA propaganda. They provided food and intelligence for the communists and, indeed, early in the Emergency a 'mass organization' (the Min Yuen) was formed throughout the country so that the supply of food and money and the gathering of information was placed on a more organized footing.

The more wealthy members of the Chinese community, the managers or owners of small estates, those employed in government service, in hospitals, schools and offices and particularly those working for the SF, were also subjects for the attention of the MRLA. A campaign of terror was directed against them and their families in order to dissuade them from playing their part in keeping the Government and the economy functioning effectively. Murder, mutilation, torture, extortion and kidnap were the measures employed.

It was into this tense situation that the Battalion was thrust. It was to occupy its attention twenty-four hours a day for the next three and a half years.

The Battalion's job was to seek out and destroy armed and uniformed units of the MRLA and the Min Yuen groups which supported them. Often companies were detached from Battalion HQ and quite frequently even platoons were based some distance from their companies. For the most part, sub-unit bases would be located on rubber estates where they found themselves occupying a block of rubber tappers' lines, the overflow of men being accommodated in tents. On occasion, schools, shops or similar buildings would be used and sometimes a European planter's house would be taken over with the surrounding lawns providing an ideal site for additional tentage.

The 'bandits', as the communist terrorists were always known, for the most part set up their camps close to the Chinese squatter settlements on whom they relied for support. Battalion operations as a result concentrated in two particular areas. Firstly in patrolling the rubber estates and peasant farming areas and, more particularly, into the jungle and swamp beyond, in order to find the bandit base camps, destroy them and kill their occupants. Secondly in laying ambushes on tracks in the jungle or on known routes in the more open estate and farming areas which lay between the local population settlements and where the bandits were believed to have sited their camps.

If these patrolling and ambushing activities were carried out without the benefit of specific information, the chances of even a contact, let alone a kill, were remote. Luck would often play a part, but the skill and determination of the patrol leader could turn a random search into a successful pursuit. Initially patrol commanders relied heavily on Iban trackers recruited from Sarawak to trace the bandits' movements through the jungle. But, with experience, they themselves became adept at picking up the scarcely perceptible signs of human movement.

As the Battalion's tour progressed and more and more information was forthcoming, so operations became less and less haphazard and more spectacular results were achieved. The best and most gripping situation for a patrol commander to be in was if he was presented with a surrendered bandit who had deserted his unit and agreed with the police to lead a patrol back to his camp. It could be that his defection was still not known to his comrades, in which case there would be a real chance of returning to the camp and finding it still occupied. Even in these apparently near perfect circumstances, so watchful were the bandit sentries, so difficult and close was the country and so noisy the jungle undergrowth under foot, that the patrol would be extremely lucky, however skilfully it surrounded the camp, to kill or capture more than four or five of the bandits in it.

By far the greatest number of operations were carried out by section and platoon patrols. But occasionally, and sometimes with co-operation from police units, much larger operations were executed. If a bandit group was known to be within a certain jungle area the whole Battalion or more would be deployed in a cordon and search, hoping to drive the CTs from their cover. Similarly, the police and army might jointly plan to cordon off a suspect group of squatters' huts and search them for bandits who might be sheltering there, or arms or obvious signs of food or medical supplies secreted for the use of the MRLA.

After the resettlement of squatters to less sensitive areas, the bandits found it increasingly difficult to obtain food and were forced to site their camps deeper in the jungle, where sufficient ground could be cleared to cultivate crops without detection. To counter this development, the Battalion patrolled deeper into the jungle, sometimes as a result of reports of open clearings seen from aircraft.

The weapons, equipment and clothing issued to the Battalion were adapted during its tour until they exactly suited the operational conditions in Malaya. The 1944 Pattern equipment (developed for the war in Burma) proved entirely suitable for Malayan conditions and the canvas-topped rubber-soled jungle boot which was light and which allowed water to drain away was worn.

The standard personal weapon for the soldier was the No 5 Rifle. It was a modification of the No 4 which had been used in the Second World War and had been modified again for the war in Burma. The butt was shortened and fitted with a rubber heel, the stock was cut back and the barrel shortened and adapted to take a flash eliminator. The magazine carried ten rounds and further ammunition was carried in a bandolier usually tied round the waist.

Section commanders were at first armed with Sten guns but these were replaced with the much more reliable but heavier Australian Owen gun. By 1951 patrol commanders were normally issued with the US Mk 2 Carbine which was light and very effective at close range in the jungle.

Each patrol would carry a Bren gun which was slung across the shoulders on a broad band of webbing. The bi-pod was normally removed, and men were taught to fire from the shoulder in the standing position in an immediate emergency.

Another weapon carried in the patrol was the Extra Yoke (EY) Rifle. The stock was reinforced with wire banding and a metal cup was attached to the muzzle. A 36 Grenade with a special base plate was fitted into the cup and, using a ballastite cartridge, the grenade could be fired up to a distance of eighty to one hundred yards. A seven-second fuse was used and then the grenade would explode either on impact or just above the enemy camp or ambush position. 36 Grenades and 80 Grenades (phosphorous smoke) were carried by all members of a patrol.

Normally the longest duration for a patrol would be four to five days without resupply. Patrols were usually issued with Compo 10-man ration packs and, in order to cut down on the weight carried, they became adept at taking only their exact requirement. Some patrols took only the meat tins and supplemented them with curry powder, rice and raisins, all of which could be carried in waterproof bags which made the packing of the necessary food and items of spare kit much easier.

Successful patrolling in a country such as Malaya against an enemy such as the MRLA necessitated the development of very sophisticated skills on the part of the patrol commander and men. A major problem was the limited range of visibility. Operating in hilly primary jungle was, from this point of view, the best, though even here the leading scout of a patrol of ten men in single file would rarely, if ever, come within sight of the rear man. As most operations were carried out close to the edge of the jungle, patrols frequently found themselves in secondary jungle. This is the term given to an area of primary jungle which has at one time been cleared or partially cleared for some kind of cultivation and then allowed to revert to natural growth. In such conditions clear visibility may be reduced to three or four yards, so thick is the undergrowth, and it was frequently necessary for the leading scout to cut a path for the patrol.

Visibility was also extremely poor in lalang, a tall coarse grass which grows the moment that cultivation ceases. In parts of Malaya land which is unused also becomes overgrown by a tough fern growing to six feet tall and while negotiating such vegetation a man would disappear from view of the next man only a yard away from him if he stumbled.

Movement in such conditions was extremely slow and patrols would not infrequently find their advance cut to a snail's pace, with progress measured at fifty to a hundred yards an hour. The constantly changing speed of a patrol also created problems with navigation.

In the jungle it was not possible to make use of the normal aids to map reading. Rarely was a patrol commander afforded a distant view and, even if, on a steep hillside, he caught a glimpse of a hazy skyline, he could never be sure of relating the hilltop he could see with the map. He was normally reduced to marching with his compass in his hand to give him a feel for the general line of movement. He then relied on his experience to relate the shape of the feature on which the patrol was moving to the contours of the map.

In totally featureless swamp he stuck as rigidly as possible to a general bearing on his compass and made a guess at his progress in terms of an approximate number of yards per hour.

A further problem to be solved in jungle patrolling centred on the question of noise. To avoid giving warning of approach to the enemy, it was necessary ideally to reduce the noise of movement to a level which could be detected only up to the distance it was possible to see. Inevitably, it was rarely possible to achieve such perfection, but experienced soldiers became experts at moving extremely quietly, recognizing which type of creeper, branch, palm frond, dead or alive, would snap or crackle if trodden on and which would not.

Problems of visibility, navigation, speed and noise could be reduced to a minimum by making use of ridge tracks frequented by animals. It was occasionally useful to move in this way, but such tracks provided the bandits with perfect opportunities to set up ambush positions.

Locating the enemy in the jungle was, of course, an easy matter if there was precise information as to his whereabouts. Yet, even after 1951 when information flowed more freely, many patrols were still sent out to search for bandit camps without anything more than a general idea of their locations. As patrol commanders built up experience, they became experts in converting what might seem an impossible, exhausting and time-consuming task into a carefully planned and meticulously executed fighting reconnaissance patrol.

If, for example, it was known that a bandit camp was located somewhere in an area of, say, six to eight map squares of jungle, then it was also clear that the bandits had to leave it and return to it and thus there must be signs of movement. While they took great care to conceal their tracks, they could not do so completely. It would be a waste of time for a patrol searching the edge of the jungle to find a track used by the terrorists to visit a local squatter settlement, as the jungle would be entered at a different point, by different men and on different occasions. However, the individual routes had to converge at some stage to gain access to the camp. If the jungle was particularly thick, the individual tracks would converge sooner. If the patrol cut into the jungle and then moved parallel to the jungle edge, but deep inside, it would in all probability eventually pick up the track running into the camp.

Another way of searching an area was systematically to follow all water courses, knowing that the bandits had to be within reasonable reach of drinking water. And yet another method of locating a terrorist camp was to patrol a ridge line a few yards below the actual ridge track. Bandits would choose to use ridge tracks for ease of movement and speed over long distances, but to drop down to their camp they would not all leave the ridge track at the same point, thereby leaving their trail for a patrol to follow. Once again, however, the individual tracks must converge and often they would do so within a few yards of the top of the ridge.

The Malayan Emergency was a 'platoon and section commanders' war'. Operations were on occasion conducted successfully at battalion and company level, but through trial and error it quickly became clear to the Battalion, for a variety of reasons, that the platoon or section was the best size of force for operating against the MRLA. Never were there enough troops available to flood areas of CT activity and, once it was realized that a platoon was of sufficient strength to tackle most situations, it made sense to deploy as frequently and as widely as possible at that level.

A major criticism of the bandits was that they would rarely stand and fight, even when grouped in large numbers. It is perhaps worth making the point that it was normally the case that at the moment of contact neither side had any real idea of the size of the enemy force opposing them, so close was the country and so circumscribed the visibility. Rather than risk being overwhelmed by a superior force, the CTs would usually run for it, to preserve themselves and their weapons to fight another day. Such a reaction allowed the Battalion to reduce the size of its patrols, sometimes even to groups of four or five men only.

Surprise was also an important factor. If a company was to deploy, the preparations for the move were obvious and so was the heavy vehicle movement to the operational area. A platoon could slip away by day or night and might well go unnoticed. Once in the jungle the problems of movement increased enormously if more than twenty to thirty men were involved. A company of eighty men in single file would trail through the jungle for some 400 yards from front to rear, and commanding such a group in an emergency situation was extremely difficult.

For all these reasons platoon and section commanders found themselves on their own, linked only infrequently with their company commanders by often unreliable radio communications. Their example would sustain morale in very difficult conditions, their determination and experience would help them locate the enemy and their skill and leadership would result in a successful operation.

Arriving in Singapore on 1 July, 1949, the Battalion was

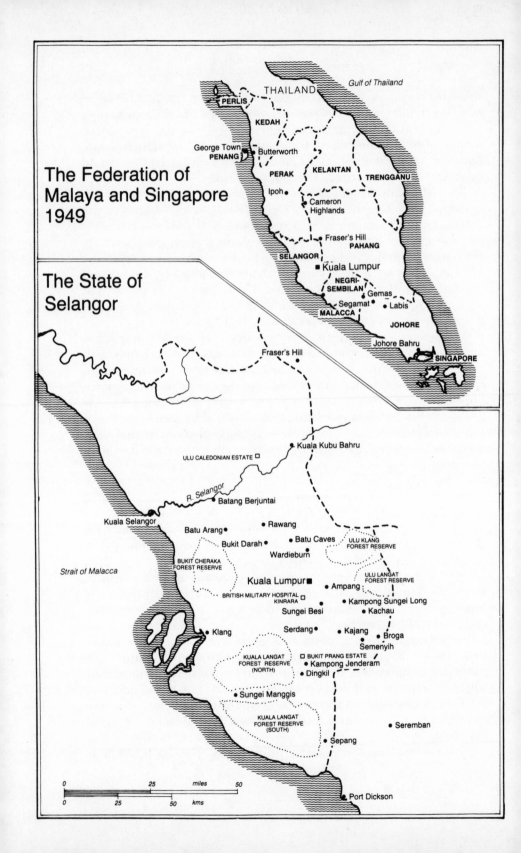

The Federation of Malaya and Singapore 1949

The State of Selangor

THAILAND

Gulf of Thailand

PERLIS

KEDAH

George Town • Butterworth
PENANG

PERAK   KELANTAN   TRENGGANU

Ipoh

• Cameron
  Highlands

• Fraser's Hill   PAHANG

SELANGOR

■ Kuala Lumpur

NEGRI-
SEMBILAN
        • Gemas
Segamat • Labis
MALACCA

JOHORE

Johore Bahru

SINGAPORE

Fraser's Hill

• Kuala Kubu Bahru

ULU CALEDONIAN ESTATE □

R. Selangor
        • Batang Berjuntai

Kuala Selangor •

Batu Arang •   • Rawang

        • Bukit Darah   • Batu Caves

ULU KLANG
FOREST RESERVE

Wardieburn

BUKIT CHERAKA
FOREST RESERVE

ULU LANGAT
FOREST RESERVE

Strait of Malacca

Kuala Lumpur ■

        • Ampang

BRITISH MILITARY HOSPITAL □
KINRARA
                • Kampong Sungei Long
Sungei Besi   • Kachau

• Klang

Serdang •   • Kajang   • Broga
                      Semenyih

KUALA LANGAT
FOREST RESERVE
(NORTH)

□ BUKIT PRANG ESTATE
• Kampong Jenderam
• Dingkil

• Sungei Manggis

KUALA LANGAT
FOREST RESERVE
(SOUTH)

• Seremban

• Sepang

0   25   miles   50
0   25   50   kms

Port Dickson

accommodated in barracks on the island for a few days, during which it trained hard for jungle operations. On 18 July it moved to a tented camp at Sungei Besi in South Selangor where a further brief opportunity for training was afforded, prior to taking over operational duties in Southern Selangor. When this happened, the Battalion Tactical HQ (Tac HQ) was established at Kajang with two companies also operating from there.

Apart from brief spells away, the small town of Kajang was to remain at the heart of the Battalion's efforts throughout its time in Malaya. A close and friendly liaison was built up with the Police and civil administration and a thorough and detailed knowledge of the surrounding country, rubber estates, hill jungle and swamps was acquired by the rifle company officers and men. These factors, coupled with a determination to maintain a high level of training and efficiency in the jungle, were to lead to a continuing run of success, which, it is generally acknowledged, was to remain unequalled by any non-Gurkha battalion until the end of the Emergency in 1960.

A decision taken early on in the Malayan tour was thought in the Battalion to have further enhanced its operational efficiency. It was to train all drafts of recruits arriving in Malaya within the Battalion. The alternative was to send them to the jungle warfare school but the advantages of 'in-house' training were considerable: new arrivals were assessed by officers and NCOs of the Battalion; they were trained quickly without delays; they were taught the Battalion's own carefully adapted drills for jungle warfare and lastly their training was done in the Battalion's operational area with which they thus immediately began to become familiar.

The Battalion remained active in the Kajang area for its first spell of duty there till May, 1950, and then, leaving a rear party in Sungei Besi, it was moved southwards to Segamat, a small town in northern Johore. The move was consequent upon a general re-deployment southwards of units within Malaya.

Once again the Battalion operational area was extremely large and companies were dispersed in remote locations well away from Battalion HQ.

In general operational achievements were less spectacular in Johore. It took time for the companies to get to know their areas and scarcely had this been achieved and successes recorded, than in October, 1950, the Battalion was taken out of operations and, travelling by train, moved north up the peninsula to the island of Penang for the first of two brief spells of rest and retraining.

Early December, 1950, found the Battalion back on operations based on a newly built camp on Wardieburn Rubber Estate, just north of Kuala Lumpur. Companies were widely dispersed around the capital city, with one, once more, taking up occupation in Kajang. This deployment remained throughout most of 1951.

In January, 1952, the Battalion's activities were once more concentrated in the southern part of Selangor. At this stage half the Battalion at a time was given a final break from operations with a brief spell in Penang. It was to be the last rest period before leaving Malaya and after a two-month tour of duty in North Selangor the remaining year's operations were to continue at a high level with one main object in everyone's mind: to destroy once and for all the MRLA unit in South Selangor, known to the Battalion as 'the Kajang Gang' which was led by a particularly brutal, but highly competent, commander Lieu Kon Kim whom everyone referred to as 'the Bearded Wonder' because of the unusual growth of beard he sported.

Success was slow in coming but gradually members of the gang were eliminated. By this stage of the Battalion's tour, patrolling expertise was of a very high order after months and years of experience. An unrivalled co-operation between Battalion Tac HQ and the Police also meant that the combined police and military resources were used to the very best advantage. The intelligence gathered by an ever more effective Special Branch meant that virtually all members of the MRLA in the area were known and, even more important, that their activities were so carefully monitored that patrols were almost always sent out on specific information, rather than as in the earlier days simply to search and ambush areas in the hope of making contact with bandit groups in them.

A major operation, mounted in the Kuala Langat Forest Reserve (South) in July, 1952, resulted in a patrol led by a National Service Officer coming on a bandit camp and killing Lieu Kon Kim. It was perhaps the highlight action of the Battalion's whole tour of duty.

For the officers and men of the Battalion, the Malayan tour was without let-up. There were never enough men to cope with the patrolling tasks that needed to be done. For most of the time rifle companies were down to two platoons each of two sections, led on patrol, normally, by the platoon commander and the platoon sergeant respectively.

Each platoon would be committed to two weeks' active operational duties which usually included two jungle patrols of anything from two to five days, one or two night ambushes and at least two days on fifteen minutes notice to move.

1. The Officers of the 1st Battalion, Palestine, March, 1946.

2. The Sergeants of the 1st Battalion, Nelson Lines, Moascar Garrison, Egypt, 1947.

3. B Company of the 1st Battalion provided a Guard of Honour to mark the departure of the High Commissioner, General Sir Alan Cunningham, at the Damascus Gate, Jerusalem, on 14 May, 1948.

4. The Colours of the 2nd Battalion were returned from safe-keeping in Lahore Cathedral at the end of the Second World War.

5. The Officers of the 2nd Battalion in Lahore, India in 1946.

6. The final ceremonial parade of the 2nd Battalion in Lahore in India in 1947: Lieutenant-Colonel H. W. Dean (CO) and Major K.M.J. Dewar (2ic) accompany the inspecting officer.

7. Bandits killed and captured by C Company of the 1st Battalion on a jungle operation near Broga in Malaya in September, 1949.

8. The burial of a soldier of the 1st Battalion at the Cheras Road Military Cemetery near Kuala Lumpur, Malaya, in 1949.

9. If noise didn't matter, you could be comfortable in the Malayan jungle with the 1st Battalion in 1949.

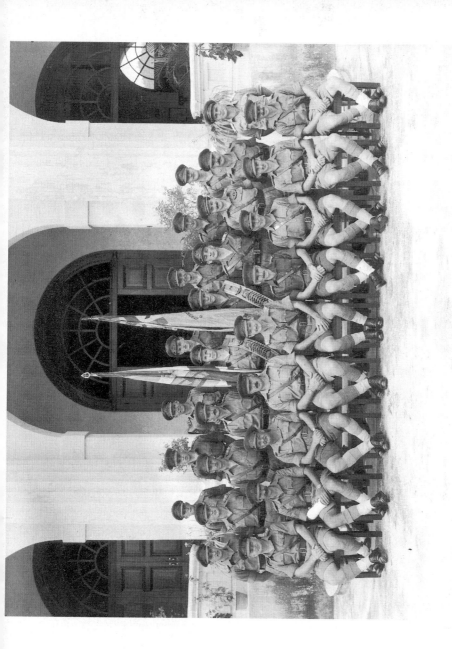

10. The Officers of the 1st Battalion in Penang, Malaya in 1950.

11. The Sergeants of the 1st Battalion in Penang, Malaya in 1950.

It was Battalion policy, not always achieved, to allow a platoon a thirty-six-hour break each fortnight, when, if in Selangor, they were allowed to spend a day and an evening sampling the somewhat primitive pleasures of Kuala Lumpur. The bigger towns in Malaya were, throughout the Emergency, largely free of threat to British troops off duty, so it was possible on these occasions to relax briefly. An alternative to Kuala Lumpur was for the platoon commander to take his platoon to camp for a night on the beautiful beaches at Port Dickson, some fifty miles from Kajang. Each of these breaks from operations also provided a chance to zero weapons and do some realistic shooting practise on specially prepared jungle ranges.

Throughout the Malayan tour a small nucleus of families of officers and men remained in Kuala Lumpur, where life was comparatively normal and where they were joined by husbands from Tac HQ and the rifle companies on their fortnightly 'exeats'!

The periods of rest and retraining in Penang were a great morale booster. Accommodated in a splendid permanent barracks over-looking the sea and a few miles only from Georgetown, the capital of the island, the Battalion briefly unwound from the tensions of operations. Training centred on shooting, the whole Battalion firing the annual range course. Plenty of sport was organized and many afternoons saw parties enjoying swimming on the idyllic tropical beaches of the island. Taken all in all, it was a real tonic in preparation for a further operational tour.

Almost all the men of the Battalion, throughout the Malayan tour, were National Servicemen. The Brigade Group system, instituted after the war, meant that they came from all over East Anglia and many, as a result, from the densely populated areas of Essex. Some, during their brief tours of perhaps only a year or eighteen months, achieved great distinction whilst with the Battalion and all gave of their best. It was in no small part due to their effort that the Battalion achieved such a great reputation in Malaya.

When in January, 1953, the time came for the Battalion to leave Malaya, it was given a splendid farewell. It marched triumphantly through the streets of Kuala Lumpur where the High Commissioner, General Sir Gerald Templer, together with the Sultan of Selangor, took the salute.

Parties were organized by the Selangor Rubber Planters and the local press described the Battalion's achievements in glowing tributes. As the Commanding Officer said, 'We hope we have done our job'. It was apparent that the people of Malaya thought this an understatement.

The Battalion embarked on the *Georgic* and sailed from Singapore on 21 January, 1953. It arrived in Liverpool on 12 February and, after an impressive welcoming ceremony, departed on block leave for a well-earned rest.

Part II

The Battalion sailed from Greece bound for Malaya on HMT *Dilwara*. Embarking at Salonika on 10 June, 1949, and calling at Port Said (where it picked up a draft of men), Aden and Colombo, it finally disembarked at Singapore on 1 July. The ship was somewhat crowded but the voyage was nonetheless pleasant for all ranks. The Band was kept busy playing concerts to entertain the passengers and ship's company during the three-week passage.

On arrival in the Far East the Battalion was seriously under-strength, numbering only twenty-eight officers and 520 other ranks. Main appointments at that time were filled as follows:

CO:	Lieutenant-Colonel I.L. Wight, OBE
2ic:	Major W.A. Heal, OBE
Adjt:	Captain G.C. Howgego
QM:	Captain J. Longstaff
RSM:	RSM B.D. Windley
OC A Company:	Major A. Parkin
CSM:	CSM Gingell
OC B Company:	Major W.W. Cook
CSM:	CSM Ramplin
OC C Company:	Major J.C. Devy
CSM:	CSM Keeble
OC D Company:	Captain A.F. Campbell
CSM:	CSM Randall
OC HQ Company:	Major O.K. Leach
CSM:	CSM Winter

The Battalion was accommodated in Nee Soon Transit Camp from its arrival in Singapore till 18 July. While there it carried out two weeks' weapon training and a jungle fighting familiarization course.

The Advance Party from Greece had already completed its course and had been sent north to begin taking over the Battalion's operational commitment. It was to be based near Sungei Besi, a small tin-mining town in the State of Selangor, some eight miles south of the State capital Kuala Lumpur, which was also the capital city of the whole of the Federation of Malaya.

On 18 July, travelling on the night train, the Battalion left Singapore bound for Sungei Besi, which was reached in the mid-morning of the next day. It was to come under command of the 2nd Guards Brigade and would eventually take over an operational commitment from the 3rd Battalion, the Grenadier Guards.

In Sungei Besi Camp, officers and men were accommodated in tents known in Ordnance terms as EPIP (European Personnel Indian Pattern) which were erected on concrete slabs and lit by electricity. Offices, messes and stores were housed in huts which were constructed out of palm-leaf panels, fixed to a timber frame, which were known as *bashas* (the Malay word for a shelter) and a few Nissen huts, used to house armouries and other valuable stores.

On leaving Greece, the Battalion's AF G1098 equipment was handed over and it had to draw a complete set on arrival in Malaya. At first the Ordnance Branch at GHQ Farelf ordered the QM to indent individually for all items (well over a thousand different pieces of equipment were involved). But, after the CO intervened, it was agreed that the stores would be issued using the AF G1098 equipment ledger which greatly simplified the process.

The Battalion's operational tour proper did not start until 20 August and the intervening month based in Sungei Besi was used to good effect to further the limited training already undergone. The Left Flank of the 2nd Battalion, the Scots Guards shared the camp and spent the month very helpfully passing on their knowledge of jungle warfare by means of lectures and demonstrations. A newly arrived draft of nine NCOs and 136 private soldiers (essential to build up the strength of the rifle companies before committing them to operations) was put through a two-week weapon and jungle training cadre. Then, with the new draft posted to companies, all four rifle companies completed a further fortnight's training designed finally to prepare them for operations. This fortnight was devoted almost completely to learning to live and move in the jungle and to practising the Immediate Action (IA) drills which were designed to respond to the sudden encounter with the enemy, which was so typical of operations in the jungle, where visibility was so circumscribed.

On 20 August, 1949, D Company moved to the small town of Kajang, nine miles to the south of Sungei Besi and took over operational responsibility for the Kajang Police District from the Right Flank of the 2nd Battalion, the Scots Guards.

Kajang was, for much of the Battalion's tour of duty in Malaya, to be its main base of operations and it was in this district, and slightly further afield in south Selangor, that it was to gain its greatest successes.

The first successful operation came quickly. On 24 August a small patrol of four to five men from 10 Platoon of D Company, under the command of 2nd Lieutenant J.G. Starling, killed three bandits in the area of Kampong Sungei Long, six miles south-east of Kuala Lumpur. 2nd Lieutenant Starling, with his group, including Sergeant Bradshaw, had been sent out to rendezvous with the remainder of his company, already deployed on an operation. Moving into the jungle, where they expected to find the company, they walked straight into a group of twenty bandits resting on a track. A brief fire fight ensued, during which the three bandits were accounted for, while the remainder ran off.

On 28 August B Company came under command of the 2nd Battalion, the Scots Guards and moved to Kuala Kubu Bahru for Operation Lemon, which was aimed at clearing bandits from a large area some miles north of Kuala Lumpur. In addition, a platoon of C Company, remaining at Sungei Besi, was earmarked as a reserve for this operation.

On 30 August a patrol from 12 Platoon of D Company under 2nd Lieutenant J.N. Kelly, operating with a number of Police Agents near Kajang, ambushed three bandits, killing two and wounding one.

On 6 September the Battalion Tac HQ moved to Kajang, together with C Company, to conduct more intensive operations in the Kajang Police District and came under command of Central Malaya Sub-District. A Company remained in Sungei Besi and was responsible for the training of a new draft and provision of a platoon on stand-by for Operation Lemon. B Company continued on Operation Lemon. The Operations Staff of Tac HQ moved into Kajang Police Station where the CO worked closely with the Officers Commanding the Police District (OCPD).

The C-in-C Far East Land Forces, General Sir John Harding, visited Tac HQ in Kajang on 12 September. He had already visited the Battalion at Sungei Besi on 25 August.

As a result of information received from the police on 25 September, C Company, with a platoon from D Company, carried out a sweep in the area of Broga, a remote village east of Kajang. A party of seven bandits was destroyed: four were killed and three captured.

On 28 September the Battalion suffered its first losses. A patrol of A Company was ambushed and two soldiers, Private L.R. Payne and Private D. Nobbs, were killed in the incident.

1 October saw A Company relieving D Company at Kajang, the latter returning to Sungei Besi.

Tac HQ, A and C Companies in Kajang reverted to the command of the 2nd Guards Brigade on 9 October and the remainder of the month was spent patrolling and ambushing throughout the Kajang Police District. It was at this time that the personalized nature of the campaign developed and the Battalion began to see Lieu Kon Kim, the bearded Chinese leader of the Kajang district MRLA, or the Kajang Gang as it came to be known, as their number one enemy.

On 1 November, however, the area of operations was changed. The Battalion temporarily took over command of Operation Lemon in North Selangor from the 2nd Battalion, the Scots Guards, and Tac HQ with C and D Companies moved to Kuala Kubu Bahru to join B Company, leaving A Company in Kajang. This disposition was to be shortlived, as on 5 November B Company was sent on detachment to Batu Arang, in the main to guard the coalmine there, and on 10 November command of the operation changed to the 2nd Battalion, the Coldstream Guards, which took B, C and D Companies under their command. As a result Battalion Tac HQ returned to Sungei Besi.

On 22 December C and D Companies returned to Sungei Besi and B Company at Batu Arang came under the command of the 2nd Battalion, the 7th Gurkha Rifles. The period from 1 November to 22 December saw operations continue with great intensity, though with little reward to show for the determined effort put into patrolling. A number of contacts were made with bandits, but only two were killed.

On 30 November, however, 2nd Lieutenant J.G. Starling earned the first Military Cross awarded to the Battalion in Malaya. His patrol was ambushed by bandits, but 'by dint of his courage, skill and leadership' he turned the tables on the enemy and routed them, causing them to flee, leaving behind much of their equipment.

The period 23 to 31 December saw the bulk of the Battalion free from operations and able to celebrate Christmas while preparing for the next deployment against the bandits.

Early in 1950 the Battalion was once more committed to intensive operations. Initially, little reliable information on the MRLA was forthcoming, and patrols and ambushes were largely based on an intelligent appreciation of the ground and the likely areas in which bandits might be camped or on the move. Successes were slow in coming, but the general operational expertise of the Battalion was developing apace.

The arrival in Malaya in April of Lieutenant-General Sir Harold Briggs, to take up the newly created post of Director of Operations, was to have a dramatic effect as the year progressed. Two of his innovations made an immediate impact on the Battalion's operations. In the first place, the expansion of the Special Branch led to more and better information being made available to patrols, and secondly the resettlement of remote 'squatter' settlements considerably narrowed down likely areas of operation of the MRLA groups and forced them to expose themselves through taking greater risks to collect supplies and information from the outlying peasant communities and rubber tapper lines that remained available to them.

On 4 January, 1950, B Company moved from Batu Arang down to Kajang to relieve A Company which returned to base at Sungei Besi.

During the period 15 to 21 January A, B and C Companies were committed to operations out of Sungei Besi and Kajang in South Selangor. C Company had two contacts with the enemy, killing two bandits and wounding two more.

For a short while, from 22 to 26 January, the CO was responsible for operations throughout Selangor, with two companies of the 1st Battalion, the Coldstream Guards, under command. Tac HQ briefly moved to Kuala Kubu Bahru during this period. Then, the 2nd Battalion, the Green Howards, took over responsibility for North Selangor and Tac HQ returned once more to Kajang.

In February a patrol from 12 Platoon of D Company located a bandit camp in the Kachau area to the north-east of Kajang. The patrol attacked the camp and resistance was offered by the bandits. In the fight which followed, three bandits were killed. For gallantry in this action 2nd Lieutenant J.N. Kelly was awarded the Military Cross and Lance-Corporal D.E.R. Wicks the Military Medal.

The deployment out of Kajang and Sungei Besi continued until the middle of May. Companies were rotated between the two places during this period. Usually one company was based at Sungei Besi and was responsible not only for operational commitments there, but also for the training of newly arrived drafts.

From 5 to 14 February and again on 22 February, a troop from the 26th Field Regiment, RA, carried out artillery 'shoots' against areas known to be used by bandit groups.

On 11 March B Company killed one bandit and wounded and

captured another in an action six miles north of Kajang. The following day, in an action near Broga, ten miles to the east of Kajang, D Company killed three more.

In the latter half of March a major operation called Jack Pot, involving several battalions in the States of Pahang, Selangor and Negri-Sembilan, was carried out. The operation continued for several weeks, with company patrols often being re-supplied by air. The aim was to pressurize the enemy by such large-scale action that he would reveal his whereabouts, but it scarcely succeeded. The enormous effort involved in such large-scale operations rarely if ever paid off, at least in terms of concrete results.

22 March saw C Company, together with three Police Jungle Squads, involved in searching an area of thick scrub (balouka) behind the Cheras Road Cemetery, four miles south of Kuala Lumpur. Two members of C Company, Sergeant G. Thomas and Corporal Harris, were slightly wounded during this operation, but three bandits were killed after a lengthy and very tense search of the dense undergrowth. Sergeant Thomas was awarded a C-in-C's Certificate for gallantry displayed during this and other operations.

During the first three months of 1950 the constant loss of NCOs and men returning to the United Kingdom on posting or at the end of their National Service began to cause major problems for the Battalion. New drafts arrived but very few NCOs came with them. Over the period seventeen Junior NCOs left and only four arrived to take their places.

In March the Battalion achieved a major sporting success by winning the Far East Land Forces Inter-Unit Hockey Championship. Considering the pace of operations at the time it was a splendid achievement. The team had played only two or three matches prior to going to Singapore for the final and on each occasion most members of the team were almost literally plucked from the jungle in order to play.

April saw another example of a major operation involving careful and detailed planning. It was called Operation Blast and lasted from the 11th to the 20th of the month. A, C and D Companies took part, with two companies of the 1st/7th Gurkhas. A troop of 26th Field Regiment, RA, a troop of the 4th Hussars and four Police Jungle Squads were under command.

Several pieces of information led to the conclusion that a concentration of over a hundred bandits was gathered at the time of the operation to the north-east and east of Broga. The intention of the operation was to seal off the area, then to bombard it for three days, then to sweep through it. C and D Companies, with one company of the 1st/7th Gurkhas, were to sweep the area with A Company and the other Gurkha Company remaining in ambush after the bombardment. The Battalion's 3" Mortars and the field guns of the Artillery provided only a minor element of the bombardment, for which the Royal Air Force used a squadron of Lincoln Bombers, a squadron of Brigands, a squadron of Tempests and Spitfires and a Sunderland Flying Boat.

Elaborate precautions were taken to ensure surprise for the operation. A Company was moved into the area at night in civilian lorries with Malay Police drivers dressed in civilian clothes. D Company was routed in a very roundabout way to the point where it left its vehicles and no information was released to the press until after 18 April.

Despite all the effort put into the operation little success was achieved though further intelligence concerning bandit movements in the area was gathered.

As if to demonstrate the futility of large-scale operations four small patrols on 4, 9 and 10 May achieved dramatic results.

On 4 May the Mortar Platoon, used as an infantry patrol, and a party from C Company under Sergeant Ashdown, together with a Police Jungle Squad, were sent out on information to search an area some miles from Kajang. A group of bandits was encountered and a fire fight developed in which the mortars killed five bandits and C Company killed one and captured four. The determined action by the Mortar Platoon led to the loss of Lance-Corporal H.R. Simmonds who was killed in the assault on the bandit group.

On the morning of 9 May a patrol from C Company, acting on information, searched an area of the Brookside Rubber Estate near Kajang, together with a Police Jungle Squad. An occupied bandit camp was located and three of four bandits were killed. Two pistols, a shotgun and a grenade were recovered.

The same evening, following the surrender of a bandit in the afternoon, a D Company patrol searched part of the Dominion Rubber Estate, a few miles east of Kajang. They located a camp and killed four bandits in it. Two rifles, grenades and ammunition were recovered.

Early the following morning, 10 May, 8 Platoon of C Company with 12 Platoon of D Company searched the area of a tin mine four miles east of Kajang and killed one bandit during the operation. A rifle and ammunition were recovered.

Another of General Briggs's plans was now to affect the Battalion directly. He felt that a large concentration of the Army in one part of Malaya, with the idea of flooding the area with troops, might eliminate terrorism from it once and for all. The scheme was put into effect and tried over a period of some months, but then it was dropped. The area chosen was the Southern State of Johore and Army units already there were reinforced by the Battalion as well as the 1st Battalion, the Green Howards, the 2nd Battalion, the 2nd Gurkha Rifles and elements of two other Gurkha Battalions.

The Battalion got its orders to move in the middle of May and, with the exception of D Company, had concentrated in Sungei Besi by the 18th. A small rear party, largely comprising the Band, was to remain there, while the rest of the Battalion moved by road and by train down to Johore between 18 and 23 May.

The Battalion now came under command of the 26th Gurkha Infantry Brigade, based in Johore Bahru on the north side of the causeway to Singapore Island. The Battalion HQ was located in Segamat in northern Johore and the companies were, on arrival, deployed in company bases. A Company was detached some eighty miles away under command of the 2nd/6th Gurkha Rifles. B Company was located at Tenang on Voules Estate, C Company on a large Dunlop Rubber Estate a few miles north of Segamat and D Company to the south of the town on a rubber estated at Bekok.

For some while after arrival in Johore companies sent out patrols generally, in their operational areas of responsibility, in order to build up a detailed knowledge of the ground. Incidents in the Battalion area were very frequent, including the murder of rubber estate workers, thefts of workers' identity cards and the burning of estate buildings and vehicles. The night trains running between Singapore and Kuala Lumpur were frequently shot at, within the Battalion's area.

That there were plenty of bandits in the district was not in question, but information about their organization and methods was practically non-existent. Part of the problem stemmed from difficulty in establishing a close working relationship with the police in the area. Whereas the most excellent co-operation had been built up with the police in Kajang, it seemed in Segamat that they resented the arrival of the military on the scene. As the weeks went by, however, this unhappy situation did improve and some successes were achieved.

A number of incidents in D Company area early in June suggested that a large MRLA group was operating there and, as a result, a large operation – Operation Dunmow – involving B Company, D

Company, 7 Platoon C Company, the Mortar Platoon and three Police Jungle Squads, was mounted from 6 to 9 June, with the aim of tracking them down.

On the first day of the operation a police party had three contacts with the bandits and recovered five bandit packs. Then, on 7 June four bandits walked into an ambush laid by Sergeant Dunne's section of 5 Platoon of B Company. One bandit was killed and an American Mk 1 Carbine was recovered.

On 14 June D Company moved from Bekok to Labis where they were based on the Johore Labis Estate. A successful ambush laid by 2nd Lieutenant G.F.N. Charrington, with a patrol from 10 Platoon of D Company on 17 June, resulted in two of a party of three terrorists being killed and one wounded, and the recovery of three rifles and ammunition.

On 19 June C Company base was moved to a small rubber estate close to the village of Batu Anam, to the north of Segamat on the main north-south Malayan trunk road.

A section of 4 Platoon of B Company, under 2nd Lieutenant the Hon T. Ponsonby, killed two bandits in an ambush on 30 June. A Thompson sub-machine gun and a rifle with ammunition were recovered. The ambush was sprung just as darkness fell, only thirty-five minutes after it had been laid.

At the end of June, Lieutenant-Colonel I.L. Wight, OBE, handed over command of the Battalion. The Battalion's successful tour in Malaya owed much to Lieutenant-Colonel Wight's leadership at the outset; his insistence on high standards of training and his determination and enthusiasm certainly inspired those who worked under him. The award of the DSO to him was published in *The London Gazette* on 4 July. The citation for the award is demonstrative of Colonel Wight's leadership and also shows how well the Battalion's tour of duty in Malaya had started. The citation reads:

Lieutenant-Colonel Wight commanded the 1st Battalion, the Suffolk Regiment during operations between 4 and 11 May, against the bandit forces in South Selangor. As a result of these operations, contact was made with them on four separate occasions, during which fourteen bandits were killed and seven others captured or surrendered. In addition, from the information obtained from the latter, fifty-eight known bandit supporters were arrested.

These outstanding successes have undoubtedly caused serious disruption of the bandit organization in South Selangor.

A principal cause of these successes has been Lieutenant-Colonel

Wight's most able leadership of his Battalion. He backed up skilful planning and execution of the operations entailed by leadership of a very high order. On more than one occasion he assumed direct command when contact had been gained and set an example of cool leadership which was the inspiration of all ranks.

The tremendous enthusiasm, speed of action and determination to close with the enemy, which was the outstanding feature displayed by his Battalion, and which in several cases made all the difference between success and failure, have directly resulted from his personal drive and the offensive spirit which he has maintained in his men over a very long period of operations.

Lieutenant-Colonel P.A. Morcombe, OBE, succeeded Lieutenant-Colonel Wight in command of the Battalion.

The month of July saw the rate of incidents in the Battalion area persist at a high level and in consequence operations of great intensity forged ahead. All companies sent out a constant stream of patrols and ambushes. One or two larger operations involving up to two companies were also carried out. The Mortars were involved in a number of 'shoots', on several occasions linked to bombing sorties by the Royal Air Force.

Of particular interest, in view of the good long-term results that followed, the CO was in mid-July ordered to locate Tac HQ in Segamat police station. Initially the move caused dismay in police ranks, but, working side by side from then onwards, a mutual trust built up between the Battalion and the police which fostered success.

Following the change of command, senior appointments in the Battalion were held as follows:

CO:	Lieutenant-Colonel P.A. Morcombe, OBE
2ic:	Major W.A. Heal, OBE
Adjt:	Captain G.C. Howgego
QM:	Captain H.S.R. Case
RSM:	RSM B.D. Windley
OC A Company:	Major A. Parkin
CSM:	CSM Collen
OC B Company:	Major C.J.V. Fisher-Hoch
CSM:	CSM Ramplin
OC C Company:	Major J.C. Devy
CSM:	CSM Keeble
OC D Company:	Major L. Field, MC
CSM:	CSM Randall
OC HQ Company:	Major O.K. Leach
CSM:	CSM Winter

On 5 August 8 Platoon of C Company went out on a two-day patrol in jungle some ten miles from the company base in the Ulu Jementah Forest Reserve. On 6 August a bandit camp was found which had been used in the last forty-eight hours; it was destroyed. On the way out to the jungle edge to return to base, contact was made with a party of five Min Yuen. A brief fire fight ensued and Sergeant J.A. Ashdown, 8 Platoon Commander, was shot and killed. One bandit was wounded, but he escaped, leaving behind his pack.

Early in August A Company, less 1 platoon, returned from a ten-week period under command of the 2nd/6th Gurkha Rifles and on 8 August they were committed to operations in the Battalion area. The last platoon did not return to the Battalion area until 30 August.

The remainder of August and September was spent in intensive patrolling and, except for one occasion, no contact was made with the enemy. It seemed that the Battalion was always within reach of the bandits yet they managed somehow to escape. A number of very large bandit camps was found, in one case with accommodation for 250 men, including over fifty well-constructed 'atap' huts.

At this time the Battalion was unexpectedly able to deploy more troops on the ground than previously. As a result of the outbreak of the Korean War the Government had been forced to increase the period of National Service from eighteen months to two years. National Servicemen with only days to serve were less than happy with the news, which, to make matters worse, was first heard on Radio Malaya! The increased strength of the Platoons in Rifle Companies which resulted, however, was of great benefit to the Battalion.

A patrol from 12 Platoon of D Company made contact on 17 September. A fire fight broke out as the patrol attacked a bandit camp and continued for over twenty minutes. One bandit was killed and one was wounded. Two rifles, a bren gun magazine and ammunition were recovered. The camp was capable of holding 100 men and most fled when the sentry opened fire on the patrol. The final bandit withdrawal was signalled by a call on a bugle. Tracks from the camp were followed for two days and patrols from A and C Companies were sent into the area in the hope of cutting off the bandits' retreat, but nothing more was seen of them.

Operations continued without any fresh contacts until 2 October when the Battalion area of responsibility was handed over to the 1st Battalion, the Worcestershire Regiment, and it left for the island of Penang in the north for a period of rest and retraining.

The Intelligence Officer, Lieutenant D.E. Hookham-Miller, with a small convoy comprising his own car, two jeeps and a Humber scout car mounting twin Vickers 'K' machine guns, was the last to leave Kajang on 3 October.

On arrival at Semenyih the convoy was stopped at the Police Station by a CQMS from the Malay Regiment, who reported that he had been fired on by an ambush a few minutes before on his way south from Kajang towards Semenyih. Lieutenant Hookham-Miller sent the scout car northwards along the road to shoot up the position and followed with the rest of the convoy a couple of minutes later. The bandits did not fire at the scout car, but did at the remaining vehicles. The two bren-gunners on the jeeps, Private Tobin of D Company and Private Gutteridge of C Company, returned heavy and accurate fire on the bandit positions and the convoy escaped unscathed. The Intelligence Officer deployed the bren-gunners to fire back into the ambush positions and the scout car, under command of Corporal McNally of HQ Company, drove several times to and fro through the position, bringing heavy fire to bear on the enemy. He fired eight drum magazines into the ambush during this period and was fired on continuously by the bandits until, after approximately half an hour, as dusk was descending, the bandits withdrew. A Police Jungle Squad and armoured vehicle then arrived and, as darkness fell, the convoy continued its journey, somewhat shaken but none the worse for the experience.

During the rest and retraining period which lasted for two months, the Battalion was housed in Minden Barracks six miles from Georgetown. The barracks were built just prior to the Second World War and were originally named Glugor Barracks, but had been appropriately enough recently renamed Minden Barracks by the 1st Battalion, the King's Own Yorkshire Light Infantry, another Minden Regiment, whose main base it still was.

The time spent in Penang was thoroughly enjoyed by the whole Battalion. There were no active bandits on the island and, for the first time for a year, it was possible to relax without the fear of being caught off guard.

Training was concentrated on improving shooting and all companies fired the annual range course on the very good ranges at Butterworth on the mainland opposite the island. With constant ferries operating, this was achieved with little trouble and a gratifying high standard of shooting resulted.

After classification was complete, a final day on the ranges saw the Battalion Rifle Meeting. Major C.J.V. Fisher-Hoch, OC B Company, won the individual championship and his Company also won the company shoot. It was later to go on to come third in the Malaya Shooting Shield.

With the Battalion together for this brief period, a major effort was also expended in a series of inter-platoon and inter-company sporting activities. Unfortunately, the stay in Penang came to an end before all leagues and knock-out competitions were completed. C Company demonstrated considerable prowess on the football field, winning the inter-platoon knock-out football competition and, surprisingly, looking set, after beating the Band and Signals team, to win the hockey league.

Minden Day, which could not be celebrated in August with the Battalion split up and heavily committed to operations, was also enjoyed in Penang. 24 November was the day chosen and it began with a Drum Head Service. A swimming gala, however, was the central event of the day.

Both the Officers' and Sergeants' Messes pursued active social programmes in Penang. Two formal dinners were held in the Officers' Mess at which the Commander HQ Malaya, Major-General R.E. Urquhart, the Commander 18th Infantry Brigade, Brigadier R.J.K. Pye, and the Chief Police Officer of Penang were entertained. The main event in the Sergeants' Mess was the Minden Ball, to which the Officers and their wives were invited.

Above all, the stay in Penang was a time for relaxing. Married members of the Battalion were accommodated with their families in Leave Hostels in Georgetown and they and everyone else had constant opportunities for enjoying the marvellous swimming on the lovely beaches of this beautiful island.

Well before the end of the rest and retraining period, it was learned that the Battalion would be returning to operations in the State of Selangor. It would be part of the 18th Infantry Brigade which had been born out of the 2nd Guards Brigade, now that only one Guards Battalion, the 2nd Battalion, the Scots Guards, remained. The area of responsibility was to be the South Selangor Police Circle with a base in Kajang and the Central Selangor Police Circle with Battalion Rear HQ located in a newly refurbished hutted and basha camp on Wardieburn Estate, just north of Kuala Lumpur.

Arrangements for the move went ahead and the Battalion took leave of Penang on the last day of November, 1950.

On 1 December Tac HQ was established in the same Kajang School building as before and operational responsibility was assumed from 1400 that day. A, B and D Companies went to Kajang initially, but on 3 December B Company moved out on detachment to the Tarun Estate to the east of Kajang, while D Company took up residence on the Bukit Prang Estate west of Kajang, five miles north of the village of Dingkil. This left A Company based in Kajang at readiness to provide a reserve in the other company 'framework' areas, but also with a small area of responsibility of its own around Kajang itself.

Battalion Rear HQ moved into Wardieburn Camp which was only partially rebuilt and prepared for it, and C Company went immediately out on detachment to Bukit Darah Estate at the 19th Mile on the main road north-west out of Kuala Lumpur, leading to Kuala Selangor.

Operations now recommended in earnest with all platoons entering the general cycle of twelve days' operations followed by thirty-six hours' rest wherever possible!

On 6 December the Brigade Commander visited all detachments and the next day the GOC South Malaya District, Major-General R.C.O. Hedley, CBE, DSO, did the same. They were both surprised and pleased to find so few men at any of the detachments!

The first contact after returning to operations was made by 1 Platoon of A Company under 2nd Lieutenant Black on 6 December when his patrol saw a small party of bandits at 200 yards' range. Fire was opened on the group but they escaped.

Two days later a platoon from C Company operating out of Bukit Darah came on three bandits in the Bukit Mayang area, killing one of the three and recovering one rifle and ammunition.

On 17 December a party of forty bandits committed three murders and set fire to some newly constructed labour lines on the Galloway Estate, about two miles south of D Company's base. A patrol to follow up the bandits was sent out by D Company. A small group of bandits (three were seen) was found and attacked at the western extremity of the estate, where the rubber gave way to the vast swamps of the Kuala Langat Forest Reserve (North). Two were killed in this action and two rifles, a shotgun and three packs were recovered.

Christmas Day, 1950, passed uneventfully. No leave was granted to rifle companies which, although they did not actively patrol, retained a stand-by section with everyone else resting between operations in Company bases.

At 1930 on New Year's Eve a moving ceremony took place at the Cheras Road Military Cemetery, just south of Kuala Lumpur. A memorial service to the men of the Battalion who had died or been killed on operations since arriving in Malaya in 1949 was held. One hundred men of the Battalion paraded under the command of Major O.K. Leach. The service opened with a hymn and was conducted by the Senior Chaplain at HQ Malaya. The Commanding Officer read the lesson, the Band accompanied the hymns and Drummers sounded the Last Post and Reveille.

1951 opened with an intense programme of patrols and ambushes. Only too frequently patrols returned with nothing to report. But successes were slowly and painstakingly achieved as the year progressed. The very best of relations existed between the Battalion and the Police, particularly at Kajang, and information suitable for acting on by the Battalion, which became ever more frequent, was always passed to it by the Police.

With many months experience behind them, patrol commanders were now becoming much more expert in finding the enemy in the jungle. It was still difficult to bring bandits to action when they were found, however, and it would always be difficult to move silently and clearly observe the enemy positions in the dense undergrowth. Tracking in the jungle was greatly helped by the use of Ibans from Sarawak, and almost every patrol would take two of these jungle-wise experts with them.

On 11 January, acting on Police information, 3 Platoon of A Company with 10 Platoon of D Company, searched an area of overgrown rubber to the north-west of D Company's base. 3 Platoon followed a track which led to a small, occupied bandit camp. A brief fire fight led to one Min Yuen member being killed. A .32 revolver and ammunition was recovered, together with two packs containing clothing and documents.

A patrol from D Company was sent out on 22 January to search an area of secondary jungle and balouka just to the west of Kampong Jenderam. A small, deserted, but clearly still-used camp was located during the day and it was decided to ambush it at night. Just after midnight two men approached the camp. The ambush was sprung and both were killed. Both the bandits were Malay; one was discovered to be the leader of the Kampong Jenderam Min Yuen. A .32 revolver and ammunition and a 36 grenade were recovered.

This incident was to culminate in the unusual step of resettling the whole of the Malay population of Kampong Jenderam. Most MRLA members were Chinese and sought sustenance from Chinese settlements, but the Malays of Jenderam were disaffected and supported the communist cause and it was decided that they should be moved to a less sensitive area.

Operation Alka-Selza, to resettle the village, took place from 13 to 17 February. It involved the Police and Civil Government and the whole Battalion was used to provide a cordon round the village. The operation went without a hitch and removed in one fell swoop a major source of support for the MRLA in the Battalion area in South Selangor.

C Company was withdrawn from Operation Alka-Selza back to their area north of Kuala Lumpur on the 16 February and a combined patrol of 7 and 8 Platoons, acting on information, located and stormed a bandit camp in deep jungle the next day, killing four bandits and recovering their weapons.

Battalion operations in South Selangor now tended to switch to the general area west and south-west of Kajang. B Company had already moved from the Tarun Estate to establish a temporary Company base at Sepang, to the south-east of the great swamps of the Kuala Langat Forest Reserve (South).

On 18 February the Police produced information that Lieu Kon Kim, and a platoon were based in a narrow strip of swamp bordering the Sungei Limau Manis to the south-east of D Company's base. A major operation was planned in the area on 20 and 21 February. A, B and D Companies were used, with a troop from the 54th Field Regiment, RA, a troop of the 13th/18th Hussars and the Battalion 3″ Mortar Platoon in support. The Royal Air Force bombed and straffed the area in a co-ordinated fire programme, but company patrols which then searched it once again found no sign of bandit camps or movement.

On 27 February information was received that a meeting of the Communist State Executive Committee would take place the next day in a house in a village some eight miles from D Company's base. The Company surrounded the area of the house at night and one party bumped into three bandits unexpectedly. Fire was opened but no kills resulted. At first light a patrol under Lieutenant E.H. Morgan broke into the house where the meeting was supposed to have been and killed one armed bandit, the only occupant. There was every sign that a meeting had taken place, but the real quarry had flown.

3 Platoon of A Company killed one bandit in an ambush on the northern edge of the Kuala Langat Forest Reserve (South) on 28 February and recovered a rifle and ammunition.

An extremely well-executed immediate ambush was sprung by a section of 3 Platoon of A Company under the command of Lieutenant A.H.V. Gillmore on 3 March. Bandits stole some identity cards from workers on the Tarun Estate before first light that morning and Lieutenant Gillmore's section happened to be patrolling in the vicinity; he was alerted by radio to look out for the bandits. While moving through overgrown rubber, the leading scout saw a party of five bandits coming towards them. He gave the silent signal for an immediate ambush. The section took cover to the side of the track and waited. Unsuspecting, the bandits, well spaced out, moved into the killing zone, the ambush was sprung and three were killed. Three rifles, a shotgun and packs containing documents were recovered from this operation.

13 March saw companies changing location. A Company moved from Kajang to take over from D Company on the Bukit Prang Estate; C Company moved from Bukit Darah in the north down to Kajang; D Company to Wardieburn Camp to take over responsibility for Kuala Lumpur Central Police Circle and B Company, having returned from Sepang, remained at Kajang.

Not long after D Company was redeployed, it suffered a serious loss when Sergeant D. Westin, commanding 11 Platoon, was killed. On 8 April he was patrolling Bukit Cheraka Forest Reserve to the north-west of Kuala Lumpur when he came across fresh bandit tracks. The tracks led the Platoon towards an occupied camp and, as the assault went in, the bandits put up unusually stiff resistance. A battle developed in which Sergeant Westin was shot and killed. Two bandits were also killed in the engagement. B and C Companies were immediately moved into the Bukit Cheraka area to pursue the remnants of the bandit group, but no further contact resulted and patrols were withdrawn after forty-eight hours.

3 Platoon of A Company, on patrol to the south-west of the Kuala Langat Forest Reserve (South) on 19 April, found and followed fresh bandit tracks for some distance and contacted two Min Yuen. In the action which followed both bandits were killed but not before one had thrown a 36 grenade at the patrol, which fortunately failed to detonate. A .32 pistol was recovered, together with some documents after this action.

The 11 May witnessed a major action involving a section of 8 Platoon C Company, under the command of Sergeant Wright, the Platoon Sergeant. While patrolling the Ulu Langat Forest Reserve to the east of the Kuala Lumpur/Kajang road, the section was fired on by a large party of bandits from high ground. Sergeant Wright and three members of the patrol were wounded in the initial burst of fire and Lance-Corporal Price, the National Service section commander, assumed command of the patrol. He led the remaining men of the section up the hill and assaulted the enemy positions. As a result of this determined action, three bandits were killed and a quantity of weapons, ammunition and equipment was recovered. Unfortunately, one of the 8 Platoon men, Private Killick was seriously wounded and died of his wounds.

For his extremely gallant and distinguished behaviour in this operation Lance Corporal Price was awarded the Distinguished Conduct Medal.

On 3 June an ambush party from B Company succeeded in killing a senior Min Yuen member and recovering a .38 pistol and ammunition. The ambush was sprung just after last light.

9 Platoon of C Company, on patrol in jungle near the Kuala Lumpur/Kajang Road, contacted bandits on two occasions on 9 June. One bandit was killed and a .45 pistol was recovered, together with equipment and documents. A food dump was also found in the area containing eight large sealed tins of rice.

On the same day a B Company patrol shot and killed a bandit courier. A .38 revolver and several important documents were recovered.

8 Platoon of C Company continued the month's run of successes on 13 June by killing a bandit while patrolling in the Broga area. A rifle and a pack containing documents were recovered.

On 23 June a patrol from 9 Platoon of C Company, led by Corporal Thompson, shot and killed a bandit in jungle close to the 9th Mile Village on the Kuala Lumpur/Kajang road.

A Police party travelling by vehicle near Broga was ambushed at 1100 on 28 June. Six Special Constables were killed and two wounded. The stand-by Platoon at Tac HQ (7 Platoon of C Company) raced to the scene of the ambush to follow up the enemy and succeeded in killing one bandit.

On 16 July companies again changed locations (Operation Roundabout) with A Company moving to Bukit Darah, C Company to Bukit Prang Estate and D Company to Kajang where B Company remained.

In July, after an absence of two and a half years, Support Company was re-established in the Battalion, with a Medium Machine Gun, an Anti-Tank and a Mortar Platoon (the latter having been in existence independently throughout the Malayan tour). The Company was based at Wardieburn Camp and functioned as a normal operational company except for one week each month, which was set aside for specialist training with its newly acquired weapons.

It soon established its efficiency in the jungle, when, only two weeks after its formation, the Anti-Tank Platoon had its first success. Patrolling in jungle to the north of Kuala Lumpur, it came on to a newly used track which it followed until it left the jungle and entered an overgrown rubber estate. There, sitting on a log, were two bandits who fled as the Platoon came out of the jungle. A hectic chase ensued and both were killed and their weapons recovered. One of the bandits was the senior Indian member of the MRLA in Selangor. Four days after this success the Platoon registered another kill in the same area.

On 22 July the Battalion killed its hundredth bandit. A small ambush party from 8 Platoon under Corporal Meacock was just getting into position on the edge of a rubber estate overlooking a well-used track entering the estate through a patch of balouka when a party of four bandits was seen at two hundred yards' distance, moving towards the group. The ambush party froze where they were, partly exposed, but they were seen shortly afterwards and forced to open fire sooner than they would have wished. Two bandits were killed and two escaped into the balouka as darkness descended. A rifle and sten gun and ammunition were recovered.

The measuring of success in terms of a head count of enemy killed was an important element in the maintenance of morale within the Battalion during the Malayan tour of duty. Countless numbers of patrols and ambushes went out every day in a gruelling treadmill of operations which almost always achieved no result. The determination to succeed was stimulated by the competitive spirit engendered by the head count. It was a very callous business, but, then, most men in the Battalion had at one time or another witnessed at first hand the brutal murders and mutilation inflicted on the innocent by the enemy in their attempts to terrorize the population into supporting them.

On 30 July Mr Thomas E. Dewey, Governor of New York State, accompanied by Mr Malcolm MacDonald, Commissioner-General for the United Kingdom in South-East Asia, visited Tac HQ at Kajang. Their visit coincided with the return to base of a patrol from 5 Platoon of B Company, with the Company Commander, Major K.M.J. Dewar. Mr Dewey inspected the Platoon closely, talking to a number of the men and was particularly interested to meet a group of Iban trackers attached to the Battalion.

In July RSM Windley left on a home posting after two years in Malaya with the Battalion. His place was taken by RSM K. Duffy, who was to remain with the Battalion for the rest of the Malayan tour.

Minden Day, the 1st of August, provided an opportunity for most officers and men to relax if only for one day. Skeleton staff remained at out-stations while most of the Battalion assembled at Wardieburn Camp for the usual festivities.

The Companies dispersed to their bases the next day and routine patrolling and ambushing tasks resumed. On 3 August a section from 9 Platoon of C Company was placed in an ambush position on the Brooklands Rubber Estate on the northern edge of the Kuala Langat Forest Reserve (South). At 1830, just before dusk, a party of bandits entered the ambush. Two were killed and three made good their escape, though one was seen to be wounded. One rifle and an old wartime Japanese hand grenade were recovered.

On 6 August a section of 12 Platoon of D Company, operating out of Tac HQ at Kajang, under command of Sergeant Smith, was ordered to patrol the Sungei Renching Estate, south-east of Kajang. As the section moved off from its vehicles it came under fire from a small party of bandits which it had obviously surprised. In the brief fire fight which ensued, Sergeant Smith was wounded in the stomach. The bandits then made good their escape. A search of the immediate area revealed a resting place where food was still cooking on a small fire. Two bandit packs were recovered.

On 10 August a section of 8 Platoon of C Company was ordered to set up an ambush on the Brooklands Estate, between the swamp to the south of the rubber and the labour lines on the estate, from where it was thought by the Police that bandits in the Kuala Langat Forest Reserve (South) were collecting food and information about the Security Forces.

It was approximately 1830 and the Platoon Commander was just siting his men for the night ambush when the bren-gunner noticed a group of four or five cyclists in normal rubber tappers' clothes about 100 yards away, moving rapidly along the rough track which it had been intended to ambush from the direction of the swamp towards the labour lines. The first thought was that they were workers returning late. But then it was realized that all the cyclists had bandit packs strapped on the carriers. Fire was opened immediately and two of the party were killed; the remainder abandoned their cycles and fled off in the gathering dusk towards the labour lines.

The section searched the lines but, of course, failed to identify the cyclists among the other very frightened occupants. The five packs recovered contained a 36 grenade, some ammunition and a number of important letters and documents including a photograph of one of those killed (a woman) posing with Lieu Kon Kim.

On 20 August the OCPD Rawang, a town to the north of Kuala Lumpur, was killed in an ambush and A Company at Bukit Darah sent out a platoon to pursue the bandits who carried out the ambush. They moved extremely quickly and were at the scene of the ambush very soon after it occurred. Tracks were followed from the ambush position and pursued in earnest. The bandits were contacted and three were killed. On the following day fleeting contact was made again and one more bandit was shot and killed.

9 Platoon of C Company was patrolling the western edge of the Kuala Langat Forest Reserve (North) on 29 August when it came on fresh tracks and followed them. They led to a small occupied bandit camp; the camp was rushed and one occupant was killed. He was later identified as a Communist Party Branch Committee Member. A .32 pistol, ammunition and five packs were recovered.

Outside the all-consuming operational life of the Battalion, the end of August witnessed a sad occasion when the Band reverted to the home establishment and sailed for the United Kingdom. Under Band-Master Mitchenall it had been with the Battalion for two years in Malaya. It had contributed enormously to the life of the Battalion, primarily as musicians of course, but also on the sports field and even occasionally, when the pressure was really on, on operations in the jungle. Outside the unit, it had always had a very full musical programme and carried the good name of the Battalion far and wide in Malaya, often performing at the Selangor Club, the Kuala Lumpur Races and regularly supplying the dance band at the Galloway NAAFI Club in Kuala Lumpur.

On 4 September the Anti-Tank Platoon, patrolling in jungle north-east of Kuala Lumpur, unearthed a large ammunition and explosives dump which contained sticks of plastic explosive, gun-cotton primers and slabs, eight grenades, detonators, fuse wire and over 800 rounds of ammunition.

The next day a section of 11 Platoon of D Company contacted a part of five bandits in a resting place. Fire was opened at a range of two hundred yards as the bandits dashed for cover; one was killed.

Major-General R.C.O. Hedley, GOC South Malaya District, paid another visit to Tac HQ at Kajang on 6 September and on the same day 8 Platoon of C Company, detached at Sepang, was patrolling inside the eastern edge of the Kuala Langat Forest Reserve (South) swamps, hoping to locate tracks exiting the swamp into the balouka. A newly used track was found and followed out of the swamp. A shot was fired at the patrol and the leading scout returned the fire, killing what turned out to be a bandit sentry on the track. The patrol advanced rapidly along the track but other bandits had already fled. A search of the surrounding area revealed a crudely made electrically detonated land mine on a track frequently used by Police vehicles driving to a jungle practice firing range. Carefully dug and concealed slit trenches for a twenty-man ambush were also found. A rifle and ammunition were recovered from this operation. The next day a more detailed search of the area with the OCPD Sepang and a large squad of Police revealed fifteen packs hidden near the proposed ambush positions.

Reliable information given to the Police in Kuala Lumpur concerning a group of bandits operating in a large area of balouka on the boundary between the Central Selangor Police Circle and the South Selangor Police Circle was passed on to Tac HQ at Kajang for action on 11 September. 11 Platoon of D Company, under the command of 2nd Lieutenant P.D. Roberts, was immediately despatched to the area. The patrol was moving along a ridge in heavy undergrowth when a party of about nine bandits was observed moving along a track some 400 yards away. The Platoon Commander despatched one section to get beyond the bandits as a cut-off; they had been seen to halt in a thicket, presumably for a rest. He then led the other section down towards the bandit position. The track used by the bandits was quickly located and followed and almost immediately a bandit sentry opened fire on the patrol with a sten gun. The section raced forward and the Patrol Commander immediately fired on a group of four bandits, killing three of them instantly. Seven packs were recovered from this engagement.

As a result of this contact, 4 Platoon of B Company and 10 Platoon of D Company were rushed to the area to attempt to cut off the retreat of the remaining bandits. That evening after dark a 4 Platoon stop position on a track fired on two bandits, killing one of them and recovering a rifle and ammunition. A pack containing many copies of *The Vanguard*, an illegal newspaper printed in a jungle printing press, was also recovered.

Outside the jungle, September witnessed an outstanding achievement by the Battalion Shooting Team. Firing against twenty-seven other teams, including the previous year's winners, 45 Commando, Royal Marines, the team won the Malayan Major Units Rifle Championship. Top scorer for the Battalion team was CSM Moore who also went on to win the Federation of Malaya Open Individual Championship.

A very unhappy incident occurred on 3 October which served to illustrate the ever-present dangers with which men of the Battalion were confronted in their endless jungle patrolling in Malaya. 5 Platoon of B Company and 11 Platoon of D Company were sent out on information to an area of swampy jungle ten miles south of Kajang to search for a party of bandits reported seen in the area. No sign of activity was found, however, and the 5 Platoon patrol was ordered to move out of the area through dense jungle and deep swamp to a bridge over the Sungei Langat which wound its way sluggishly through the swamp. The bridge was unfortunately not found and the patrol attempted to cross the river by wading. They failed to find a safe route and one man, Private Moore, was lost. At this stage darkness fell and the remainder of the patrol, having failed to find him, spent an impossible night in the swamp. A further search at dawn failed to discover the missing man and the patrol unhappily fought its way back to safety. Later that day a fresh party of men from 4 Platoon of B Company went to the area and recovered the body of the drowned man who had clearly been weighed down by the equipment, ammunition, weapon and a wireless that he was carrying.

On 6 October Sir Henry Gurney, the High Commissioner of the Federation of Malaya, was shot and killed when the car in which he was travelling on the way to Fraser's Hill was ambushed by bandits. 18th Brigade ordered one company to stand by at fifteen minutes to move, but it was not in the end called out. The ambush occurred well north of the Battalion's operational area and three other battalions provided the troops in the follow-up operation which was to continue for over six weeks.

The Battalion was involved, however, in the provision of the escort to the cortège at Sir Henry's funeral on 8 October in Kuala Lumpur. After the funeral it also furnished a Guard of Honour and a Firing Party at the Burial at the Cheras Road Cemetery.

It was only given these duties on the afternoon of the day before and during the next twenty-four hours three officers, two senior ranks and seventy-two men were withdrawn from operations, briefed, drilled and kitted out in the necessary ceremonial uniforms. Against all the odds, RSM Duffy succeeded in producing a first-class parade for this sombre occasion which earned much praise from many sources and was highly commended by the GOC Malaya in a personal letter to the Commanding Officer.

Operation Roundabout went into action on 18 October with A Company moving to Klang with two platoons detached at Sungei Manggis, B Company moving to Bukit Darah and C Company to Wardieburn Camp. D Company moved from Kajang to Bukit Prang Estate and Support Company from Wardieburn to Kajang.

The companies rotated in this way once every three months or so. The moves injected a new interest and prevented the staleness of routine setting in. With the Battalion remaining in generally the same operational area for a lengthy period, it also had the benefit of familiarizing patrol commanders with the whole area.

The full move on this occasion was delayed when Police information was received at 1600 that a group of bandits was to collect food from a house on the outskirts of Kajang that evening. Within half an hour a Police group took up positions in the house and ambushes were laid around it by 5 Platoon of B Company and 12 Platoon of D Company. At 1940 two bandits approached the house. The Police opened fire and one was killed and the other, though wounded, escaped. About twenty minutes later two bandits approached a 12 Platoon group commanded by Lieutenant H.N. Moffitt (an RAOC Officer on a two-year attachment to the Battalion). The group opened fire, killing one of the men. Total darkness made any follow-up impossible. Two shotguns, a rifle, an 80 grenade and ammunition were recovered in this operation which served once again to demonstrate the excellent co-operation which continued to flourish between the Battalion and the Kajang Police. A third shotgun was retrieved from the area of this operation when, the next day at dawn, 12 Platoon returned to carry out a thorough search.

On 22 October, shortly after B Company moved to Bukit Darah, a 5 Platoon patrol under Sergeant Lister contacted a small group of bandits. In the brief fire fight which followed, Sergeant Lister was wounded in the leg. Fortunately, a spell in the British Military Hospital at Kinrara led to a full recovery.

The same day information came through to the Battalion of a serious MT ambush involving the Queen's Own Royal West Kent Regiment based to the north of the Battalion's area at Kuala Kubu Bahru. An officer, ten soldiers and three Ibans were killed and thirteen others injured. It was the worst set-back experienced by the Security Forces in Malaya.

A composite company made up of two platoons of Support Company from Kajang and one from C Company at Wardieburn, under the command of Major W.J. Martin, was instantly despatched to the north to assist in the follow-up operation. The next day a further mixed company, comprising the Anti-Tank Platoon, 1 Platoon of A Company and 8 Platoon of C Company, was sent as reinforcement under the command of Major M.D. O'Reilly. OC B Company, Major K.M.J. Dewar, was nominated by the CO to command the two-company group.

As was so often the case, no sign of the bandit ambush party, over forty strong, was seen, despite the rapid deployment of a total of six companies from the two battalions in an area extending outwards from the ambush on the Ulu Caledonian Estate.

By 25 October the two Suffolk companies had returned to their own locations. On the same day a patrol from 4 Platoon of B Company, operating in its own Company area, fought a battle in dense jungle with a bandit group which offered considerable resistance. In the battle Private Lewis was killed and it was little compensation that one bandit was also shot during the engagement.

On 5 November a bandit surrendered to the Police at Rawang to the north of Kuala Lumpur. On interrogation it was discovered that he had moved from a camp just north of Batu Caves to join a new group near Rawang only two days before surrendering. He agreed to lead a Police party back to the Rawang camp in the afternoon of the day he surrendered, but the occupants had, of course, fled, leaving nothing behind and no trace of their departure route. 8 Platoon of C Company at Wardieburn Camp was warned for an operation at first light the next morning, as the SEP (Surrendered Enemy Person) had agreed to lead a patrol back to his original camp.

The Platoon moved into the jungle just as dawn broke and began the slow and painstaking movement through thick undergrowth towards the camp. There was great tension within the patrol because it was highly unlikely that this bandit group would yet know of the surrender of their former gang member and thus the camp would almost certainly still be occupied.

At first, with the SEP leading the Platoon in single file through the jungle, a track was scarcely discernible. Using a Police interpreter, the Platoon Commander frequently asked the SEP how much further it was to the camp. He hoped to get adequate warning so that he could deploy a section to cut off the enemy's retreat, while the other section put in the assault. Gradually the track showed more and more signs of recent use, with individual bandit footprints clearly visible.

With, according to the SEP, still some distance to go to the camp, the Platoon Commander decided to conceal the Platoon's packs in the undergrowth beside the track on a high ridge. This relieved the patrol of an unnecessary burden and would help during the bandit camp assault. By that stage the SEP was not surprisingly in a high state of agitation, yet he still maintained the camp was at least an hour away.

Suddenly a shot rang out from ahead; it was clearly and

unfortunately the bandit sentry. The leading scout fired a burst from
his Owen gun down the track: surprise was lost. The whole platoon
charged forward down the track in single file. The dense vegetation
on both sides totally precluded opening out into extended order. The
track now entered a swampy stream bed and began to zig-zag
backwards and forwards in the usual way with tracks into a camp,
designed by the bandits to slow down a patrol's progress towards its
target. The camp was not even visible until the track climbed up
from the river bed on the other side. As the patrol ran into the camp
there was no sign of life.

The two sections of the platoon fanned out and raced to the far side
of the clearing to comb the jungle beyond. No other tracks could be
found leaving the camp and no sound of movement could be heard.
So often patrols ended in this disheartening way, but on this occasion
worse was to come.

The Platoon Commander put out sentries and told the Signaller to
erect his sky-wave aerial ready to report back to base. Sergeant Rees,
the Platoon Sergeant, was detailed off to return to the ridge with his
section to collect the packs. It was now approximately 1800, with
scarcely an hour's daylight left. Shortly after Rees's departure a
burst of heavy firing was heard in the distance from the direction of
the track along which he had returned. Leaving four men with the
Signaller, the Platoon Commander raced off back along the track
with the rest of his section, up on to the ridge where the packs were.

The Section Commander of Sergeant Rees's group was there with
six men in all-round fire positions. Apparently, as Sergeant Rees was
returning up the steep slope, the bandits had ambushed the section
from above and Sergeant Rees had been hit in the first round of fire.
Leaving him with two men of his reconnaissance group, the Section
Commander, with the remainder of his men, had left the track to left
and right and assaulted the ridge to find the bandits had once more
disappeared.

Returning down the track there was no sign of Sergeant Rees and
the two men with him. Blood traces were followed but lost as
darkness fell. Neither shouting nor rifle signal shots fired into the air
provoked a response. The Platoon Commander returned to the
bandit camp where atmospheric conditions precluded the use of the
radio, though the Signaller had earlier reported the abortive attack
on the camp and the later burst of firing.

It materialized afterwards that Sergeant Rees had been hit in the
face by two Thompson sub-machine-gun bullets, though luckily not
too severely wounded. He and his two men spent an extremely dazed

and uncomfortable night in the jungle, making their way out to the edge at first light the next day. The remainder of 8 Platoon left the jungle at almost the same spot an hour afterwards. The patrol had ended, as did so many, without success. But it highlighted the difficulties and dangers faced by the men of the Battalion throughout their tour in Malaya.

On 7 November a patrol from 9 Platoon of C Company operating in jungle to the north of Wardieburn Camp contacted six bandits, killing two and wounding two others. A 36 grenade, ammunition and packs were recovered.

Police information led to an operation on the Tarun Estate, east of Kajang near Broga, involving two platoons on 15 November. 3 Platoon of A Company and the Anti-Tank Platoon each killed a bandit as a result. A rifle and ammunition were recovered.

On 24 November 10 Platoon of D Company carried out a successful ambush on the Galloway Estate, some three miles from their Company base. One bandit was killed and a rifle, ammunition and a pack were recovered. Three days later a Malay bandit surrendered and under interrogation stated that he had been in a camp half a mile from 10 Platoon's ambush, together with Lieu Kon Kim and twenty-seven other bandits. On hearing the firing Lieu Kon Kim had immediately marched his men for five hours deep into the Kuala Langat Forest Reserve (North) swamps. That same evening the Malay bandit had shot the bandit on sentry duty and fled from the camp, or so he said.

4 December witnessed a successful ambush by 3 Platoon of A Company, south of Kajang. One MRLA section leader was killed and his carbine, ammunition and pack containing useful documents were recovered.

In December the Secretary of State for the Colonies, the Rt Hon Mr Oliver Lyttelton, made an extensive tour of the Federation of Malaya. His aim was to assess the overall situation since the death of Sir Henry Gurney. While in Malaya he spoke of the need for the 'overall direction of forces, civil and military' to be in the hands of one man. On returning to England he was quick to announce the appointment of General Sir Gerald Templer as High Commissioner. Losing no time, the General arrived in Kuala Lumpur on 7 February, 1952.

While in Malaya Mr Lyttelton visited Tac HQ at Kajang on 7 December, spending some time in the Joint Operations Room manned by Police Officers and Captain E.H. Morgan, the Intelligence Officer, and his staff. He also met the OC A Company, Major

M.D. O'Reilly, and inspected a platoon from the Company commanded by Lieutenant M.J. Benn (RAOC on a two-year attachment to the Battalion).

On 9 December all rifle companies took part in an operation in the Ampang Forest Reserve to the east of Kuala Lumpur. The operation lasted for four days and little success resulted. 2nd Lieutenant A.B. Horrex in command of 9 Platoon of C Company was wounded in the arm during this operation while leading an attack on a bandit camp.

On 14 December the I.O., Captain E.H. Morgan, with a patrol from 4 Platoon of B Company, shot and killed A.S. Maniam, the leader of the Indian Section of the MRLA in Selangor. His elimination certainly weakened the morale of the small Indian element in a predominantly Chinese bandit organization in this State.

On the same day 12 Platoon of D Company suffered a tragic loss. The Platoon was on a thirty-six-hour rest and retraining break at Port Dickson on the coast and, while engaged in 36 grenade live throwing practice, a grenade with a faulty fuse blew up as it was thrown. Private Wilson was killed and Sergeant Wilce and Corporal Bailey were both wounded, the latter only slightly.

On 19 December 3 Platoon of A Company, under command of 2nd Lieutenant M.P. Casey, ambushed two bandits, killing one and wounding and capturing the second. The ambush took place in the Sungei Long area between Kuala Lumpur and Kajang and the captured man was later identified as a local Branch Communist Party Committee Member. An old Dutch rifle and ammunition were recovered.

The Battalion was allowed a brief respite from operations on Christmas Day, 1951. A few men were able to get into main HQ at Wardieburn Camp, but for most 25 December meant a day in company bases without operational commitments. The 1st Battalion, the Cameronians, operating in the adjacent area to the south, provided a stand-by operational element for the Battalion, which was later reciprocated while the Cameronians celebrated Hogmanay.

1951 had been a very successful year for the Battalion and its reputation in Malaya was already extremely high. As if to confirm this, newspapers and magazines were constantly seeking interviews with officers and men and much publicity was given to the Battalion's exploits in the U.K. press. 'Cassandra' of the *Daily Mirror* went on patrol with a B Company platoon and wrote about his experiences in the *Daily Mirror* on 22 December, 1951, and *The Times* devoted a full two columns to the Battalion in March, 1952. Meanwhile, earlier, Harry Hopkins wrote lengthy articles about the Battalion in two consecutive editions of *John Bull*, which was at the time a mass circulation weekly in the United Kingdom.

The first contact with bandits in 1952 led to one being killed and one wounded by a patrol from 1 Platoon of A Company on 9 January. Two rifles, ammunition and packs were recovered, but the wounded bandit escaped.

His Grace the Archbishop of York, Dr Cyril Garbett, visited the Battalion on 11 January while on an extended tour of Australasia and the Far East. He was given a briefing in the Operations Room at Tac HQ at Kajang Police Station and then spoke to A and Sp Companies in the Kajang base. Following a visit to the Detachment Sergeants' Mess and lunch with the officers, in the afternoon he visited the men in their living accommodation for an informal chat.

On 21 January 12 Platoon of D Company claimed one bandit killed while patrolling on the western edge of the Kuala Langat Forest Reserve (South). This success was followed by another contact in the same area three days later which led to the death of yet another terrorist.

On 29 January 8 Platoon of C Company, under 2nd Lieutenant M. Pensotti, fought an action with bandits in the Ulu Klang Forest Reserve to the east of Kuala Lumpur. Two bandits were killed but 2nd Lieutenant Pensotti and two members of the Platoon, Privates Johnson and Norwood, were wounded in the fire-fight that followed the contact.

Information was received by the Police at Kajang on 5 February that a gang of bandits was temporarily encamped in overgrown rubber near Serdang to the west of Kajang. They were thought to be between the railway and a minor road. An operation was immediately planned involving two flights of the Royal Air Force Regiment (recruited in Malaya) and a party of fifty Special Constables, together with Sp Company and 3 Platoon of A Company. The operation was to be commanded by the OC Sp Company, Major W.J. Martin.

The troops moved into position at first light the next day, with the RAF Regiment lining the railway embankment and the Police party blocking the road. Elements of Sp Company put out stops linking the railway embankment to the road and on the fourth side of the 'box' the remainder of Sp Company and the A Company Platoon began sweeping through the area, part of which was heavily overgrown and swampy.

Two bandits were killed in the first sweep but only after one had fired his shotgun at point-blank range killing Private Walker of the Assault Pioneer Platoon. A second sweep was put through the area and a third bandit was killed. This operation was described in detail in *The Times* the next day: the paper's correspondent had been out on the operation.

6 February also saw another bandit killed by 2 Platoon of A Company patrolling in rubber near Jenderam, to the south of Kajang. B Company, operating near Rawang to the north of Kuala Lumpur, also killed a bandit on the same day. The patrol was from 6 Platoon and was commanded by Sergeant Dunne.

On 14 February the Battalion stood down for a two-month rest and retraining period and operational responsibilities were handed over to 42 Commando Royal Marines.

Senior appointments in the Battalion when the rest and retraining period began were held as follows:

CO:	Lieutenant Colonel P.A. Morcombe, OBE
2ic:	Major P.S. Clementi-Smith (Essex Regiment)
Adjt:	Captain H.H. Moore (Northamptonshire Regiment)
IO:	Captain E.H. Morgan
QM:	Captain H.S.R. Case
RSM:	RSM Duffy
OC A Company:	Major M.D. O'Reilly (Essex Regiment)
CSM:	CSM Collen
OC B Company:	Major K.M.J. Dewar
CSM:	CSM Pringle
OC C Company:	Major C.J.V. Fisher-Hoch
CSM:	CSM Keeble
OC D Company:	Major W.S. Bevan
CSM:	CSM Kerridge
OC Sp Company:	Major W.J. Martin
CSM:	CSM Miles
OC HQ Company:	Major A. Parkin
CSM:	CSM Penny

It had been hoped that the Battalion would, once again, spend the two months free from operations in Minden Barracks on Penang Island, but accommodation there was not available for the whole unit, so for the first month A, B and Sp Companies went to Penang while C and D Companies concentrated at Wardieburn Camp. On 14 March the companies changed over so that everyone had a taste of the bright lights and swimming which Penang offered.

A full training programme was implemented during the two months. Companies fired all weapons on the annual classification course and rifle companies practised jungle fighting drills including realistic jungle shooting tests. NCOs and Specialist Cadres were also organized. Inter-platoon football and hockey knock-out tournaments were played and there were many opportunities for swimming in the pools in Penang and Kuala Lumpur, as well as for trips to the seaside in Penang and at Port Dickson.

The GOC Malaya, Major-General R.E. Urquhart, inspected training at Wardieburn Camp on 25 February and the next day the C-in-C, Farelf, General Sir Charles Keightley, visited the companies in Penang. Brigadier W.H. Lambert, CBE, the newly appointed Commander of the 18th Infantry Brigade, visited Wardieburn for the first time on 25 March.

The retraining period also provided an opportunity for the 'unsung heroes' of the Battalion to catch up on maintenance of weapons and vehicles and the like. The MTO, Captain F.J. Lockett, and the QM, Captain H.S.R. Case, and their staffs worked furiously to prepare everything for a return to operations. The former achieved top marks in the whole of Malaya for a REME inspection of unit transport.

Retraining ended on 16 April and the Battalion took over the operational area of the 1st Battalion, the Queen's Own Royal West Kent Regiment, while the latter moved into Wardieburn Camp for their two months' rest and retraining.

Battalion HQ, B and C Companies were based in Kuala Kubu Bahru in the North Selangor Police Circle. D Company was detached at Rawang, while A Company moved to Klang and Sp Company to Batang Berjuntai.

Operational responsibility was assumed on 17 April and, as if to demonstrate the value of retraining, the remaining twelve days of April saw a remarkable series of successes. 3 Platoon of A Company under 2nd Lieutenant Casey killed two bandits and 4 Platoon of B Company, under their Company Commander, Major Dewar, one bandit, on 23 April. Two days later a patrol from 7 Platoon of C Company killed two more.

Then, on 26 April, the Battalion won perhaps its most important single success of the whole Malayan tour. Very high grade information from the Police led to this achievement. Five picked men from B Company were used for the operation under the command of the Intelligence Officer, Captain E.H. Morgan.

The party left Kuala Kubu Bahru just after midnight and were driven to the de-busing point. After leaving their vehicles, the patrol marched for an hour through rubber until their Police guide said they were close to the track used by the bandits. It was still dark so Captain Morgan waited till the approach of dawn gave enough light to move into ambush positions.

The positions adopted were on a slight rise and the path to be covered made its way upwards towards the ambush through a gentle depression of rubber trees, interspersed with patchy scrub.

Once individuals in the team were sited, it then remained but to wait: silent, still, sweaty and eaten alive by mosquitoes. At 0900, exactly as expected, movement was seen on the path. First came a woman, apparently unarmed and in normal Chinese dress, and then some seventy-five yards behind her a party of four armed and uniformed bandits.

The ambushers held their fire until the woman was literally only a yard or two from them and then, ignoring her, fire was opened on the four uniformed bandits beyond. All four fell dead or wounded in the first burst and the woman fled, but not before hurling a grenade at the party which, fortunately, exploded harmlessly. There was some movement among the bandits who had been hit and one or two initially returned fire which was quickly silenced by the ambush party.

When the bodies were taken back to Kuala Kubu Bahru Police Station, it was confirmed that one was Long Pin, the Commander of the 1st Regiment of the MRLA, and a member of the Selangor State Committee of the Malayan Communist Party. The other three were his close bodyguards.

The High Commissioner, General Sir Gerald Templer, sent the following signal to the Battalion on hearing of the action: 'Congratulations to all ranks concerned on your outstanding success this morning. Keep striking while the iron is hot. Well Done!'

Two days later, on 28 April, 9 Platoon of C Company, under 2nd Lieutenant Horrex, acting on information, sprang an ambush on three terrorists, killing two of them.

In these actions during twelve days the Battalion killed eleven terrorists and recovered three rifles, a carbine, a sten gun, three pistols and seven grenades.

May brought more success but also the death of an NCO in

D Company. On 10 May the Company was moving into the Serendah Forest Reserve jungle to establish a Company base from which to patrol. 12 Platoon, under 2nd Lieutenant P.R.W. Thistle-Suffern, was in the lead and came on a bandit camp. It put in an immediate assault, killing one bandit. A fire-fight ensued in which Corporal Bailey was shot and killed and Private Stevenson was seriously wounded.

On 23 May 2 Platoon of A Company under 2nd Lieutenant P.D.L. Hopper was sent out from Klang on information to ambush a track on the Bukit Tumboh Malay Reserve. The ambush produced no results, so the Platoon began to make a search of the jungle nearby. A newly constructed bandit shelter was found and just at that moment four bandits were seen, clearly returning to it. An immediate ambush was sprung and three of the four were killed, while one escaped wounded.

The actions in April and May were given considerable coverage in Malayan and Singapore newspapers and, after the success of 23 May, newspaper posters went up throughout the Federation bearing the caption 'Suffolks Do It Again'.

Despite the pressure of operations, there was also time in early May for OC B Company, Major Dewar, to train a Battalion team for the Kuala Lumpur Garrison Athletics Meeting. The team won the championship, despite only being spared from the jungle for two days before the meeting!

A shortfall of National Service recruits joining the Battalion in the early months of 1953 led to a serious drop in the operational strength of the rifle companies and in May it was decided to run down the strength of Sp Company, reducing it to a Company HQ staff with responsibility for all Battalion training. The only one of its platoons to remain in existence was the Mortar Platoon, which continued to play an important role in operations.

On 23 May, as a prelude to returning to the Kuala Lumpur and Kajang areas, the Battalion extended its operational area to include the South Selangor Police Circle, following the departure from there of 42 Commando, Royal Marines.

The Queen's Birthday was celebrated in Kuala Lumpur by a parade on 5 June. The parade was made up of detachments from all units in Malaya and the salute was taken by H.E. the High Commissioner. At the time the rifle companies were heavily engaged in operations and the Battalion's contingent was formed entirely from the Administrative Platoon of HQ Company. The QM, Captain Case, was in command, with RQMS Boast and the Pioneer

Sergeant as left and right guides. RSM's drill parades before breakfast for a month produced a first-class show and, by using HQ Company, operations were allowed to continue unabated.

The last successful operation in the Kuala Kubu Bahru area took place on 7 June near Rawang, when 12 Platoon of D Company, under 2nd Lieutenant A.K. Catchpole, acting on information, surprised two armed bandits. One was killed and the second, though seriously wounded, escaped.

On 17 June the Battalion relinquished operational responsibility in the Kuala Kubu Bahru area and moved south to take over the Central and South Selangor Police Circles. Battalion Main HQ and Sp Company returned to Wardieburn Camp; A Company remained in Klang with a detachment at Sungei Manggis; Tac HQ with B and C Companies moved back to Kajang and D Company went to Bukit Prang Estate with a platoon base at Sepang on the eastern side of the Kuala Langat Forest Reserve (South).

The end of June saw the Battalion preparing for a major operation. Over the past few months information provided by the Police Special Branch had increased both in quality and in quantity and the overall picture of MRLA units, personalities and, to some extent, current activities, had become very comprehensive and up to date. There were good reasons to believe that Lieu Kon Kim, the Commander of the 4th Independent Company of the 1st Regiment, MRLA, and the main enemy of the Battalion in the Kajang area, was based at that time in the Kuala Langat Forest Reserve swamps and it was there that the Battalion was to deploy for Operation Churchman.

For the operation the Commanding Officer had under command E Troop of the 93rd Battery, RA, B and D Squadrons of the 22nd SAS Regiment, A and Sp Companies of the 1st Battalion, the Queen's Own Royal West Kent Regiment, the Kuala Lumpur Garrison Company, a section of the 18th Infantry Brigade Provost Unit and a large contingent of Civil Police.

Operation Churchman was planned in phases with the aim of taking a small area of the swamp at a time, and flooding it with all the available forces. Likely areas of the enormous North and South Kuala Langat Forest Reserve swamp were to be searched very methodically by some of the troops with the remainder putting in a series of close stop parties.

Phase I of the operation began in the south swamp on 1 July with the SAS Squadrons, the two companies of the Royal West Kents and A Company of the 1st Battalion, the Suffolk Regiment establishing stop positions. The next morning B Company, with 10 Platoon of D Company, moved in to patrol the area using a logging train to reach their starting point. Patrolling began at 0900 that morning and within half an hour a 10 Platoon patrol came upon a camp for twenty bandits which had just been evacuated – cooking fires were still burning. During the next hour and a half five contacts were made but without kills, though seven bandits were reported likely to have been wounded. All made off in a southerly direction towards the stop positions.

Patrolling continued on 3 July, but, apart from finding several old camps, there was nothing to report and all troops were withdrawn to prepare for Phase II of the operation.

Information was received that day that Lieu Kon Kim was currently in the swamps to the south of where the operation had been taking place, near the Tumboh Malay Reserve and it was decided that B Company, led by a guide, should search this area the next day. The search was carried out by Major Dewar using only a platoon and, although there were no contacts, tracks in the area proved it was currently in use by the bandits. It was decided that B Company, in force, would return to continue the search the next day.

Thus, on 6 July the Company, deploying nine separate patrols, recommenced their search in the Batu Extension Malay Reserve to the east of the Tumboh Malay Reserve. At 1330 a patrol from 5 Platoon of B Company led by 2nd Lieutenant L.R. Hands, a National Service platoon commander, suddenly saw a lone bandit making off through the jungle to their front. The patrol opened fire and raced after him but he escaped. They ran straight into a camp just in time to see three figures leaping out of a basha. A burst of fire killed one and 2nd Lieutenant Hands raced after the other two, following the splashing noises through the swamp. He caught up with one and shot her (it turned out to be a woman armed with a shotgun) and then continued the pursuit. After 150 yards he caught up with the third and brought him down with a burst from his carbine. This last bandit was bearded and was later positively identified as Lieu Kon Kim. A rifle, a 9 mm pistol and a shotgun, plus a large hoard of very important documents were also recovered in this action. (For his part in this action 2nd Lieutenant Hands was awarded the MC.)

The elimination of Lieu Kon Kim marked a high point of the Battalion's tour of duty in Malaya. He was a major figure in the MRLA in Selangor and his death caused a setback to the bandit organization from which it scarcely recovered during the rest of the

Emergency. The Press hailed the action as a great victory and the Battalion earned yet more kudos from it. Messages of congratulation were showered on the Battalion, including a personal signal from the High Commissioner.

Operation Churchman continued phase by phase to the end of the month without any more kills but with considerable minor successes. In all, a total of twenty-two bandit camps were located and destroyed and fifteen caches containing food, documents, clothing, equipment and medical supplies were found and destroyed.

Unhappily, during the operation one soldier from A Company, Private Ansell, was fatally wounded when one morning just before dawn his patrol was mistaken for a party of bandits and fired on by another patrol from the Battalion.

Very soon after he arrived in Malaya, General Sir Gerald Templer demonstrated his rapid grasp of the Emergency situation and many innovations flowed from the High Commissioner's office. One of them was to involve the Battalion in July.

Since the beginning of the Emergency in 1948 Ibans, or Sea Dayaks as they are also known, from the interior of Sarawak had been used to excellent effect by British units in the jungle. They were at home in this primitive and dangerous environment, and their skills, particularly in the art of tracking, were invaluable to patrols. The Battalion had quickly recognized the quality of these wise and practical men. Happy to live in the jungle and thoroughly at home in it, they helped teach the Suffolk patrol commanders how to maximize the value of their forays against the enemy.

Templer, too, saw their value and asked why they should not be trained as soldiers themselves. In consequence, two experimental platoons were formed, one with the Battalion and a second with the 1st Battalion, the Cameronians, in Johore.

The Suffolk Platoon was commanded by Lieutenant F.A. Godfrey, MC, who, together with a Platoon Sergeant, two Corporals and a Signaller from the Battalion, began training the Platoon on 1 July. The Iban Platoon was committed to operations in early October and achieved considerable success in the three months before the Battalion left for England.

On 1 August the whole Battalion, less skeleton staffs, was relieved from operations to celebrate Minden Day in Kuala Lumpur. The day began with a ceremonial parade at HQ Malaya where the salute was taken by Brigadier W.H. Lambert, CBE, Commander of the 18th Infantry Brigade.

Immediately after the parade a swimming gala was held. D Company won the swimming cup.

The next day companies returned to their distant 'out-stations' and operations were resumed.

On 6 August 8 Platoon of C Company claimed another lucky kill, when the sentry posted at the rear of the patrol while it was having a short break, observed a bandit making his way towards the section along the track which they had used. The sentry signalled the approach of the bandit and all froze till he was within four or five yards of the patrol. He was shot and his rifle, ammunition and some valuable documents were recovered.

15 August witnessed another Operation Roundabout with A and D Companies moving to Kajang, C Company to Sepang and B Company to Klang with a Platoon at Sungei Manggis.

A successful night ambush was sprung by a section of 9 Platoon of C Company under Sergeant Evans on 23 August at Sepang. A party of five bandits, well spread out, entered the ambush just after 2000. Two were killed and a rifle and mauser pistol and ammunition were recovered. It was later confirmed that a third member of the party had been wounded and that he had died.

On 11 September a patrol from 7 Platoon of C Company, operating in the Kuala Langat Forest Reserve (South), west of Sepang, located a small occupied camp for two to three people. An immediate assault was put in and two bandits were killed. Two rifles, ammunition, packs and documents were recovered.

At the end of September D Company registered two more kills. On the 26th 11 Platoon under 2nd Lieutenant D.A. Chamberlain was sent out on Special Branch information to ambush a group of disused buildings on the Saringgit Estate, east of Kajang. Two bandits approached the ambush, moving very cautiously and well apart. Fire was opened and one was killed and a shotgun with ammunition was recovered. Two days later, in the follow-up to this incident, 10 Platoon under 2nd Lieutenant Catchpole contacted and killed a second bandit. A Japanese Second World War rifle and ammunition were recovered.

2nd Lieutenant Crowe, commanding a patrol from 1 Platoon of A Company, captured and killed one bandit just north of Dingkil on 6 October. The terrorist threw a grenade at the patrol which exploded harmlessly and a further grenade was recovered, together with some documents.

A further successful engagement was registered by C Company on 9 October, when 9 Platoon located an unoccupied camp for fifteen to twenty persons in swampland a few miles north of Sepang. As the Platoon entered the camp, one bandit also entered it from the opposite direction. He was killed and a rifle, ammunition and documents were recovered.

Towards the end of October it was announced that the Commanding Officer, Lieutenant-Colonel P.A. Morcombe, OBE, had been awarded the Distinguished Service Order in recognition of gallant and distinguished services in Malaya. The whole Battalion was delighted with the news. The citation for Lieutenant-Colonel Morcombe's award spoke of the consistent success of the Battalion under his command and of the high morale and fighting spirit with which he had infused it. It described how his complete disregard for his own safety had set a fine example to his men and how his leadership, drive and inspiration had resulted in his Battalion achieving outstanding results among both British and Gurkha battalions.

The Iban Platoon had its first contact with the enemy on 4 November. A section under Corporal Laver located a camp occupied by three bandits in the Sungei Long area. The camp was attacked and two bandits were killed. A rifle, ammunition, a grenade and packs containing documents were recovered.

On 9 November, again in the Sungei Long area, 12 Platoon of D Company under 2nd Lieutenant R.L. Farmer contacted and killed one bandit armed with a rifle which was recovered. This action was followed on 13 November by one close to Kajang in which 11 Platoon of D Company, acting on information, killed one bandit and recovered a Dutch rifle and ammunition, together with two grenades and packs containing a quantity of documents.

Further to the west, B Company Commander took out an ambush party from 6 Platoon, commanded by 2nd Lieutenant P.B. Bird, to the Tanjong Duablas area on 15 November. Led by an informer, the group contacted and killed one bandit and recovered his rifle, equipment and documents.

6 Platoon of B Company were again successful on 21 November when they killed a member of the Min Yuen operating in the Sungei Manggis area. A Japanese grenade and some documents were recovered.

On 22 November, operating on Special Branch information in overgrown rubber in the Sungei Merabu area, off the Kajang to Kuala Lumpur Road, 11 Platoon of D Company with their Company Commander, Major E.T. Lummis, contacted two bandits while returning from an unsuccessful ambush. One bandit was killed and was later identified as a Platoon Commander of the local MRLA unit. A rifle and packs containing valuable documents were recovered.

A major engagement occurred on 25 November in jungles of the Tanjong Duablas Malay Reserve Extension, to the west of the Kuala Langat Forest Reserve (North). A and B Companies with Artillery Support had launched an operation backed by good Police information. It was believed that elements of the 4th Company MRLA were in the area. At 1100 a section of 6 Platoon of B Company, commanded by 2nd Lieutenant Bird, contacted two bandits. One was killed by the first burst of fire from the leading scout and the other was pursued as he fled and he too was shot. A carbine and a rifle, plus two grenades, were recovered.

While carrying the bodies of the two bandits back to their base camp for identification, the patrol met the OC B Company, Major Dewar, with 5 Platoon under the command of Sergeant Smith. Major Dewar sent 6 Platoon back to base with the two dead terrorists and went on to patrol the area with 5 Platoon. At approximately 1430 this patrol came under fire from a group of at least ten bandits, including one armed with a bren gun. The patrol instantly charged the enemy and killed two during the attack. A further carbine, a 9mm pistol, a rifle and three grenades were recovered in this engagement.

During the next two hours the Platoon was harassed by continual bursts of small arms fire from long range, but it was unable to locate the enemy who kept on the move. During one of these bursts of firing Lance-Corporal Mallows of 5 Platoon was hit and killed.

One of the terrorists killed that day was later identified as Kong Har, who had taken over from Lieu Kon Kim as Commander of the 4th Company of the MRLA.

On 29 November the Iban Platoon achieved its second success when a section located a bandit camp and stormed it, killing one of its two occupants.

On 30 November the run of successes in A and B Companies' operations west of the Kuala Langat Forest Reserve (North) prompted the CO to move Tac HQ from Kajang to Telok Datoh to control operations in that area more directly. Troops from outside the Battalion, including A Company, 1st Battalion, the Worcestershire Regiment and A Squadron, 22nd SAS Regiment, also came under command for operations there. D Company and the Iban Platoon remained in Kajang with C Company still located to the south in Sepang.

On 6 December a section of the Iban Platoon located a clearing being prepared for cultivation which the Platoon Commander had observed from an Auster aircraft during a reconnaissance flight. A single hut just off the clearing was seen and it was surrounded and attacked from fifteen yards after movement had been observed in it. All three occupants were killed. A rifle and ammunition and two grenades were recovered from this action.

A Patrol from 8 Platoon of C Company contacted a party of terrorists on the edge of the Kuala Langat Forest Reserve (South) swamp, just north of Sepang on 8 December. One bandit was killed and his rifle and ammunition recovered.

On the same day a patrol from 6 Platoon of B Company contacted and killed one bandit on the western edge of the Kuala Langat Forest Reserve (North). A Colt automatic pistol and ammunition was recovered. On 16 December, acting on information, a patrol from 10 Platoon of D Company commanded by Major Lummis, the Company Commander, located a group of five terrorists in the Ulu Langat Forest Reserve. One was killed but the others made good their escape. A Dutch rifle and ammunition were recovered.

Christmas Day, 1952, was celebrated with a stand-down from operations, except for one section standing-by at each company base. There were now only twelve more days of operations before the Battalion withdrew for the last time.

On 28 December 12 Platoon of D Company, acting on information, set up an ambush on the jungle edge at Cheras east of the Kuala Lumpur Kajang Road. Two bandits walked into the ambush and both were killed. A rifle, ammunition and a grenade were recovered.

On 28 December also, a memorial service was held at the Cheras Road Military Cemetery for the men of the Battalion who had died in Malaya during the present tour of duty. At one point in the service RSM Duffy read out their names.

The honour of the final successful action in the Malayan Campaign fell to D Company. Acting on information, a patrol from 10 Platoon, under 2nd Lieutenant Catchpole, established an ambush on the edge of a rubber estate just outside Kajang on 2 January. A bandit came out of the jungle to meet another man. The ambush was sprung and both were killed.

On the same day General Sir Gerald Templer, the High Commissioner, visited Kajang and Sungei Manggis to say farewell to the Battalion.

The Advance Party of thirty men under the Quartermaster,

Lieutenant G.S. Jasper, sailed for the UK on 5 January and operational responsibility for the Battalion area was handed over to the 1st Battalion, the Somerset Light Infantry on 7 January.

Senior appointments at the time the Battalion handed over operational responsibilty were filled as follows:

CO:	Lieutenant-Colonel P.A. Morcombe, DSO, OBE
2ic:	Major W.S. Bevan
Adjt:	Captain H.H. Moore
QM:	Lieutenant G.S. Jasper
RSM:	RSM Duffy
OC A Company:	Major M.D. O'Reilly
CSM:	CSM Collen
OC B Company:	Major K.M.J. Dewar
CSM:	CSM Hutchings
OC C Company:	Captain E.H. Morgan, MC
CSM:	CSM Keeble
OC D Company:	Major E.T. Lummis
CSM:	CSM Kerridge
OC HQ Company:	Captain F.J. Lockett
CSM:	CSM Norman
OC Sp Company:	Captain A.G.B. Cobbold
CSM:	CSM Miles

The final total of bandits killed and captured stood at one hundred and ninety-six when operations ceased. It was a record which was to remain unbeaten by any other British Battalion through to the end of the Emergency in 1960.

On 8 January in the early evening the Battalion marched ceremonially through the streets of Kuala Lumpur thronged with all races of the community. The CO led the parade and the Colours of the 2nd Battalion were carried by Lieutenant A.B. Horrex, MC, and Lieutenant P.D.L. Hopper. The salute was taken outside the Secretariat by the High Commissioner, General Sir Gerald Templer, who was accompanied at the saluting base by the Sultan of Selangor, the GOC Malaya, General Sir Hugh Stockwell, and other senior Government, Police and Service Officers.

The march continued to the war memorial where a wreath was laid by the CO and thence to the railway station where the Battalion entrained for Singapore.

The High Commissioner, the Sultan and the GOC bade farewell to the Battalion at the station, shaking hands with all the officers before the train moved off. It was a noisy, exciting and emotional occasion and all members of the Battalion were highly elated at this rather special send-off.

On arrival in Singapore the Battalion was temporarily accommodated in Selerang Barracks.

A memorial service was held at Kranji Military Cemetery in Singapore for the men of the 4th and 5th Battalions, the Suffolk Regiment and the 1st and 2nd Battalions, the Cambridgeshire Regiment, on 14 January, 1953. The service was conducted by the Reverend Leigh-Wood, CF, MA, and the C-in-C Farelf, General Sir Charles Keightley, KBE, DSO, MC, was present.

The Battalion embarked for England on HMT *Georgic* on 20 January and sailed the same evening at 1830. The ship docked in Liverpool on 13 February, 1953.

As the Battalion left Malaya *The Times* published a leading article in which it extolled the successes it had achieved. It was a fitting recognition of the Battalion's deeds in Malaya and included a tribute to the National Servicemen of the Battalion.

> The young men were always careful to regret loudly their National Service, but they had a youthful enthusiasm which made light work of jungle patrolling. To assess this enthusiasm it must be remembered that according to estimates they marched two million miles in three years and wore out 15,000 pairs of jungle boots.
>
> They also pursued with a deadliness not usually associated with young men the so-called Kajang gang, an armed gang which once terrorized South Selangor. When they left the gang leaders had been killed and their surviving followers scattered.

CHAPTER V

THE FIRST BATTALION:

HOME AND TRIESTE 1953–1954

'Summer Sunshine and Autumn Storms'

Part I

The Battalion arrived home from Malaya on board HMT *Georgic*, docking in Liverpool on 11 February, 1953. It was greeted by a large reception party led by the Colonel of the Regiment, and after the welcoming ceremony was over the whole Battalion dispersed from Liverpool on a month's leave.

The stay in England was to be very brief; even before the ship docked it was known that the Battalion was to be posted to Trieste in May. For this short stay in the UK accommodation was found in Meanee Barracks in Colchester. It was as well to be stationed close to Suffolk, because the County was determined to honour the Battalion on its return to the UK for the first time since it left home to participate in the D-Day landings in June, 1944. The whole three months were to be packed with activity, with the Battalion being feted by the people of Suffolk wherever it went.

Disembarkation leave over, the Battalion reassembled in Colchester to prepare for a series of parades. On 25 April, 1953, it was granted the Freedom of Sudbury and on the 29th it was accorded an official welcome home in Ipswich and the next day a civic welcome at Bury St Edmunds.

Then it was time to prepare for the move to Trieste. The Battalion entrained at Colchester Station on 15 May, 1953, crossed from Harwich to the Hook and, travelling across Europe by train, arrived in Trieste on 17 May. There it was located in Rossetti Barracks which provided excellent accommodation for the duration of its stay until August, 1954.

The Battalion was posted to Trieste to form part of the British Element Trieste Force (BETFOR). The Force, made up of American as well as British troops, had been formed at the end of the Second World War, consequent upon the eruption of a dispute between the Italians and the Yugoslavs who both claimed sovereignty over the city and its surrounding territory.

A temporary agreement with regard to the dispute had divided the Trieste area into two zones: Zone A and Zone B. The former embraced the City of Trieste itself and a few square miles of outlying territory in which the inhabitants were largely of Italian origin. Zone B, to the east, was in the main populated by Slovenes, one of the Slav peoples which make up the population of Yugoslavia.

The agreement to divide Trieste into the two administrative zones also allowed for a joint British and American force to be stationed in Zone A. Both the United States and Great Britain were entitled to station five thousand troops there, whose task it was to maintain law and order until the whole problem of sovereignty was resolved. The force also served as a guarantee that neither the Italians nor the Yugoslavs would attempt any external moves against Trieste.

When the Battalion arrived, the US and British Garrisons had been considerably reduced and all was peaceful in Zone A. Zone B, controlled by Yugoslav forces, had been already virtually incorporated into Yugoslavia itself.

Initially the situation looked set fair for a bout of peacetime soldiering and this feeling was reinforced when, immediately after arrival in Trieste, drill parades began in preparation for a parade on 2 June, 1953, to mark the Coronation of HM The Queen.

On the eve of the Coronation came the announcement that Her Majesty The Queen had appointed HRH The Princess Margaret to be Colonel-in-Chief of the Suffolk Regiment. It was an honour greeted within the Battalion with much excitement and pleasure.

Training facilities were somewhat limited in Trieste, but they were utilized to the full while the Battalion was there. Lieutenant-Colonel W.A. Heal, OBE, who acceded to command of the Battalion in Colchester, now discovered he had an interesting paradox to resolve. He found that the Battalion he had taken over had the highest morale of any he had served in, yet it was, after three and a half years in Malaya, almost totally ignorant of the basic tactics and procedures involved in European warfare as it had evolved in the post-Second World War years, with the coming of nuclear weapons.

During the summer and autumn of 1953 he strove to put this right by achieving a high standard of training whilst retaining the Malayan spirit alive.

The training programme encompassed everything from individual up to battalion level and culminated in August and September with a number of battalion exercises in the conventional phases of war.

This tough but successful régime was enlivened in July, 1953, by a three-week training period away from Trieste for field firing and low-level tactical training in the Schmelz Training Area, high in the mountains of Austria.

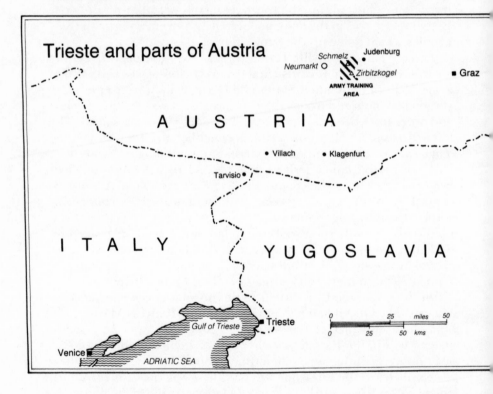

At the end of September political forces began to make themselves felt. In an attempt to put pressure on the Italian and Yugoslav Governments and finally to resolve the Trieste problem, the British and US Governments announced on 8 October, 1953, that their garrisons would be withdrawn from the territory in the immediate future. Within six days it was confirmed that the Battalion would be moving to BAOR, and on 19 October the Advance Party left Trieste bound for a barracks in Wuppertal in the Ruhr region of Germany. All families were also evacuated straightaway.

Continued uncertainties as to the future of Trieste led to a series of strikes and a number of large-scale riots in Zone A in November, during which month the Battalion was actively engaged in keeping the peace in support of the Police.

Thereafter, following the restoration of order, the days, weeks, and months went by with everyone assuming a move to Germany was imminent. Christmas passed and the 'peacetime' routine got into its stride once more in the New Year.

The Spring and early Summer of 1954 saw a full programme of training and sport, including another visit to Schmelz in Austria for field firing.

The Colonel of the Regiment, Brigadier E.H.W. Backhouse, paid a ten-day visit to the Battalion in May. He came, in the main, to see the Battalion at work and meet as many officers and men as possible, but he also brought with him the Regimental Brooch, which had been purchased by subscription within the Regiment for the new Colonel-in-Chief, for all to see.

Training and sport, as usual, continued throughout June and July and then in August, 1954, at last the Battalion moved out of Rossetti Barracks on route for Harding Barracks in Wuppertal, where it arrived by 22 August. Soon after the Battalion's departure Zone B effectively became part of Yugoslavia, as also did a slice of Zone A above the city. The Italians were left with the city itself, plus a coastal strip of land.

Part II

On 13 February, 1953, the Battalion, commanded by Lieutenant-Colonel P.A. Morcombe, DSO, OBE, docked at Prince's Landing Stage at Liverpool aboard HMT *Georgic*. It was greeted on arrival by a large welcoming party representing the Army, the Regiment and the County of Suffolk. Those at the dockside included General Sir Cameron Nicholson, GOC-in-C Western Command, Brigadier E.H.W. Backhouse, Colonel of the Regiment, the Mayor of Ipswich, Alderman James Chalmers and the Mayor of Bury St Edmunds, Alderman G.H. Pemberton. Other members of the Regiment included Colonel W.N. Nicholson, Brigadier R.E. Goodwin,

Brigadier I.L. Wight, Colonel. G.H.M. Harper, Lieutenant-Colonel F.A. Milnes, Lieutenant-Colonel K.J.K. Pye and Lieutenant-Colonel W.A. Heal.

The Battalion Band played on the quayside and also aboard the ship before the speeches of welcome by the Colonel of the Regiment and the Mayors of Ipswich and Bury St Edmunds.

One would-be visitor to welcome the Battalion home was unhappily denied access to the ship by an over-zealous Military Policeman. The famous Conductor, Sir John Barbirolli, working at the time with the Liverpool Philharmonic Orchestra, had started out on his musical career as a member of a Suffolk Regiment Band and was anxious to renew his acquaintance with the Regiment and add his congratulations on the Battalion's homecoming.

Immediately on disembarking, the Battalion dispersed on a month's leave.

On 12 February Major W.H. Brinkley of the Royal Norfolk Regiment was posted to the Battalion as Second-in-Command.

At a meeting of East Suffolk County Council on 3 March, 1953, a resolution of congratulation and welcome was passed commending the 'brilliant and courageous manner' in which the Battalion had carried out three and a half years of active service in Malaya. Six days later, on 9 March, Colonel J.H. Harrison, TD, MP, former CO of the 4th Battalion, paid tribute in the House of Commons to the men of the Battalion during the Malayan tour.

The Battalion reassembled at Meanee Barracks in Colchester on 16 March on the completion of leave. The next few weeks were spent on administration, with a large number of officers and other ranks posted in and out of the Battalion.

Early in April preparations went ahead for ceremonial parades in Sudbury, Ipswich and Bury St Edmunds at the end of the month.

On 25 April the Battalion paraded in Sudbury, where on the Cricket Ground on a lovely Spring day they were to receive from the Lord-Lieutenant an address of welcome and also the Honorary Freedom of the Borough.

The Battalion, 250 strong, was drawn up in a hollow square and was flanked by a contingent of seventy-five men from the Depot, a contingent of the Army Cadet Force from Sudbury Grammar School and over 200 members of the Old Comrades Association.

Shortly before 3pm the Mayor of Sudbury, Councillor C.E. Grimwood, arrived at the dais accompanied by the Colonel of the Regiment. Then the Lord-Lieutenant, Commander the Earl of

Stradbroke, RN (Retd), arrived. Both parties were received by a General Salute.

An inspection by the Lord-Lieutenant and the Mayor followed and then the Lord-Lieutenant made a speech of welcome. Speaking, as he said, for everyone in the County, he praised the Battalion's magnificent record in Malaya, where it had added fresh lustre to an already long and glorious history. He then, on behalf of the Officers of the Lieutenancy, presented the Battalion with two silver bugles.

His Worship the Mayor of Sudbury made an address of welcome and the Town Clerk read out the resolution conferring the Honorary Freedom of the Borough on the Suffolk Regiment. The Mayor then presented the Regiment with an illuminated copy of the resolution and two silver bugles. In his reply the Colonel of the Regiment thanked the Mayor for the honour bestowed on the Regiment and, on behalf of the Regiment, presented two claret jugs to the Borough. The Lord-Lieutenant then departed and the Battalion marched through the Borough, where at the Market Hill the Mayor took the salute for the March Past.

To conclude the day, the Battalion and Depot contingents were entertained to tea by the Borough.

On 29 April a further parade took place in Ipswich. The Parade was to receive from the Borough an official welcome home from Malaya and, as the Battalion were already Honorary Freemen of the Borough, they marched with Band playing, bayonets fixed and Colours flying through the town to Christchurch Park where the parade was held. There the Mayor inspected the Parade and made his welcoming speech. He then presented two silver bugles to the Battalion as a memento of the occasion.

The CO replied to the Mayor, thanking him for the presentation. The Colonel of the Regiment then presented a two-handled silver cup to the Mayor as a gift to the Borough from the Regiment. After the presentation, the Battalion marched to the Cornhill where the Mayor took the salute before large crowds of spectators. Afterwards the Battalion was entertained to tea in large marquees outside Christchurch Mansion.

In the evening the officers and sergeants of the 4th Battalion entertained the officers and sergeants of the Battalion in their respective messes at Great Gipping Street.

On 30 April the final welcoming home parade took place at Bury St Edmunds. It was a memorable and moving occasion, the first time the Battalion had paraded in its home town since receiving the Honorary Freedom of the Borough on Minden Day in 1944.

The parade went ahead despite incessant rain, before a large gathering of spectators including all the Mayors of Suffolk, the Chairmen of East and West Suffolk County Councils and of all the Urban and Rural District Councils in the County.

The parade, formed up in the Abbey Gardens, began with an inspection by the High Sheriff of Suffolk, Lieutenant-General Sir Harold Carrington, KCB, DSO, accompanied by the Mayor. There followed speeches by the High Sheriff, the Commanding Officer, the Mayor and the Colonel of the Regiment. There were presentations, too, of two silver bugles from the Borough to the Regiment and of a pair of silver claret jugs from the Regiment to the Borough.

At the conclusion the Battalion marched through the Borough to the Corn Exchange where it was entertained to tea as the guests of the Borough.

In the evening a welcome home dance, in honour of the 1st Battalion, was arranged in the NAAFI at Blenheim Camp. The Master of Ceremonies was Sergeant Mowle of the Depot Staff, and a buffet supper for 800 was prepared by Sergeant Gleeson and his staff from the Depot cookhouse.

On 3 May the Battalion provided a Guard of Honour for the official opening ceremony and dedication of the Suffolk Regiment War Memorial Homes (a fuller account of this occasion may be found in Apendix VI).

On 10 May, Lieutenant-Colonel P.A. Morcombe, DSO, OBE, handed over command of the Battalion to Lieutenant-Colonel W.A. Heal, OBE, at Meanee Barracks, Colchester. Lieutenant-Colonel Morcombe had taken over command of the Battalion in 1950 and, building on his predecessors' successes, he had with equal success led it for two and a half years in Malaya, during which time its operational record had gone from strength to strength, until at the end its achievements stood as an example to all other Battalions to emulate.

A farewell parade for the Colonel of the Regiment was held in Meanee Barracks on 1 May, prior to the Battalion's departure for Trieste. Long Service and Good Conduct Medals were presented to RSM Duffy, CSM Kerridge and CSM Fenner at this parade.

The Battalion entrained at Colchester Station en route for Trieste on 15 May, 1953. Crossing from Harwich to the Hook of Holland on the *Empire Parkeston*, it boarded two military trains of the MEDLOC Express which arrived in Trieste after a comfortable journey on 17 May. The first train carried the Colour Party, the Band and B, C and D Companies. This contingent marched from the station to Rossetti

Barracks where the Band of the 1st Battalion, the Loyal Regiment, was formed up on the square to welcome the Battalion.

On arrival in Trieste the Battalion came under command of the 24th Independent Brigade Group, which effectively made up the British Element Trieste Force (BETFOR). The Brigade Commander was Brigadier V. Boucher, CBE. The GOC of the combined British and American Forces in Trieste was Major-General Sir John Winterton, KCMG, CB, CBE.

The day after the Battalion arrived it was assembled for an address by the Brigade Commander and this was followed in the next day or two by a number of briefings on the role of BETFOR and the Battalion within it.

20 May saw the first rehearsal for the BETFOR Coronation Parade to be held on 2 June and two days later, on 22 May, the GOC-in-C visited the Battalion.

Senior appointments in the Battalion soon after arrival in Trieste were held as follows:

CO:	Lieutenant-Colonel W.A. Heal, OBE
2ic:	Major W.H. Brinkley (Royal Norfolk Regiment)
Adjt:	Captain H.H. Moore
QM:	Lieutenant G.S. Jasper
RSM:	RSM Duffy
OC A Company:	Lieutenant W.C. Deller
CSM:	CSM Collen
OC B Company:	Major K.M.J. Dewar, OBE
CSM:	CSM Chenery
OC C Company:	Major L.W. Allan, MBE (Essex Regiment)
CSM:	CSM Fenner
OC D Company:	Major W.S. Bevan
CSM:	CSM Kerridge
OC Sp Company:	Major C.A. Boycott, MBE
CSM:	CSM Calver, BEM
OC HQ Company:	Major C.E. Britten (Bedfordshire & Hertfordshire Regiment)
CSM:	CSM McColl

On 1 June 1953, Her Royal Highness, The Princess Margaret, CI, GCVO, was appointed Colonel-in-Chief of the Suffolk Regiment and the Commanding Officer sent a telegram to Her Royal Highness, expressing the deep appreciation of all ranks of the Battalion of the honour.

On 2 June the Coronation Day of Her Majesty Queen Elizabeth II was celebrated in BETFOR by a parade commanded by the GOC-in-C. The Battalion paraded with the Colours of the 2nd Battalion as its own Colours were carried by the Battalion contingent at the Coronation Parade in London, which was commanded by Major W.S. Bevan.

The Battalion provided a Guard of Honour commanded by Major E.T. Lummis when the Commander of the US Sixth Fleet visited Trieste on 8 June.

B Company, with elements of HQ and Sp Companies, moved out to Bassovizza Ranges, five miles from Trieste, on 9 June to fire the annual range course. They were followed on 16 June by D Company and on the 21st by C Company. Range organization was in the hands of the Weapon Training Officer, Lieutenant W.C. Deller.

In July, 1953, the Battalion was allotted the Schmelz Field Firing Area near Judenburg in Austria for a period of field firing and tactical training. It left Trieste on 6 July and, after bivouacking for one night at St Viet, arrived in Schmelz the next day. The journey was by motor transport except for the last eight miles which climbed four thousand feet up into the mountains and were completed on foot.

The Battalion returned from Austria to Trieste on 28 and 29 July, just in time to celebrate Minden Day. 1 August, 1953, was the first Minden Day for many years that the Battalion was together and not on active service. It was planned to be, and was, a memorable occasion. The day started with a loud and 'ad hoc' reveille, played by the band split up, so that all Companies on all floors of the great barracks were woken. All members of the Battalion were then served with tea in bed.

The Minden Day Parade was held at 9 o'clock and the Colours of both the 1st and the 2nd Battalions were on parade adorned with the customary roses. The inspection was carried out by Major-General B.M. McFayden, Commanding General of the US Forces in Trieste. He then took the salute at the March Past and concluded the ceremony by making an excellent speech.

After the parade, the officers entertained a number of guests in the mess and the last guest had scarcely left when the Sergeants' Mess arrived en masse for drinks.

A special lunch had been prepared by Sergeant Atkinson in the cookhouse and it was served to the men by the officers and sergeants while the Band played. This was followed in the afternoon by a very successful Minden Fair which was organized with a wide variety of sideshows and amusements. In the evening a very good variety show was put on by professional artists recruited from the nightclubs of Trieste. The day ended with a buffet supper prepared by the Cook Sergeant and his staff and then a Band Concert plus entertainment by various members of the Battalion, organized by the Regimental Sergeant-Major.

During the remainder of August the Battalion was kept very busy with a period on the Bassovizza Ranges where companies practised for the Battalion Rifle Meeting and fired Decentralized Army Rifle Association competitions. A number of exercises at company and battalion level was conducted during the month, and provided the opportunity for the Battalion to get to grips with the conventional phases of war which would now form the basis of all its training.

In August, too, companies held swimming competitions which culminated in the Battalion Swimming Sports on 17 August, which were won by HQ Company. The prizes were presented at the end of the meeting by Mrs W.A. Heal, wife of the Commanding Officer.

The GOC BETFOR, Major-General Sir John Winterton, visited the Battalion at Rossetti Barracks on 26 August and on 10 and 11 September, the Commander 24th Independent Brigade Group, Brigadier H.A. Borrodaile, DSO, set a Brigade exercise, 'Exercise Fairway II'. The Battalion took part in this exercise which was designed to test battle procedure and the command structure. The whole unit was deployed and the test was completed, but in the most fearful weather conditions imaginable. Gale-force winds blew unabated and they were accompanied by heavy thunder and lightning and a continual and torrential downpour of rain.

A Battalion Rifle Meeting took place on 19 and 20 September on Bassovizza Ranges. HQ Company won the Inter-Company Competition and Sergeant Ridout, REME, the Battalion Armourer Sergeant, was the Champion Individual Shot.

A few days afterwards, on 24 September, the Battalion acquitted itself very well in the BETFOR Rifle Meeting, winning the Rifle and the Pistol Open Championships and coming second in the SMG Competition. Major Brinkley, the 2ic, won the Individual Pistol and Captain Lockett came second by a hair's breadth in the SMG with Sergeant Ridout obtaining third place in the Individual Rifle Shoot.

6 October saw the Battalion engaged in a two-sided Brigade exercise 'Exercise Durmy I', which also involved the 2nd Battalion, the Lancashire Fusiliers. The exercise was cut short on 7 October owing to the deteriorating political situation in Trieste.

The following day came the announcement that British and

American forces would be withdrawn from Trieste. As a preliminary step, families would leave forthwith, to be followed later by all BETFOR troops. Within a few days it was learned that the Battalion's new station was to be Wuppertal in Germany and, on 17 October, the 2ic, Major Brinkley, left for Wuppertal to command the Advance Party. The next day twenty-one families left for BAOR on a special train. On arrival in Wuppertal they moved into quarters with the much-appreciated help of the 1st Battalion, the Northampton-shire Regiment.

The Battalion Advance Party, which left Trieste on 19 October, was established in Harding Barracks in Wuppertal by the 21st. It included representatives from all companies and also the Band. Officers of the Advance Party in addition to Major Brinkley included Major Lummis, Lieutenant Deller and 2nd Lieutenant Wilson.

The remainder of October saw all families leaving Trieste. One group of seventeen stayed for a week in Villach in Austria, while the wives of five officers drove their own cars from Trieste to Germany. By 31 October all women and children, of whom there were over 100, were safely quartered in Wuppertal.

Tension in Trieste rapidly increased in early November and on the 4th the state of alertness changed from 'green' to 'yellow' and the Battalion prepared itself to support the Venezia Giulia Police.

The Italian population in Zone A feared that the allies were about to bow to Yugoslav pressure and allow the latter to take over some part, or all, of the Zone. A general strike was mounted and trouble-makers began to roam the streets. At 1720 on 5 November, Alert State 'red' was ordered, consequent upon large crowds assembling in the city, demonstrating vociferously their opposition to any 'sell-out' to the Yugoslavs.

Shortly after 1800 three guards of two NCOs and six men were sent to the three hotels on the waterfront, the Devonshire, the Corso and the Excelsior, which were used to provide hostel accommo-dation for Army families. They had all been attacked and entered by rioters. At the same time one company was placed at immediate notice to move in support of the Police. During the night Captain F. J. Lockett visited the three guards and his vehicle was stoned by rioters on the Via Candueri.

At 0940 on 6 November the guard on the Corso Hotel reported a disturbance outside the hotel. It was decided that the guards should be commanded by officers, and the Adjutant, Captain Moore, left barracks with three officers to take over these duties. He arrived at the Devonshire Hotel at 1100 and then set out for the Corso.

However, a large and angry crowd had assembled during the morning outside the Corso Hotel near the Banco di Napoli and, despite attempts by Police Units to disperse it, the Adjutant was unable to get to the hotel. After reporting the situation back to the Battalion from HQ BETFOR, he again tried to reach the Corso but once again failed. Large crowds were still assembled and his vehicles were repeatedly stoned. Small-arms fire was heard in the area of the Piazza Unita where the Corso Hotel was located. AT 1215 the Adjutant's group returned to Barracks, having failed to reach their destination.

At 1225 B Company was placed at immediate notice to move and at 1245 the Commanding Officer, with B Company under Major K.M.J. Dewar, left Barracks for the Hangar Club (an American Other Ranks Club) which was centrally positioned to provide a base for operations.

The Company arrived there at 1300 and Major Dewar left soon afterwards to report to the Commanding Officer of the US Infantry Battalion at the Prefecture building under whose command B Company was to come.

Shortly after 1330, as part of a plan agreed with the US Battalion Commander, B Company formed up by platoons and marched at the 'slope' with bayonets fixed and magazines charged to positions in front of the Prefecture on the Piazza Unita. Twenty minutes later, still following the pre-arranged plan, the Company moved by platoons at the port arms position, to seal off the civil administration buildings from rioters. It took five minutes to deploy and then for the next half-hour, while crowds remained gathered in force, the Company stood its ground between the rioters and their target.

Stones were hurled at the men of the Company and the crowd, in an ugly mood, jeered and booed at their presence. One attempt by a car and several by youths riding motorcycles to break through the cordon were thwarted. By 1440 the crowd began to show signs of breaking up and the Company reformed outside the Prefecture and marched back to the Hangar Club. Meanwhile 2nd Lieutenant A.J. Scott finally assumed command of the Corso guard and Lieutenant J.P. Macdonald of the Excelsior guard at 1405.

At 1550 the Excelsior guard reported small-arms firing in the Piazza Unita and, shortly afterwards, a crowd, some fifty strong, attacked an Intelligence Corps Officer in his car outside the hotel. Lieutenant Macdonald and the hotel guard put the attackers to flight by prompt action.

By 2030 that evening the Police were back fully in control of the streets and alert situation 'red' reverted to 'yellow' at that time.

7 November saw C Company, commanded by Major L.W. Allan, take over from B Company and, in turn, D Company, commanded by Major W.S. Bevan, took over from C Company on the 8th. By 1815 that day the Duty Company was stood down from immediate readiness to half-an-hour's notice to move.

On 9 November the crisis was past and officers were withdrawn from the hotel guard.

A flotilla of Royal Naval frigates visited Trieste from 12 to 16 November and the Battalion acted as hosts to HMS *Magpie*. Despite the need for a continued patrolling programme in the city owing to the recent unrest, the four days provided an attractive break for all ranks. Men from the ship joined patrols on the streets and soldiers from the Battalion in turn toured HMS *Magpie*. A full programme of sports and reciprocal entertainments was also organized.

By the end of November tensions had completely subsided and all town guards and patrols ceased and life returned to normal.

There were to be no more serious outbreaks of unrest, though the routine of training was constantly enlivened by brief moments of alertness which were not without their amusing aspects.

From time to time the Battalion was required to mount observation posts on the border of Zone A overlooking both the Italian and Yugoslav frontiers. On one such occasion a young officer on watch, looking out towards the Yugoslav side, reported back in a state of some excitement that he could see tanks deploying in the woods to his front. The CO was sufficiently interested to go and look for himself, but found on arrival at the observation post that the tank guns were in fact tree trunks being moved about by logging workers operating a very noisy crane!

Another occasional responsibility which came the Battalion's way was to retain a company on stand-by to be deployed astride the main road from Italy into Zone A, where there was always an observation post to warn of the approach of Italian forces. B Company, under Major Dewar, was ordered to deploy there once, consequent on the observation post reporting back to Brigade HQ that 'two battalions were approaching the frontier'. The Company arrived, together with their American supporting tanks, to find no sign of any Italian movement. On investigation it transpired that the message should have read 'two Italians are approaching the frontier'!

Hopes remained that the orders to leave Trieste would shortly be issued, but it was not to be and the Battalion settled down to normal routine training, resigned that there would be no move to BAOR until after Christmas.

By December, 1953, postings had led to the following changes in the senior appointments in the Battalion:

CO:	Lieutenant-Colonel W.A. Heal, OBE
2ic:	Major W.H. Brinkley
Adjt:	Captain H.H. Moore
QM:	Lieutenant G.S. Jasper
RSM:	RSM Gingell
A Company:	formed only as a training organization
OC B Company:	Major K.M.J. Dewar, OBE
CSM:	CSM Chenery
OC C Company:	Major H.C. Harvey
CSM:	CSM Fenner
OC D Company:	Major W.S. Bevan
CSM:	CSM Collen
OC Sp Company:	Major C.A. Boycott, MBE
CSM:	CSM Mayhew
OC HQ Company:	Major W.C. Smith
CSM:	CSM McColl

A number of exercises and study days were held in December, including one on the 11th for officers which dealt with Sp Company weapons and was run by OC Sp Company, Major Boycott. A foretaste of what was to come in BAOR was experienced by the CO and Majors Smith, Boycott and Harvey, when they attended 'Exercise Grand Slam' run by HQ BETFOR on 17 and 18 December. The exercise involved a study of the use of atomic weapons in a North-West European setting.

Christmas, 1953, was a somewhat subdued affair, although, because of the departure of the families, both the Officers' and Sergeants' Messes were much fuller than normal in a peacetime station. The officers and sergeants served Christmas Day lunch in the men's dining hall in the traditional manner.

1954 began with some extremely inclement weather. The Northern Adriatic is subject in the winter to a ferocious north-easterly wind known locally as the 'Bora'. Temperatures fell dramatically and storms of snow whipped through the Barracks. Tiles were torn from the roofs and chimney pots tumbled down. On one night in January the gale was so furious that no less than a hundred heavy double-glazed windows were blown out.

RSM Duffy was posted back to the Depot at the turn of the year and his place was taken by RSM Gingell. The former had been with the Battalion since July, 1951. In Malaya intense operations had rarely provided him with a chance to exercise the normal RSM's duties in the Battalion, but he worked tirelessly in the background to maintain proper standards and a high morale. When men were at a premium he had often gone out on escort duty with vehicles to collect patrols in from the jungle (and taken the chance, with a twinkle in his eye, to chide those whose jungle shaving was not up to his standard).

Another arrival in January, 1954, was the new Padre, the Reverend T.W. Metcalfe, MA, CF. He was to stay with the Battalion for the next five years.

The return from Germany of much of the Battalion's heavy baggage in the New Year was viewed with mixed feelings. Life was more comfortable with it but did it mean that the impending move to BAOR was postponed still further? Some cynics, particularly in the Sergeants' Mess, felt that such a major administrative operation could only mean one thing, that departure was imminent. But time was to show they were wrong.

The strength of the Battalion had dwindled since leaving Malaya and, even with A Company reduced to a Training Cadre and then put into suspended animation, the other rifle companies could barely muster by the New Year a strength of forty officers and men. With the inevitable requirement for guards and duties reducing numbers still further, it was extremely difficult to implement a full training programme. Yet it did go ahead.

In January a Battalion attack exercise was carried out which involved a long approach march and the breaching of a minefield. The two-day exercise was completed in dense fog and interminable cold rain.

February saw preparations for the annual administrative inspection. The CO inspected companies between the 3rd and the 6th, and the inspection itself, carried out by the Commander, 24th Infantry Brigade, Brigadier H.A. Borrodaile, DSO and his staff, was on 18 February.

The Band rejoined the Battalion when it returned from Malaya and went to Trieste. When the Advance Party left for Wuppertal in October, half the Band went with it and half was retained in Trieste to assist with the numerous requirements for guards and duties. During this period the only musical duties carried out were fulfilled by the Dance Band, which did much to make the Advance Party Christmas celebrations go with a swing. At the end of February, however, the Band was reunited in Trieste where it remained with the Battalion.

The first quarter of 1954 saw much sporting activity and the Battalion achieved considerable success in both hockey and rugby. The 2nd Battalion, the Lancashire Fusiliers were beaten in the final of the BETFOR Hockey Tournament after a very hard game and the Battalion Rugby Team reached the finals of the Inter-Unit Competition, having convincingly beaten both the other Battalions of the Brigade on the way.

In March training forged ahead and early in the month the Anti-Tank Platoon spent a fortnight in BAOR at the Hohne Ranges where it was able to engage in live firing practices with the seventeen-pounder anti-tank gun, something it was not possible to do with the limited ranges available in Trieste.

The annual range course was fired at Bassovizza during March, despite ominous signs of civil unrest in the town of Trieste. The Battalion was placed on immediate notice for internal security duties in the city on 19 March, but it was stood down after thirty-six hours when the situation calmed down without the necessity for the military to intervene.

April saw a continuing focus on sport. The BETFOR Seven-a-side Rugby Competition was held on the 2nd and 3rd, when the two teams fielded by the Battalion were unlucky to be knocked out in the semi-finals. Then, on 6 April the BETFOR Six-a-side Hockey Competition was held. The Battalion A Team won the competition and, unfortunately, because of the draw, knocked out the B Team in the process.

From 3 to 11 May the Battalion played host to the Colonel of the Regiment, Brigadier E.H.W. Blackhouse, DL. His stay turned into something of a marathon with a very full programme and the whole Battalion was delighted to see him on his first overseas visit since being appointed Colonel of the Regiment.

Brigadier Backhouse travelled on the MEDLOC train and stopped en route at München Gladbach station in Germany to meet a party of wives from the Battalion who had travelled from Wuppertal. He was able to show the party the Regimental Brooch which was to be presented to Her Royal Highness, The Princess Margaret, the new Colonel-in-Chief, later in the year.

During his ten-day stay in Trieste the Colonel of the Regiment was able to watch training in progress and he also carried out an inspection and took the salute at a formal parade in his honour. He attended a Regimental Guest Night and a cocktail party in the

Officers' Mess and was also entertained at a formal dinner in the Sergeants' Mess.

When he first arrived in the Officers' Mess he was cornered by a group of officers and pressed to display the brooch. Undoing his tunic and shirt buttons, he withdrew a small package suspended round his neck. It was indeed the brooch, kept, as he said, in the safest place he could think of!

Brigadier Backhouse was present on 4 May to witness a decisive win by the Battalion Team in the BETFOR Athletics Championship. The Team took 114½ points, with its nearest rivals, the 1st Battalion, the Loyal Regiment mustering a mere seventy-one.

After Brigadier Backhouse's visit came the highlight of the Battalion's annual training cycle, when it moved on 16 May to Austria to engage in field training and live firing on the ranges at Schmelz. As in 1953, the training began with companies marching the last eight miles into the mountains where the camp was located.

The first few days were spent in repairing the ravages of the winter inflicted on the range roads and then the more serious business of training was begun. Companies fired live ammunition on a battle practice range prepared by the Weapon Training Officer while the MMG and Mortar Platoons of Sp Company perfected their battle drills and also carried out live firing.

There were many opportunities to engage in less serious but nonetheless energetic pastimes as well. Several parties climbed to the summit of Zirbitz Kogel, including one from B Company which took the Padre with it. The Reverend T.W. Metcalfe was armed with his cine camera to prove, as *The Gazette* notes suggested, that they made it to the top!

On 7 June, as a climax to the training period a company attack demonstration was executed by a composite company from B and D Companies, supported by the Mortar Platoon and the MMG Platoon. The GOC BETFOR, Major-General Sir John Winterton, was visiting the Battalion at the time and sent highly complimentary messages to those taking part in the demonstration.

At the end of the Schmelz training a plan was put into effect which the Commanding Officer had had in his mind since the previous visit. The Battalion left the training camp and marched down the mountains to the small town of Neumarkt where it camped on 10 June.

That evening at 1730 a Guard of Honour with the Band and Drums was formed up in the main street of the town. The CO, together with the Burgomaster of Neumarkt, arrived by car at the saluting base to the sounding of a General Salute. The Burgomaster then inspected the Guard of Honour drawn up by Sp Company and commanded by Captain W.D.G. Fairholme, after which the CO made a speech, which, as the *Regimental Journal* recorded, was made in German, to the delight of the Austrians and the amazement of the Battalion!

Lieutenant-Colonel Heal then presented the Burgomaster with a letter from the Chairman of Newmarket Urban District Council in Suffolk. In reply the Burgomaster also made a speech and presented the CO with an album of photographs of Neumarkt. The Band and Drums them beat retreat (the first public parade of the Drums since disbandment for the Malayan tour in 1949) on the main trunk road through Neumarkt which the Burgomaster had ordered to be closed for the occasion! The remainder of the evening was spent with the Battalion joining their Austrian hosts in various guest houses in the town.

Soon after return to Trieste, the period of uncertainty as to the future of the Battalion was brought to an end upon receipt of firm orders for its move to Germany in August.

There was one further brief moment of tension, when political developments over Trieste led to both the Italian and Yugoslav armies threatening the territory with a show of force. The Battalion deployed a Company on the Italian frontier on this occasion and found itself confronted by an overwhelming array of Italian armour in the presence of which it felt extremely vulnerable. Fortunately, the crisis passed without incident.

A particularly happy event for the Advance Party in Germany occurred on 15 July. The new Colonel-in-Chief, HRH The Princess Margaret, was on a visit to BAOR and she had earlier indicated that she would much like to meet the families of the Battalion already based in Wuppertal. Bad weather precluded her flying to Wuppertal for the occasion, so the families were transported by bus to Dusseldorf where they assembled in the ballroom of the Rhine Centre.

On her arrival the Commanding Officer was presented to the Colonel-in-Chief by the GOC 2nd Infantry Division, Major-General B.A. Coad, CB, DSO. The Princess then inspected a small Guard of Honour from the Advance Party commanded by Captain H.D. Sutor. Mrs Heal, the Brigade Commander and his wife were then presented to Her Royal Highness.

Accompanied by the CO and Mrs Heal, the Princess then went into the ballroom to meet the families. All officers and wives present were presented to Her Royal Highness and she then chatted with a number of wives. The ceremony lasted for half-an-hour and was particularly significant as the first occasion of a visit to any part of the Regiment by the Colonel-in-Chief since her appointment.

Meanwhile, in Trieste, the last few weeks for the Battalion sped by and, when Minden Day arrived, packing for the move was well advanced. The day was spent in the usual manner. It began with a ceremonial parade which was taken by the GOC BETFOR, Major-Geneal Sir John Winterton, KCMG, CB, CBE. Following the parade, the whole Battalion moved to the barracks of the 1st Battalion, the Loyal Regiment, at Lazaretto where a swimming gala was held. In the evening there was a cabaret organized by the PRI.

Within a week after Minden Day the Battalion was on the move. The journey was made on MEDLOC military trains with companies being despatched separately over a period of several days. C Company left first and B Company last, with the final group of men arriving in Harding Barracks in Wuppertal on 22 August. Feelings on leaving Triests were mixed. It was a good peacetime station to which to be posted and it would have been enjoyed by everyone had the political situation been more temperate and allowed a full tour to go ahead uninterrupted and without the necessity to despatch the Advance Party and the families early to Wuppertal.

CHAPTER VI

THE FIRST BATTALION:

BAOR 1954–1956

'A small part in the Army of the Rhine'

Part I

The Battalion arrived back in Germany some nine years after it had left in December, 1945, to go to the Middle East. In those years the situation in Germany had changed dramatically. Where it had been a land torn and ravaged by war, it was by 1954 well on the way to assuming a prosperous, productive and confident air. Where its people had earlier barely scratched a living in their conquered land, they were now a newly sovereign and independent nation, soon to form its own army.

Yet another even greater contrast was evident – one which was to dominate the Battalion's tour of duty as part of the 6th Infantry Brigade of the 2nd Infantry Division. When the Battalion was in Gutersloh at the end of the War, the Soviet Union was an ally, but when it returned to Wuppertal in the heart of the Ruhr industrial area of Germany, it was to form part of a NATO army deployed against a massive Soviet army, seemingly bent on encroaching further westwards into Europe, having secured its dominance over the countries of Eastern Europe which it had occupied since the downfall of Hitler in 1945.

Training and preparations to repel such a threat were to be central to the role of the Battalion in BAOR for the next two years. For the first time since the War, it found itself a small cog in an enormous war machine, and yet there was something of a paradox in the whole situation. Wherever else it had been since 1945, the Battalion had been frequently confronted by a threat which in universal terms was

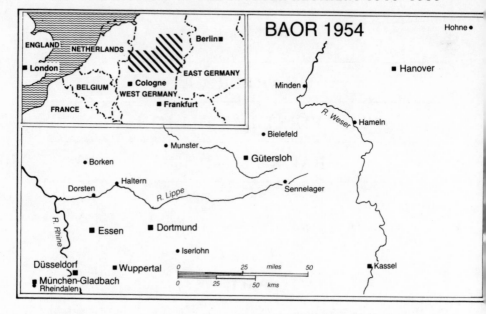

limited, (even in Malaya this was so) and yet life had been filled with excitement and often fraught with danger. Now, in Germany and with the advent of nuclear weapons, the Battalion was faced with the greatest possible potential threat, and yet in the daily round of life this threat seemed scarcely discernible. The two years in Germany were to be the nearest thing to peacetime soldiering that the Battalion would experience in the period covered by this history.

The cog in a machine analogy was the most apt description of life for a unit in the British Army of the Rhine at that time. Each year the Army completed a strictly ordered cycle of training which culminated in September and October with large-scale manoeuvres designed to test the ability of NATO's Northern Army Group of which it was a part, to take to the field in response to a threat emanating from the East.

The arrival of the Battalion in Wuppertal in August, 1954, meant it had to enter the annual cycle of training just before the major manoeuvre season and it was fortunate that, despite the shortages of manpower and the plethora of routine administrative duties in Trieste, training in the phases of war as currently envisaged in Northern Europe had been conducted wherever and whenever possible.

Almost immediately on arrival in Germany large drafts of recruits were posted into the Battalion to bring it up to the current BAOR

12. Lieutenant-Colonel I.L. Wight, DSO, OBE, Commanding Officer of the 1st Battalion in Greece and Malaya from 1948 to 1950.

13. By May, 1952, the 1st Battalion's success in the Malayan Emergency was such that it was trumpeted on the streets of Malaya and Singapore.

SUFFOLKS DO IT AGAIN

SINGAPORE, SUNDAY, MAY 25

Sunday Times

14. A 1st Battalion patrol making its way through Malayan jungle torn apart by RAF bombs.

15. The B Company patrol led by Captain E.H. Morgan which ambushed and killed the Commander of the 1st Regiment of the so-called Malayan Races Liberation Army, on 26 April, 1952.

16. The Officers of the 1st Battalion at Sungei Manggis in Malaya in 1952.

17. General Sir Gerald Templer, High Commissioner of the Federation of Malaya, saying farewell to officers of the 1st Battalion at Kajang on 2 January, 1953.

18. General Sir Gerald Templer and the Sultan of Selangor (accompanied by the Commanding Officer, Lieutenant-Colonel P.A. Morcombe, DSO, OBE,) speeding delighted soldiers of the 1st Battalion on their way to Singapore and the UK at the end of the extremely successful Malayan tour of duty.

19. Captain F.J. Lockett and CSM Collen leading their company past the
    Mayor of Sudbury after the 1st Battalion received the Freedom of the
    Borough on returning from Malaya in 1953

20. The Mayor of Ipswich takes the salute as the 1st Battalion marches through
    the Borough on return from Malaya in 1953.

21. The 1st Battalion party for the Coronation of HM Queen Elizabeth II in June, 1953.

22. Major K.M.J. Dewar, OBE with a detachment of B Company faces an ugly demonstration on the Piazza Unita in Trieste on 6 November, 1953.

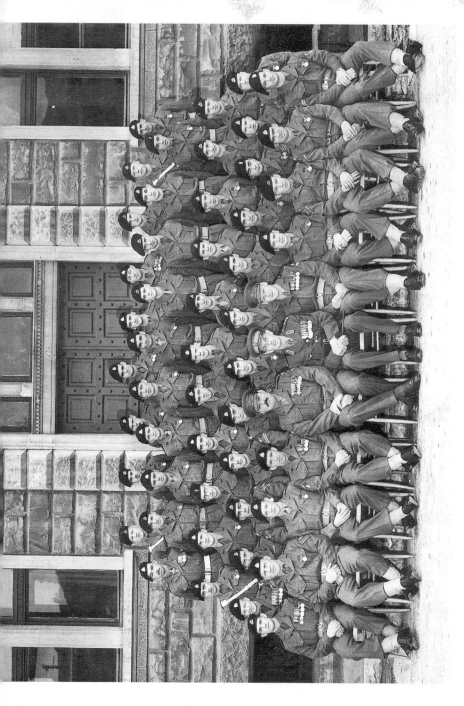

23. The Corporals of the 1st Battalion with the Colonel of the Regiment in Trieste in May, 1954.

24. The Colonel-in-Chief inspected the 1st Battalion when she presented new Colours in Wuppertal on 23 May, 1955.

25. Lieutenant J.R. Heath receives the new Queen's Colour from the Colonel-in-Chief with Major G.R. Heyland, OBE, MC in attendance.

establishment for an infantry battalion. A Company was reconstituted as a training organization and all the other rifle companies and specialist platoons were brought up to full strength.

The Autumn manoeuvres of 1954, named Battle Royal, were designed to test the ability of the Northern Army Group to respond to a Soviet advance into Western Germany. To play its small part in this giant scheme, the Battalion had but a few weeks in which to prepare. In that short space of time the whole Battalion underwent an intensive period of watermanship training and participated in early September, in a 2nd Infantry Division exercise, Phoenix II.

All of this went well enough and at the end of September, with some confidence, the Battalion moved out for Battle Royal keyed up with a feeling of great anticipation. In the event, the exercise was something of an anti-climax: just when plans were prepared for a night approach march to, and an opposed crossing of, the River Lippe in which the Battalion was directly involved, it came to a halt.

The Battalion returned to Harding Barracks and settled down to the beginning of the new twelve-month training cycle. Throughout the winter months the emphasis was on individual training. The rifle companies concentrated on weapon training, fieldcraft and shooting and the Support Company platoons on their own particular tasks. It was also the season for cadres for junior NCO's, drivers, signallers and other specialists. These latter were run by A Company which, as the Battalion's own expert training organization, was also responsible for short induction courses for newly arrived drafts of recruits from the United Kingdom.

In the Spring of 1955 the training moved forward to field training and minor tactics starting at section and platoon level and advancing to company exercises involving battle drills for deployment and action.

Finally, in preparation for exercises run by higher formations later in the summer and autumn, the Battalion complete deployed and tested itself in all the phases of war.

On these exercises the CO frequently took the opportuniy to 'kill off' commanders at various levels in order to test the ability of the unit to function, despite suffering major losses. While it was clearly invaluable to test the responses of those suddenly put in command in such circumstances, their consternation often provided considerable amusement for those not so involved!

The Battalion completed two such annual cycles of training while in BAOR and its state of training by the end of its two and a half years in Germany was at a very high level.

Such a cycle of events inevitably meant that a large part of the year was spent out of barracks and away from Wuppertal on the various ranges and training areas which abounded in Germany and which were of a very high standard.

When in barracks, however, life took on the air of peacetime soldiering. The Barracks themselves, built before the Second World War for the German Army of the time, were rather grim in appearance but provided all the facilities that could be wanted. The Officers' and Sergeants' Messes were of a high quality and the barrack rooms light and airy and with plenty of baths, showers and drying rooms. Training facilities in the barracks were excellent and sports grounds throughout the garrison of the highest order.

Wuppertal lay in the Ruhr industrial area, but at the south-eastern edge of it and the countryside beyond was very attractive. Harding Barracks was built on the hills outside the town.

The Headquarters of the 6th Infantry Brigade was close by as were the Barracks of the other battalions in the Brigade.

Throughout the stay in Germany the Band and Drums played a vital and full role in the peacetime activities of the Battalion. The stability of two and a half years in one barracks afforded an opportunity which the Bandmaster and the Drum Major seized on to improve and perfect their musical and military skills. Constantly in demand for official and private functions, they also had to perform frequently in massed concerts at Brigade, Division and BAOR level.

In previous stations since 1946 life for the families with the Battalion had had its ups and downs. Now, in Wuppertal, the number of families began to multiply. Conditions were on the whole good for them, apart, of course, from the long absences of husbands on exercises. Married quarters varied from good to excellent, shopping was good and the general amenities in the garrison area of a very high order. The presence of the families also did much to enhance the life of the Battalion on its various social occasions.

Leave was enjoyed to the full by everyone while in Germany. It was easy to get home to the United Kingdom and, for the more adventurous, Wuppertal was well situated geographically to explore the rest of Germany and further afield.

Sport featured prominently in the daily life of the Battalion. The competitive spirit reigned both within the unit and beyond. Inter-Company and Inter-Platoon knock-out and league competitions in football, hockey and cricket followed their course throughout the year. Companies entered various Brigade Minor Units competitions and the Battalion fielded teams in Brigade, Divisional and BAOR championships.

Being stationed in Germany provided the first opportunity for many to learn something of winter sports. A considerable number of officers and men attended winter warfare courses and many others availed themselves of a chance to take a short leave at Winterburg, the British Army's own ski resort in Germany.

There is no doubt, however, that the principal event for the Battalion during its sojourn in BAOR came in May, 1955, when HRH The Princess Margaret, Colonel-in-Chief of the Regiment, came to Wuppertal to present new Colours.

The old six-foot Colours had been in service for one hundred and six years and an opportunity to receive new Colours to replace them had been sought for some time. As far back as 1949 in Greece, when the Colours achieved their centenary, the then Commanding Officer Lieutenant-Colonel I.L. Wight, OBE, had hoped to arrange for new Colours to be presented, but the sudden orders to move to Malaya prevented the ceremony from taking place.

The tour of duty in Germany was to provide the ideal opportunity. The Colonel-in-Chief could travel with reasonable ease to join the Battalion, it was at full strength and in May the manoeuvre season had yet to start in real earnest and there was thus an opportunity to prepare properly for the occasion.

The Commanding Officer made the Officer Commanding HQ Company responsible for arrangements. Planning got under way early in 1955, although the final confirmation that the presentation would be made only came through in April.

An article from the *Regimental Journal* for the third quarter of 1955 described the occasion in detail and is reproduced in its entirety at Appendix IX.

By the end of 1955 the Battalion was nearing the end of its tour in BAOR. It had reached a peak of efficiency and morale was high with many successes, both military and in the field of shooting and sport, behind it.

Early in December news was received that its next posting would be in August, 1956, to the troubled island of Cyprus. The Battalion left Wuppertal on 1 July bound for the UK.

Part II

Soon after arrival in BAOR from Trieste senior appointments in the Battalion were held as follows:

CO:	Lieutenant-Colonel W.A. Heal, OBE
2ic:	Major W.H. Brinkley (Royal Norfolk Regiment)
Adjt:	Captain W.C. Deller
QM:	Lieutenant G.S. Jasper
RSM:	RSM Gingell
OC A Coy:	Captain A.L. Willdridge
CSM (SMIM):	CSM Lyon
OC B Coy:	Major P.H.A.L. Franklin (Essex Regiment)
CSM:	CSM Loveday
OC C Coy:	Major L.W. Allan, MBE, (Essex Regiment)
CSM:	CSM Norman
OC D Coy:	Major C.E. Britten (Bedfordshire & Hertfordshire Regiment)
CSM:	CSM Robinson
OC HQ Coy:	Major W.C. Smith
CSM:	CSM McColl
OC Sp Coy:	Major H.C. Harvey
CSM:	CSM Mayhew

The Battalion's arrival by train in Germany can best be described as a trickle which began with the arrival of the bulk of C Company with elements of HQ Company at the end of the first week of August, 1954, and continued until 24 August when B Company finally drove in through the gates of Harding Barracks in Wuppertal.

Everyone quickly settled in, agreeably surprised by the spacious and functional accommodation which the pre-war German barracks provided. It was as well that the settling-in process was achieved without a major hitch, as training began almost immediately after arrival, it being essential that the Battalion should have a chance to prepare itself for the Army manoeuvres scheduled for the end of September.

In preparation for the probability that the Battalion would be involved in river crossings in the forthcoming manoeuvres, it was necessary initially for everyone to be trained in basic watermanship. Companies in turn spent three days on the River Lippe at the Dorsten Training Area where they received instruction in the use of collapsable assault craft by day and by night.

All watermanship training was completed before the end of August and in September a series of minor exercises culminated in a 2nd Infantry Division exercise called Phoenix II. This exercise was by way of being a prelude to the Northern Army Group exercise, Battle Royal, which was to involve the Battalion as part of the 6th Infantry Brigade, in completing an approach march to a river by night, followed by an opposed river crossing.

Phoenix II completed, the Battalion found itself back in barracks towards the end of September, making careful preparations for Battle Royal. When the big exercise finally took place early in October, as is so often the way of things, the Battalion met with little to challenge it. It completed a series of night moves into harbour areas and then into concentration areas, but not once did it come face to face with the enemy! Just as things looked set for the long-awaited opposed river crossing, against which enterprise so much training and heart-searching had been involved, the end of the exercise was announced and the Battalion made its way back to Harding Barracks.

On 5 October A Company was reformed as a training company with responsibility for all cadres for platoon commanders, senior and junior NCOs and for new drafts from the United Kingdom before posting to companies.

Early in the month the Battalion joined the others in the Brigade in lining the route to say farewell to a very popular Brigade Commander, Brigadier C.A.R. Neville, CBE, DSO. He was succeeded in November by Brigadier R.E. Goodwin, CBE, DSO, to whose arrival all in the Battalion looked forward.

9 October witnessed a new departure in the Sergeants' Mess. A feature of Suffolk Regimental life had long been the Sergeants' Mess Past and Present Annual Dinner, held at Bury St Edmunds every year since first inaugurated in 1906. In Wuppertal the Sergeants' Mess decided to hold a dinner in 1955, on the same day as that in Bury St Edmunds and it was named the Sergeants' Mess Dinner (Past and Present) Abroad. The Commanding Officer was invited to be Chairman of the dinner and four other officers were invited as guests.

Sadly, the next day it was learned that Sergeant R.C.J. Taylor of the Band had died at BMH Iserlohn. Sergeant Taylor had enlisted in the Regiment as a Band Boy in 1926, serving with the 2nd Battalion in China and India until 1934 when he returned to the United Kingdom and joined the 1st Battalion at Plymouth. He remained with the 1st Battalion thereafter, going to Malta and returning to the United Kingdom in 1939. He was taken prisoner while serving with the 1st Battalion in France and after the War stayed with the 1st Battalion in all their postings until his death. A fine history of service to the Regiment died with him.

With individual training in full swing from the middle of October, a great deal of time was spent on the ranges and on the 28th and 29th of that month the Battalion Rifle meeting was held at Erbschlo Ranges near Wuppertal. 645 members of the Battalion fired the rifle and Private Malyon of D Company scored 115 out of a possible 120 to become Champion Shot. C Company won the Company Championship Shield.

On 7 November the Battalion joined the other Battalions of the Brigade (1st Battalion, the Durham Light Infantry and the 1st Battalion, the Royal Ulster Rifles) for a Remembrance Day Service held in the Wuppertal Opera House.

In the two months up to Christmas, 1954, a heavy programme of sports was arranged. An Inter-Company knock-out football competition was hastily organized, hoping that it would reveal talent for a Battalion team to play in the BAOR Cup competition. Unfortunately, the cup was lost in the first game of the season and to make matters worse the team was also defeated in the first round of the Brigade Major Units knock-out competition. The Inter-Company league continued through the season as the best means of working up talent to try for the cup again next year.

The rugby team fared scarcely better in their run for the Army Cup, drawing an early game with the previous year's divisional finalists. It remained for the Battalion team to play a series of enjoyable, hard-fought friendly matches, while hatching plans for the following year.

The hockey team, too, found the going tough and was knocked out after a closely fought game in the first round of the Army Cup.

It was generally acknowledged by the sportsmen that the standard of games in BAOR was high and that great efforts were required to perform better in the future. But it should be added that it was deliberate policy, welcomed by all, not to build up teams of gladiators for any particular sport, but rather to strive for maximum participation in all sports at all levels, from platoon upwards, an aim which was certainly achieved.

The Battalion church, which had been renamed St Edmunds by the Battalion when it arrived in Wuppertal, had been attractively refurbished under the supervision of the Padre, The Reverend T.W. Metcalfe, with the help of the QM's Pioneers. It was well used every

Sunday and at Christmas the celebrations were in traditional manner with Midnight Communion on Christmas Eve and a six-lesson Carol Service on Christmas morning, which was accompanied by the Band.

In 1955 training recommenced with determination. On 4 January the CO took Battalion HQ, together with Company and Sp Platoon Commanders, out on a wireless exercise, and on the 10th a Platoon Commanders' tactics course, run by A Company, began.

The Commander-in-Chief of the Northern Army Group, General Sir Richard Gale, GCB, KBE, DSO, MC, ADC, descended on the Battalion during a heavy snowstorm towards the end of the month and made a tour of inspection of every company and every department.

27 January witnessed the Inter-Company Drill Competition which to the very last minute seemed likely to be cancelled. However, RSM Gingell and his gang of 'snowmen' (as they were described in one company's notes for the *Regimental Gazette*) managed to clear the parade ground by dint of Herculean efforts and it went ahead with D Company runners-up to B Company on the day!

In February a number of Brigade and Divisional exercises was held which demanded participation only by key personalities from the Battalion. Heavy falls of snow during the month meant that company training was a chilly affair. It did mean, however, that the 2nd Infantry Division skiing championships, in which two officers and nine men from the Battalion participated, went ahead without a hitch.

To end the month the Brigade Commander, Brigadier Goodwin, carried out the annual administrative inspection. It was the first such formal inspection since 1949 when the Battalion was in Greece, on the point of departure for Malaya. It went well enough and the Band correspondent writing in the *Regimental Gazette* summed up the general feeling when he wrote, 'It was a pleasure to meet Brigadier Goodwin and to find his interest in the Battalion still as keen as it was when he served with the Regiment'!

Aside from training, February also witnessed two events worthy of note. When the Battalion arrived in Harding Barracks the only shortcoming found there was the lack of a large enough room for the various social functions likely to be held. It was decided to convert the attic of the NAAFI building into a club room and the chosen theme for decoration was the cabin of an 18th Century Man-of-War. When it was ready, Mrs Heal named the ship HMS *Suffolk* and launched it with the traditional bottle of champagne at the opening night ceremony which was declared a full house with a gathering of some 350. The Regimental Dance Band played during the evening and the PRI, Major Lockett, with his usual flair, produced an excellent cabaret from the nightclubs of Wuppertal.

Agatha Christie's play, *Ten Little Niggers*, produced and directed by Captain H.D. Sutor, with a cast drawn from the officers and their families, was so successful on its first production in February that it played again for Wuppertal Garrison and then was taken to the 2nd Infantry Divisional HQ Barracks for a charity show in aid of SSAFA.

With the advent of March, the level of training was stepped up and more time was spent in the field. The early part of the month was taken up with platoon marches which each lasted four days. Platoons were required to adhere to a route of approximately sixty miles, otherwise they were left to their own devices and all found the hospitality of local German farmers overwhelming and thus slept comfortably in hay lofts and barns en route.

The whole Battalion moved to the Sennelager Training Area on 12 March for two weeks' field firing and, though the weather was cold and snowy, a comprehensive programme both for rifle company and sp platoons was completed.

The early part of April saw companies visiting the Borkenburg Training Area where they practised day and night platoon and company attacks. This was in preparation for the first Battalion exercise of the season – Exercise Netheravon – which was conducted by the Commanding Officer and which pursued the same theme from 11 to 21 April. The opportunity was also taken at this time to train the stretcher bearers for the Connaught Shield, a competition for all units in BAOR which took place at the end of April. In the event the Battalion team came sixth out of twenty-one teams competing.

Late in April a Battalion Rifle Meeting was held with the object of selecting teams for the Brigade and BAOR Rifle Meetings. In this, the first full training season in BAOR, hopes were high of winning similar success to that last achieved in Malaya and as events were to prove, this enthusiasm was not misplaced.

On 1 May a trial reorganization of the Battalion into four rifle companies, each of four platoons and with the MMG Platoon the sole support element, was implemented. A Company was reformed as a rifle company and its training functions were taken over by a small Regimental Training Centre.

The next day the Battalion Shooting Team successfully fired a match to qualify for the BAOR Rifle Meeting to be held in June.

Apart from a brief two-day spell of watermanship training, the remainder of May was almost exclusively reserved for preparations for the presentation of new Colours by the Colonel-in-Chief, The Princess Margaret. Final confirmation that the presentation would be made on 23 May only came in April, so that little time was left and the pace of preparation soon quickened. The Commanding Officer, the Adjutant and the RSM were, of course, closely involved in rehearsing the Battalion for the parade itself, while OC HQ Company, Major W.C. Smith, assisted by a committee including the QM and outside agencies, dealt with the overall planning arrangements which included working out the timetable of the parade and other events associated with it, preparing and dispatching invitations to an extremely elaborate guest list and arrangements for receiving and accommodating guests from elsewhere in BAOR and from the United Kingdom. Major Smith and the QM also supervised a major campaign to smarten up the Barracks.

On 16 May a full-dress rehearsal for the presentation parade was taken by the Brigade Commander, Brigadier Goodwin, at which the opportunity was also provided for him to present the insignia of a Member of the Most Excellent Order of the British Empire to the OC C Company, Major L.W. Allan, and Military Medals to Colour Sergeant R. Fowler and Sergeant R. Evans for gallant and distinguished services in Malaya.

A detailed description of the Colour Presentation Parade on 23 May and associated events was written by the Battalion sub-editor of the *Regimental Gazette* and is to be found in Appendix IX.

Main appointments on the Presentation Parade included:

CO:	Lieutenant-Colonel W.A. Heal, OBE
Adjt:	Captain W.C. Deller
RSM:	RSM Gingell
No 1 Guard Commander:	Major G.R. Heyland, OBE, MC
No 2 Guard Commander:	Major L.W. Allan, MBE
No 3 Guard Commander:	Captain H.J. Chisnall
No 4 Guard Commander:	Major H.C. Harvey
Old Colour Party:	
Queen's Colour	Lieutenant J.P. Macdonald
Regimental Colour:	2nd Lieutenant J.G.M. North
Escort:	CSM McColl, Sergeant Drew and Sergeant Evans, MM

New Colour Party:
Queen's Colour	Lieutenant J.R. Heath
Regimental Colour:	Lieutenant J.D. Churchill
Escort:	CSM Bates, Sergeant Aspinall, Sergeant Mowle

The whole occasion was a marvellous success and an inspiration to the Battalion, although, as well, a moment of sadness at the passing out of service of the, by then, old and unique Colours carried by successive generations since their presentation at Weedon in 1849.

Two days after the parade B, C and D Companies moved to Soltau Training Area for five days to carry out infantry/tank co-operation with the 8th Royal Tank Regiment. A Company went to Soltau on 28 May for the same training and the next day B, C and D Companies moved to Sennelager to join up with Battalion HQ and complete further training at company level. With the arrival of A Company from its Soltau training on 1 June, a battalion exercise was conducted over the next three days covering the advance to contact, a dawn attack, defence and withdrawal.

On returning to Wuppertal on 4 June, it was learned that the Battalion Shooting Team had won the Rhine Army Championship Shield against stiff opposition from thirty-six other teams, of which twenty-two were from other infantry battalions. It was, indeed, a great victory for the Team in which it defeated two battalions of the King's Royal Rifle Corps (renowned for their shooting) and the 1st Battalion, the Worcestershire Regiment (rivals from Malayan days).

Wuppertal Garrison held a parade on 9 June to celebrate the birthday of Her Majesty the Queen. Along with the other battalions of the Brigade, the Battalion provided a contingent of seventeen officers and 200 men, together with the Drums. The salute was taken by Brigadier Goodwin.

An amusing sequel to this parade came a few days later in an article published in a local Wuppertal paper. When the Parade formed up it was necessary for the contingent of the 1st Battalion, the Royal Ulster Rifles, to come on to the parade ground after the other two Battalions, since they moved, as usual, in double time. The correspondent for the paper praised the parade fulsomely, but added that it was a pity that one contingent was late and had to run!

On the same day the Band lent its weight to the 4th Guards Brigade at Dusseldorf for a celebration of the Trooping of the Colour in which the Colours of the 2nd Battalion, the Scots Guards, were trooped. The end of a busy day found the Band playing in the evening at a garden party at the British Embassy in Bonn given by H.M. Ambassador, also in honour of the Queen's birthday.

Ten days later the Band and Drums were out in force to combine with other Bands and Drums of the 2nd Infantry Division to give a mass display for 40,000 spectators at the Dusseldorf stadium. One section of the stadium was filled with British servicemen and their families but the vast majority of the spectators were Germans, clearly hugely entertained by the spectacle.

All four rifle companies were out on Borkenburg and Haltern Training Areas engaged in platoon and company training from 20 to 25 June, and the month ended with Exercise Silent River, which involved A, B and C Companies in an assault river crossing of the River Rhine, using assault boats manned by men of the Royal Marines Volunteer Reserve.

While this exercise was in progress, D Company had perhaps the less glamorous and certainly the most onerous task of constructing a defence position, using new techniques about to be introduced into the Northern Army Group, to provide proper cover against the use of atomic weapons.

With a view to selecting two platoons to compete in the Nijmegen Marches in Holland at the end of the month, an inter-platoon marching competition was organized on 2 July. The platoons marched a distance of sixteen miles and marks were awarded for speed and bearing, as well as for completing the course together. 3 Platoon of A Company commanded by 2nd Lieutenant D. Mullock won, with 2nd Lieutenant C.J.N. Trollope, 8 Platoon of C Company, coming in second. These platoons were earmarked for three weeks' intensive training before dispatch to Holland.

For the rest of the Battalion the remainder of July was used to perfect patrolling techniques for the Battalion and Brigade patrolling competitions which took place on 26 and 27 July. The former was won by 2nd Lieutenant Hill's Platoon from B Company, and this Platoon represented the Battalion the next day.

2nd Lieutenant Trollope led the Nijmegen March contingent to Holland on 26 July and, along with some 400 officers and men from BAOR, among the thousands who entered, endured sore feet and completed the four days of marching in fine style.

Minden Day was suddenly upon the Battalion. With an over-full training programme, time was squeezed in to rehearse for a ceremonial parade which took place in the morning. The parade took the form of a Trooping of the Colours of the 2nd Battalion (prior to laying them up at Bury St Edmunds). The salute was taken by the GOC, 2nd Infantry Division, Major-General J.H.O. Wilsey, CB, CBE, DSO, supported by Brigadier Goodwin, who could hardly have been expected to miss the opportunity of parading with the Battalion wearing Minden roses.

After the parade the day was spent in the traditional manner. The Officers and Sergeants joined forces to serve lunch to the men and then all adjourned to the parade ground to enjoy a light-hearted sports meeting and a Minden Fair. Once again the PRI, Major F.J. Lockett, turned up trumps and organized an excellent cabaret which followed a buffet supper for the men in the evening.

Such a brief account of this Regimental occasion scarcely paints a true picture of the entirely self-generated pleasure of the day, in which the Battalion showed, as so frequently in the years gone by, a real family identity.

With little time to recover from the holiday, the Battalion climbed back on to the never-ceasing treadmill of training and moved to Sennelager on 3 August for another ten-day stint. The first exercise involved advancing to contact through a heavily wooded area, and the second was a dawn attack in cooperation with the 8th Royal Tank Regiment, following the use of an atomic missile. The third tested the Battalion in a river crossing (imaginary, there being no rivers in the training area) and an attack launched on an enemy deployed well beyond it. Consternation reigned at one point when Battalion HQ found, having deployed in the night, that it was sited in the middle of a nudist camp!

It was during this last exercise that the CO, Lieutenant-Colonel Heal, introduced what was to become his notorious code word, Bungo. Whoever was Bungo-ed was presumed to be a casualty and could take no further part in the battle. Such a departure concentrated the minds of 2ic's wonderfully, as the CO seemed to take a delight in eliminating commanders just when the battle was at its thickest.

On 7 September the 6th Infantry Brigade performed a Searchlight Tattoo in the Wuppertal stadium before a British and German audience of 12,000. The evening opened with a noisy firework display and then came a series of events performed by the three Battalions involving music, drill and dancing (by the Royal Ulster Rifles). The drill contingents of the Battalion and the 1st Battalion, the Buffs, were dressed in scarlet tunics and the appropriate helmets and made a fine sight.

The remainder of September was taken up with the two major

exercises of the collective training season, Pied Piper and Full House. Pied Piper was a 2nd Infantry Division exercise lasting from 13 to 18 September, involving the three Brigades of the Division. It comprised a successful crossing of the River Weser near Hameln by the 4th Guards Brigade and the 5th Infantry Brigade, with the 6th Infantry Brigade in reserve. The two forward Brigades were then held up by an atomic missile and the 6th Infantry Brigade crossed the Weser and moved into defensive positions. As Reserve Battalion of the Reserve Brigade, the Battalion saw scarcely any action, but learnt much about night movement and the taking up of concentration areas in total darkness!

In the 1st British Corps exercise, Full House, which ran from 19 to 27 September, the Battalion played a much more active part. The scenario of the exercise was similar to that for Pied Piper. Initially the 2nd Infantry Division was in reserve with the task of exploiting a bridgehead over the Weser established by one of the other Divisions of the Corps. The 4th Guards and the 5th Infantry Brigades crossed the Weser on the 22nd and made good progress. The 6th Infantry Brigade, with the Battalion and the 1st Battalion, the Buffs, forward, crossed the next day and advanced to seize their objectives. At this point the enemy countered with an atomic missile, wiping out the Buffs and also virtually eliminating the Battalion, leaving but a composite Company made up from Battalion HQ personnel under command of the Battalion 2ic, Major G.R. Heyland, the CO, Ajutant and IO having been killed off by the exercise directing staff.

The exercise ended on 26 September, leaving a very weary but satisfied Battalion to make its way by road back to Wuppertal, having completed another major exercise season.

The summer had, despite the heavy training commitments, witnessed a full programme of sports, in which, while not achieving any outstanding victories, the Battalion held its own in Brigade and Divisional competitions.

A good all-round performance of the 2nd Infantry Division Athletics Meeting on 1 July was followed by taking third place in the Divisional Inter-Unit Swimming Championships on 26 July at Dortmund.

In tennis Lieutenant R.H. Champion (the RMO) and 2nd Lieutenant Wortley reached the final of the Divisional Men's Doubles, only being defeated by the current BAOR champions.

Following the victory in the BAOR Shooting Championships, the Battalion Shooting Team journeyed to Bisley in July, but the high hopes were not realized on the day. However, Private Malyon and

Corporal Chatten gained forty-seventh and seventy-first places respectively in the Army Hundred.

With the end of the exercise season, the Battalion returned to the individual training cycle. A number of cadres for specialists started in October and the rifle companies spent many days on the ranges firing the annual range course.

A Company reverted to a training organization after exercise Full House, but also held under its command the nucleus of the support weapons of the Battalion, including the Mortar and the MMG Platoon.

On 16 October a detachment of twenty men under Lieutenant J.P. Macdonald, together with the Band and Drums, was sent to Holland to represent the Battalion at the annual memorial ceremony at Overloon, remembering the battle there in October, 1944, in which the Battalion participated, sustaining heavy casualties in fierce fighting. Other units who had taken part in the battle also sent detachments and the whole parade was commanded by Major D.U. Fraser, MBE. Brigadier and Mrs Goodwin and the Commanding Officer and Mrs Heal attended the ceremony, at which the salute was taken by General Sir Lashmer Whistler, who had commanded the 3rd Infantry Division at the battle.

On 20 October the CO, Lieutenant-Colonel W.A. Heal, OBE, presented a specially bound set of the three volumes of the History of the Regiment to the Colonel-in-Chief, The Princess Margaret, at a ceremony at Clarence House. The gift from the Battalion was to commemorate the Princess's visit in May to present new Colours.

At the end of October the MMG Platoon under 2nd Lieutenant J.D. Churchill joined the annual Northern Army Group MMG concentration at Sennelager where live firing and other training took place.

5 November witnessed a grand celebration of Guy Fawkes night. Searchlights played on the Band and Drums while they beat retreat. There followed a torchlight procession and then a marvellous firework display to accompany the lighting of the traditional bonfire.

A more sombre note was struck the next day to celebrate Remembrance Sunday. The Battalion paraded on the square and then, with other units of the Brigade, marched to the Wuppertal-Elberfeld Opera House for a Garrison Remembrance Day Service.

Range work went ahead in November, with companies continuing to classify their men on the annual range course and also firing the outstanding non-central Bisley matches.

For some time rumours had been rife as to the Battalion's next posting, and on 3 December notification was received that it would move to Cyprus in August, 1956, staging in the United Kingdom en route.

On 5 December a Battalion Signals Exercise, Winter Wheat, was held. Battalion and Company HQs in skeleton form took to the field for it.

There followed a brief spell of frantic preparation for the Brigade Commander's annual administrative inspection, which took place on 15 and 16 December. Brigadier Goodwin expressed himself well pleased with what he found, and in his report spoke of the exceedingly high standard he felt the Battalion had achieved in BAOR.

The year came to an end with a wide variety of Christmas activities, which included a Families' Club dance and an Inter-Company barrack room decorating competition which was won by C Company, who created a Suffolk pub with beams, a bar and a very life-like hearth with a blazing fire.

A Nativity play was performed by children in the Battalion in St Edmunds Church on 18 December and a nine-lesson Carol Service was held on the 21st. The Church choir, with the Band, sang carols on two nights in the married quarters and Christmas Day was celebrated by a midnight communion and a morning service on Christmas Day itself.

The arrival of 1956 was marked by a serious deterioration in the weather. Most of January saw freezing conditions accompanied by heavy and frequent falls of snow. For the most part individual training had to be completed indoors. With the exception of skiing, outdoor sports were curtailed and basketball and badminton in the gymnasium gained many supporters.

Two exercises did, however, take place during the month. The first, Exercise Cold Feet (very appropriately named), was run by the Battalion on 10 January and was designed to test Signals and Command Groups in the attack. The second, organized by Brigade HQ, was supposed to run from 31 January to 2 February and was designed to test the Brigade in a rapid advance to contact. However, temperatures dropped to a freak level, resulting in eleven cases of frostbite in the Battalion and one or two burst vehicle radiators, despite their having the recommended level of anti-freeze in them. The Battalion was feeding from fresh rations and on the first morning of the exercise breakfast was somewhat curtailed. Bread, milk and even eggs were frozen solid. Those members of Battalion HQ sporting moustaches turned white, as their breath froze and coated the hair with frost.

The Brigade was effectively brought to a standstill and the exercise was eventually cancelled, leaving many to ponder on the likely effectiveness of BAOR should it need to take to the field in earnest under such intolerable conditions.

Those lucky enough to get on to skiing courses were the only ones to benefit from the severity of the weather. The Divisional Ski Championships were also held in January and, though the Battalion team did not gain a place, the individual championship was won by 2nd Lieutenant J.L. Bazalgette.

The Battalion ran a knock-out badminton championship competition between 14 and 16 February. Captain R.H. Champion (RMO) and Captain H.J. Chisnall won the mens' doubles and the RMO, playing with Mrs Norman (wife of CSM Norman), the mixed doubles.

Major General C.L. Firbank, CB, CBE, DSO, Director of Infantry, paid a visit to the Battalion to observe individual training in progress on 17 February.

On 20 February the Band and Drums combined with the other Bands, Pipes and Drums of the Brigade to perform a musical concert in the Wuppertal-Elberfeld Opera House before an Anglo-German audience.

Throughout the winter the Sergeant-Major Instructor of Musketry, CSM V.G. Lyon, had worked hard in the realms of small-bore shooting. Inter-Company competitions led to the formation of a very good Battalion team, which won the Divisional Cup and, from 20 to 22 February, fired in the BAOR Championships at Sennelager. The team shot well to reach the final but then was narrowly defeated by the 1st Battalion, the Manchester Regiment.

On 8 March the Signal Platoon won the Brigade Inter-Unit tests which were conducted in the form of a signals exercise.

Training continued through March with all companies shaking off the winter gloom, with a brief spell, in turn, at Borkenburg Training Area to carry out section and platoon tactical training. In the latter half of the month A Company took the MMG, the Anti-Tank and the Mortar Platoons to Putlos Ranges on the Baltic coast for a fortnight's field firing.

The Band was put through its paces on 13 March, when it was given a very testing inspection by the Director of Army Bands. A good report was achieved, so the effort of preparation was well rewarded.

23 March saw a Guard of Honour from the Battalion parading at München-Gladbach, accompanied by the Band and Drums. The

occasion was to mark a visit by the Dutch Minister of Defence to HQ Northern Army Group. Also on parade were troops from the Royal Marines, the Belgian Army and the British and Dutch Royal Air Forces.

A further parade on 4 April took place to commemorate the formation of NATO in 1949. It was held in Dusseldorf and comprised contingents from Belgium, Holland and Canada, as well as from the British Army of the Rhine. The newly formed German Army was represented for the first time by a Military Band.

Beyenburg Range was the venue on 10 April for the Battalion Rifle Meeting. B Company won the Inter-Company Championship and Colour Sergeant R. Evans, MM, of C Company won the individual rifle championship by two points from the runner-up, Captain E.H. Morgan, MC.

Immediately following the Rifle Meeting all companies left for Sennelager to carry out seven days of live field firing.

The latter half of the month was a busy time for Captain Champion, the RMO. Working with the Medical Sergeant, Sergeant Newett, he conducted an intensive training course for the Battalion stretcher bearers, in preparation for the BAOR Inter-Unit competition for the Connaught Shield. The competition took place from 23 to 26 April and the Battalion team came fifth out of all the teams from every Battalion and Regiment in BAOR.

The end of the month saw a number of events organized to bid the Commanding Officer farewell at the end of his tour of command. Lieutenant-Colonel Heal took over in England prior to the departure of the Battalion for Trieste, and now was leaving after almost exactly three eventful years at the helm. A beating retreat was performed by the Band and Drums in the CO's honour on 25 April, after which he and Mrs Heal were entertained in the Sergeants' Mess.

He was dined out of the Officers' Mess on 27 April and the next day, at a ceremonial parade, he formally handed over command to the new CO, Lieutenant-Colonel W.S. Bevan. The Bandmaster, Mr G.A. Holben, was presented with his Long Service and Good Conduct Medal by Lieutenant-Colonel Heal during the course of this parade.

The next morning, Sunday 29 April, the CO and Mrs Heal were towed out of Barracks by the officers and sergeants to the accompaniment of the Band and cheering from the men lining the route.

The bleak winter weather had savagely curtailed football, hockey and rugby programmes. The Battalion football team were runners-up in the Brigade league and B Company's team won the Brigade Minor Units knock-out competition. Two friendly hockey matches only were played, of which one was won and the other lost. In the latter game against a Sapper team, it snowed so heavily that the two umpires could not even see each other!

Similar conditions precluded the playing of rugby altogether. By the time the Divisional Seven-a-sides were played in April the weather was better and the Battalion team reached the semi-finals against stiff opposition, losing 5–0 to the 1st Battalion, the Buffs, who went on to win the competition.

One figurative ray of sunshine pierced the winter gloom, when Corporal Taylor of B Company boxed his way at welterweight to the BAOR finals and then to the Army Boxing Championship in which he reached the quarter-finals.

On 3 May an Inter-Company Patrolling Competition, Exercise Silent Snatch, was staged. The results were close with A Company the winners and D Company runners-up.

A week later the Battalion shooting team won the Brigade Rifle Meeting held on the Sennelager Ranges for the second year running. CSM Hazelwood fired well to win the Individual Rifle Championship and Lieutenant T.D. Dean was Best Officer Rifle Shot.

The Inter-Company Athletics Meeting was held in the Wuppertal Stadium on 16 May. The competition was won narrowly by HQ Company from C Company. The final outcome was in doubt until the very last event, the 4 × 400 metres relay. C Company won the race but HQ Company came second and thus gained enough points to clinch the trophy.

With only a month to go before departure for England, June saw everyone packing in preparation for the move. The cycle of training ran down and thoughts were turned to plans made for Minden Day in England, when Princess Margaret would be visiting the Battalion in Colchester, prior to the Battalion's move to Cyprus.

Senior appointments in the Battalion following the assumption of command by Lieutenant-Colonel Bevan, included:

CO:	Lieutenant-Colonel W.S. Bevan
2ic:	Major G.R. Heyland, OBE, MC
Adjt:	Captain W.C. Deller
QM:	Captain T.C. Warren
RSM:	RSM Gingell
OC A Company:	Captain A.L. Willldridge
CSM (SMIM):	CSM Lyon
OC B Company:	Major F.D. Ingle

CSM:	CSM Hazelwood
OC C Company:	Major G.T.O. Springfield
CSM:	CSM Norman
OC D Company:	Captain H.J. Chisnall
CSM:	CSM Smith
OC HQ Company:	Major D.U. Fraser, MBE
CSM:	CSM McColl
OC Sp Company	Major H.C. Harvey
CSM:	CSM Robinson

There remained two events of note to record before the departure from BAOR. The Battalion Shooting Team went to Sennelager from 4 to 8 June to fire for the Rhine Army Shield. Hopes were high that it would repeat the success of 1955 and bring the shield back to Wuppertal, but it was not to be. The Team fired competently but failed to achieve the really high scores necessary. It came seventh out of thirty-six – a creditable enough performance, but nevertheless a disappointment. Four members of the team won a place in the Rhine Army Hundred, with the CO topping the list in third place.

The 6th Infantry Brigade Sports were held in Wuppertal on 16 June and the Battalion team won a well-deserved victory in this the last competition of its tour of duty in Germany.

There now came a series of events to mark the departure from BAOR. First, on 17 June, a Drumhead service was conducted by the Padre, the Reverend T.W. Metcalfe, to give thanks for the successful completion of the tour of duty in BAOR. Then, two days later, the new Divisional Commander, Major-General C.A.R. Neville, CBE, DSO, paid a farewell visit to the Battalion. After visiting the Sergeants' Mess and lunching with the officers, he addressed the Battalion paraded on the square.

On 21 June the Brigade Commander, Brigadier Goodwin, also came to say goodbye. Following a parade on the square, he addressed the Battalion, congratulating them on their performance under his command in BAOR and wishing them well in Cyprus. That same evening the Brigadier was the guest at a farewell dinner in the Officers' Mess.

Two days before leaving, the Corps Commander, Lieutenant-General Sir Hugh Stockwell, KBE, KCB, DSO, paid a final visit to the Battalion, thus repeating his last visit when it left Malaya in 1953 when he was GOC Malaya and saw the Battalion off at Kuala Lumpur railway station.

On the morning of 1 July, headed by the Corps of Drums, the Battalion marched out of Harding Barracks for the last time, heading for Steinbeck Station where it was to entrain. The Drums of the 1st Battalion, the Buffs, played from the middle of the column to add musical weight and beat to the occasion and, as it passed the HQ of 6th Infantry Brigade, Brigadier R.E. Goodwin, CBE, DSO, took the salute.

A large crowd of well-wishers gathered at the station and, as the train left, it was played out by the Band of the 1st Battalion, the Royal Ulster Rifles.

The crossing to England was made on the night trooping ferry from the Hook of Holland to Harwich and thence by train to Colchester North Station.

CHAPTER VII

THE FIRST BATTALION:

HOME AND CYPRUS 1956–1959

'The final overseas tour of duty'

Part I

The Battalion returned to the United Kingdom on 2 July, 1956, and remained there until it sailed from Southampton for Cyprus on board the *Dilwara* on 10 August.

The first part of this five-week staging period was taken up with a brief spell of disembarkation leave, which was followed by a concentrated effort to prepare for the visit of HRH The Princess Margaret, Colonel-in-Chief of the Regiment, to Roman Way Camp on 1 August, Minden Day.

Despite the worst endeavours of the English weather and a constant drizzle, intermingled with periods of steady rain, the Minden Day visit went well (it is described in more detail in Part II of this Chapter). The parade was watched by large numbers of spectators from the 4th Battalion, the Depot and the Old Comrades' Association as well as the Battalion. After the parade Her Royal Highness, accompanied by the Colonel of the Regiment, visited the Sergeants' Mess and then had lunch with the officers and their wives.

With Minden Day over, the whole Battalion, save some unfortunates who had been on the Rear Party in Germany and were now on the Advance Party to Cyprus, went on embarkation leave prior to sailing on 10 August.

The situation on the island of Cyprus, after simmering for several years, had blown up into a major crisis towards the end of 1954. For a long time there had been a movement among the Greek Cypriots who made up four-fifths of the island's population (the remainder being largely Turkish) for union with Greece (Enosis) and when the British Government announced in June, 1954, that it intended to transfer the Headquarters of its Middle Eastern Forces from Egypt to Cyprus, the statement triggered off an instant response from the supporters of Enosis, led from the pulpit by their champion, Archbishop Makarios.

The Greek Cypriots were not alone in seeing their chances of union with Greece fading with the arrival of the British HQ from Egypt. The Greek Government itself immediately appealed to the United Nations to consider its claim to the island. In December, 1954, the UN General Assembly refused even to debate the request, thereby triggering off an outbreak of violence in Cyprus.

But worse was to come. A guerrilla force calling itself Eoka had been formed by young Greek Cypriots. Led by George Grivas, a former Colonel in the Greek Army who adopted the legendary name of Dighenis, its activities were to become a serious menace to the Government of Cyprus and led over the next eighteen months to a major build-up of Army units in the Colony.

Eoka operated in two ways. Its agents stirred up trouble in the towns on the one hand, while its gangs of armed guerrillas ambushed security forces and attacked Police stations in the rural areas on the other, aiming to weaken the resolve of those Greek Cypriots who served as Policemen and Government Officials. Once an action was carried out, the terrorists, as they were known by the security forces, simply faded away. Those in the towns were quickly lost among the general population and the armed gangs had the rugged terrain of the Kyrenia Mountain Range in the North and the main central Troodos Mountains, dominated by Mount Olympus, in the heartland of the island, in which to hide.

It was into this situation that the Battalion was plunged on arrival in Cyprus. Little was as yet known of the movements or organization of Eoka, though the Security Force intelligence-gathering procedures were slowly coming to grips with the situation.

The best that could be hoped for was that the Battalion would succeed in dominating its area of responsibility and, by close cooperation with Police and Civil Government Officers, gradually build up a sufficiently accurate picture of the enemy for more positive results to be achieved. It was simply a question of getting to know the area intimately and reacting forcefully and effectively to initiatives taken by the terrorists.

The Battalion was to experience the problems and frustrations of

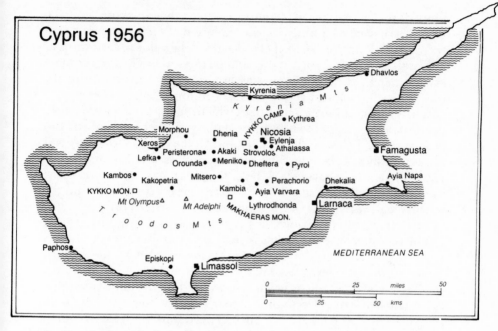

Cyprus 1956

dealing both with the unlawful gangs in the streets and alleyways of the old city of Nicosia and with the more efficiently organized guerrilla groups operating out of the mountains and remote villages in the foothills.

On arrival in August, 1956, it took over a tented and hutted camp from the Gordons at Xeros near Lefka on Morphou Bay, to the north of the Troodos Mountains.

Despite the necessity to set aside large numbers of men for the provision of guards and escorts, the Battalion was able to put a good percentage of its forces into the field in search of the elusive enemy. In many ways operations during this period of the Battalion's tour in Cyprus added up to a mixture of what had been experienced in earlier years in Palestine and Malaya. On the one hand long hours were spent patrolling roads and checking bridges and culverts for enemy booby-traps and ambushes and in cordoning and searching suspect villages, while, on the other, companies were dispatched into the hills and mountains actively to seek out the enemy by continuously patrolling and ambushing in the mountains.

For the men of the Battalion this was a mixed experience. The success rate in locating the enemy or his materiel was low in the villages and cordoning and searching was frequently a tedious business. Likewise, checking roads for booby-traps was rarely rewarding and extremely time-consuming, though those few who had experienced an ambush or the explosion of a mine under or near their vehicles were more likely to recognize the value of the exercise.

Rural patrolling was more interesting, though rarely more rewarding. In the foothills it was hot and dusty work and in the mountains it was a physical slog, negotiating steep and rocky re-entrants and climbing along ridges which, as the crest was reached, never failed to reveal yet another slightly steeper one ahead. But here, as down below in the villages and on the roads, the enemy was always elusive. Eoka guerrillas were fit and used to the mountains and, unlike jungle-covered Malaya, the mountain sides were, apart from occasional trees and bushes, bare of vegetation, allowing the terrorists an early view of the approach of Security Forces.

Thus it was that, during this period based on Xeros, apart from one or two spectacular successes such as the ambushing of Markos Drakos, a senior figure in Eoka, by D Company in January, 1957, there was little to show for a huge and sustained effort on the part of the Battalion. Few felt sufficiently rewarded by the knowledge that the enemy was curtailed in the scope of his activities by the military presence on the ground, but such indeed was the case. If other reward is sought, it must be said that the Battalion had never been more physically fit than when in May, 1957, it found itself transferred from Xeros to Kykko Camp, just outside Nicosia on the road to the airport.

Here the Battalion was to remain until the end of its tour in Cyprus in May, 1959. In those two years it was to experience many a rise in tension and its relaxation, as political initiatives to resolve the Cyprus problem waxed and waned and the Eoka enemy stepped up or moderated his varied activities as a result. Eoka's methods ranged from brutal thuggery and murder to carefully planned ambushes relying on detailed knowledge about the movements of the Security Forces.

Such was the situation that the Battalion was rarely able to seize the initiative, but rather was forced most frequently to stand waiting to respond to moves made by Eoka. Its time was almost equally divided between duties as Internal Security (IS) Battalion in the Old City of Nicosia and as Rural Battalion in the low-lying plains which surround the city in the heart of the island.

At moments of high tension in the Old City, as for instance when the Turkish Cypriot riots broke out at the end of January, 1958, the whole Battalion was heavily committed and companies were constantly deployed on the streets to restore order among the stone-throwing mobs. At other times companies and platoons, at varying stages of notice to move, would wait for days and sometimes weeks for a call which never came. The Central Police Station compound in Nicosia will be remembered by men of the Battalion with mixed feelings, depending on whether they recall long hours of waiting inside it or brief moments of feverish activity outside it!

For a soldier to stand still is anathema. It is always good to be on the move, thus almost invariably he dislikes guard duties and delights in patrolling. It was therefore a great relief for the Battalion when it came to the end of a tour of duty as IS Battalion in Nicosia and took over as the Rural Battalion, for although there were still guards to be done it meant that there would also be a heavy programme of patrolling both on foot and in vehicles and this comparatively attractive routine would frequently be additionally enlivened by specific operations further afield which resulted from intelligence acquired by the Police Special Branch. Sometimes the whole Battalion would deploy, but more often the operation would be at a lower level with much scope given to platoon and section commanders to use their own initiative and pit their wits against the enemy. If he was not very often brought to battle, it was not the fault of the Battalion, but rather because he was not there to be found.

Life for the officers and men of the Battalion in their off-duty hours varied according to the degree of tension existing at any given time. If the pressure was on, it was not possible even to leave camp off duty, but when the security situation allowed more freedom of movement, Cyprus was a wonderful island on which to live. Winters were mild, though cold in the hills and happily brief, and Spring, Summer and Autumn were a succession of long, sunny days. Beautiful beaches abounded all round the coast and when it came to taking local leave there were leave centres at Famagusta and Kyrenia which would have been the envy of those who in more recent times have flocked to the crowded coasts of Spain.

In the first few months of the tour families were not allowed to join the Battalion, but from the beginning of 1957 they came in a steady trickle until, by the end of the year, well over fifty officers and men had been joined by their wives and children.

The families, of course, shared the alternating freedoms and restrictions imposed by the security authorities. At one moment they were free to enjoy the island and at another tied down and not infrequently required to adhere to a curfew imposed over the area in which their homes were situated.

The impending amalgamation of the Regiment with the Royal

Norfolk Regiment overshadowed the whole Cyprus tour. Outwardly it was accepted as something that had to come, but inwardly all felt a degree of apprehension about the future and already were nostalgic for a past in which the Battalion had surely lived and worked as a really successful family entity.

The prospect of returning to the United Kingdom in 1959 was thus greeted with mixed feelings. The Battalion's experience in Cyprus had frequently been a frustrating one and what achievements there had been were not always immediately obvious to officers or men, even if, according to the powers that be, the job had been done well.

On the other hand, Cyprus was a beautiful island and everyone found much to enjoy there when the opportunity presented itself. The countryside was attractive and varied, the beaches as good as anywhere in the world and some had even learnt to ski on the snowy winter slopes of the Troodos Mountains.

But now amalgamation was just round the corner and if the future looked a little uncertain it was generally felt best to get on home and start to make it as happy and successful as the past had always been.

Part II

The Battalion arrived in Colchester from Germany on 2 July, 1956. The train from Harwich pulled into Colchester North Station and there the Colonel of the Regiment, Brigadier E.H.W. Backhouse, DL, waited to greet them on their return to the United Kingdom. He spoke to many officers and men as they alighted on the platform and, after companies had formed up outside the station, he made a brief address of welcome.

The Battalion, led by the Corps of Drums, then marched up North Hill into Colchester where, in the High Street, the Mayor of Colchester took the salute outside the Town Hall. Thence the march continued to Roman Way Camp.

As soon as everyone was settled in, the majority of officers and men went home on short leave, leaving behind key personnel with the responsibility for preparing for the Minden Day visit of HRH The Princess Margaret, Colonel-in-Chief of the Regiment.

The Officer Commanding HQ Company, Major D.U. Fraser, MBE, was in charge of arrangements for the big day and he was kept extremely busy from the time the Battalion arrived in Colchester. Apart from all the detailed preparation for the parade – timings, invitations, catering arrangements and the like – he also had the enormous task of supervising the complete refurbishment of Roman Way Camp itself which had lain empty for many months prior to the Battalion's arrival. RQMS Calver, BEM, and Sergeant Gilbert, the Pioneer Sergeant, provided first-class support and, with the willing cooperation of the Garrison Engineer and his staff, a great transformation was made. Grassland became lawn, weedy areas became flower beds and the various buildings to be used or even seen were tidied up and painted. Finally, a dais was erected on the square, spectator stands were positioned and marquees pitched.

It was very much a Regimental occasion and invitations were sent out to the Depot and the 4th Battalion and also to all members of the Old Comrades Association. Many members and former members of the Regiment responded and a very large gathering of spectators assembled on the day.

Because of a shortage of No 1 Dress, it was decided that a Guard of Honour only would be formed up in ceremonial order, together with the Band and Drums, and that the remainder of the Battalion would parade unarmed and in battle dress. The Guard of Honour was to be commanded by Major G.T.O. Springfield, with a Colour Party comprising Lieutenant J.P. Macdonald, 2nd Lieutenant J.Y. Morris, CSM Robinson, Colour Sergeant Wilce and Sergeant Lawrence. The remainder of the Battalion on parade was to be commanded by Major D.U. Fraser, MBE.

After leave, the Battalion reassembled and rehearsals for the parade went ahead at full swing. The Garrison tailors were kept busy with fittings and alterations to uniforms, and parties of men worked on the last-minute preparation of the square, the stands, marquees and the general barrack area.

Finally, 1 August arrived and all was ready. The day dawned overcast and unhappily the forecast was for rain. Sure enough, just before the Royal guest was due to arrive at 1130 a drizzle set in which, by the time the Princess's car drove up, had turned into a steady downpour which was to continue throughout the day. The wet weather programme was nonetheless rejected and the parade went ahead as planned.

The Colonel-in-Chief stepped down from her car looking charming in navy blue and wearing the Regimental brooch, to be greeted by the Colonel of the Regiment and the Commanding Officer. The Orderly Officer, 2nd Lieutenant R.P.H. Mermagen, was also in attendance carrying a large but very necessary umbrella. After greeting the Princess, Lieutenant-Colonel Bevan presented her with a bouquet of Minden Roses which she carried with her throughout the parade.

The Royal Salute was received on the dais, and then the Colonel-in-Chief inspected the Parade. On returning to the dais after the inspection, Her Royal Highness addressed the Battalion. She spoke first of the significance of the Battle of Minden and then of the Battalion's forthcoming tour in Cyprus. Finally, she congratulated the Battalion on the high standard of the Parade, speaking of the great pleasure the occasion had given her.

In his reply the Commanding Officer thanked the Colonel-in-Chief for her kind words and for being with the Battalion on Minden Day. He spoke also of the Battalion's determination to do its duty in Cyprus in the coming months. The Guard of Honour then marched past to the strains of the Regimental March, Speed the Plough, after which the Parade gave three cheers for the Colonel-in-Chief. With a final Royal Salute, Her Royal Highness left the parade ground.

There followed a visit to the Sergeants' Mess, where Mess members and many of their wives were presented to Her Royal Highness. After this, twelve Junior NCOs and men were also presented to the Colonel-in-Chief and then she proceeded to the Officers' Mess where she spoke informally to the officers of the Battalion and their wives and then had lunch with them.

After lunch the Princess sat for photographs with the officers and sergeants and then took her leave. Preceded by the Band and Drums playing the Regimental March, Her Royal Highness drove slowly out of the Barracks past the cheering throng of soldiers and their families lining the route in the still damp afternoon.

That evening the men of the Battalion dispersed for embarkation leave. The Officers were entertained to cocktails later in the evening, as guests of the 4th Battalion at their Mess in Ipswich, while Minden Day was celebrated by the Warrant Officers and Sergeants in their Mess at Roman Way Camp.

Final preparations were now set in train for the move to Cyprus. The Advance Party under the 2ic, Major M.G. Eliot, had already sailed from Southampton on 27 July on board the *Nevassa*, which was on her maiden voyage, and the main body of the Battalion was due to sail, also from Southampton, nine days later on board the *Dilwara*.

The Battalion embarked on 10 August. The Colonel of the Regiment and Colonel Senior, the Brigade Colonel of the East Anglian Brigade, were at the quayside to say goodbye, together with many friends and families of the Regiment. The Band of the 5th Battalion, the Royal Hampshire Regiment, played as the ship moved off from her berth, proudly flying the Regimental Flag at the yardarm.

The voyage passed enjoyably and productively, though under somewhat cramped conditions, as the ship was shared with another Battalion, the 1st Battalion, the Oxfordshire and Buckinghamshire Light Infantry. A considerable amount of training was accomplished in preparation for the Battalion's role in Cyprus.

The ship called unexpectedly at Algiers and while in port the Band gave a concert on deck.

Once in the Mediterranean battle dress was discarded and replaced by khaki drill uniforms.

The ship arrived in Limassol harbour on 21 August and, because the Port was too shallow to come alongside, the Battalion was ferried ashore on lighters.

The Commanding Officer of the 1st Battalion, the Royal Norfolk Regiment, Lieutenant-Colonel W.H. Brinkley, well known to the Battalion as 2ic in Trieste and Officer in Command of the Advance Party in Wuppertal, and a number of other representatives of his unit, met the Battalion on arrival. The Drums of the Royal Norfolks played on the quay during disembarkation.

It had been expected that the Battalion would take over from the Royal Norfolk Regiment in the Limassol area on arrival and it was only on reaching Cyprus that it was learned that plans had been changed. All the careful and detailed preparation and briefing for expected tasks was unfortunately wasted.

Instead, the Battalion was ordered to take over from the 1st Battalion, the Gordon Highlanders, on the northern side of the island at a tented camp at Xeros on Morphou Bay. To get there the Battalion, less B Company, was driven, as the *Regimental Gazette* notes said, 'in local buses of great age and much discomfort' almost a hundred miles to Xeros via Nicosia, with a brief halt at Waynes Keep Camp in Nicosia for a meal.

B Company was to be on detachment at the village of Kakopetria, nestled on the northern slopes of the Troodos Mountains, linked by a twisting road some twenty miles from Battalion HQ. They drove in similar buses straight over the top of the mountain and down to Kakopetria.

On arrival in Cyprus, main appointments in the Battalion were held as follows:

CO: Lieutenant-Colonal W.S. Bevan
2ic: Major M.G. Eliot
Adjt: Major P.D.F. Thursby

QM:	Captain T.C. Warren
RSM:	RSM Gingell
OC B Coy:	Major F.D. Ingle
CSM:	CSM Hazelwood
OC C Coy:	Major G.T.O. Springfield
CSM:	CSM Evans, MM
OC D Coy:	Captain H.J. Chisnall
CSM:	CSM Richardson
OC Sp Coy:	Major F.J. Lockett
CSM:	CSM Bates
OC HQ Coy:	Major E.T. Lummis
CSM:	CSM Jones

Aberdeen Camp at Xeros was rather primitive but adequate. It lay on land belonging to the Cyprus Mining Corporation and next door to that Company's copper mine. The Company was American-owned and the mine was managed by Americans and for the most part run by British mining engineers. The Company was very helpful and a happy relationship quickly developed between the Battalion and its expatriate staff.

The Battalion's area of responsibility embraced the Lefka District which covered the coastal region around Morphou Bay, including the Greek Cypriot town of Morphou and stretched inland up on to the northern slopes of the mountains, to just short of Kakopetria (B Company was under command Troodos Sub-Area). The District Officer and the Officer Commanding the Police District had their offices in the small Turkish Cypriot town of Lefka, just outside which Xeros lay.

The Commanding Officer was the Military Area Commander in Lefka and, as such, established the necessary close contacts with the District Officer and the Officer Commanding the Police District. All planning and allocation of tasks to the Battalion was co-ordinated and agreed by a District Committee involving all three.

Within a few days of arrival the Battalion was visited by a number of senior figures including the Cyprus District Commander, Major-General A.H.G. Ricketts, CBE, DSO, the Commander 50th Independent Brigade, Brigadier K.H. Collen (the Battalion was under command of this Brigade which had its headquarters in Nicosia), the Chief of Staff to the Governor, Brigadier G.H. Baker, CB, CBE, MC, and the Commissioner of Police, Lieutenant-Colonel G.C. White.

The most important visitor, however on 8 September, was His Excellency the Governor, Field-Marshal Sir John Harding, GCB,

CBE, DSO, MC. On arrival, HE inspected a Quarter Guard with the band in attendance, and was introduced to the officers and sergeants in their respective messes. He then addressed those members of the Battalion who were not out on operations.

Operationally, the Battalion soon discovered, at least those who had served there, that the situation in Cyprus was quite unlike that encountered in the Malayan Emergency. The enemy, though fewer in number, operated in towns and villages as well as in the rural areas. Moreover, the Cypriot population went unchecked about their daily business wherever it took them and, unless caught with incriminating evidence, there was absolutely no way of determining whether any one person was a member of the terrorist organization Eoka or not. Success in such circumstances was to be extremely slow in coming.

While stationed in Xeros, the Battalion's operational responsibilities were two-fold. It was required to guard certain vulnerable points and its own installations and protect its own administrative road movements. What troops remained after this heavy commitment were available for active operations against Eoka.

Initially, within this general framework, two companies were employed providing a guard on two police stations (one at Morphou which was always a potential trouble spot), the explosives magazine and main mine shaft of the Cyprus Mining Corporation, camp guards, vehicle escorts and a stand-by platoon at five-minute readiness to move. With one company attached at Kakopetria, this left only one company available for active operations. Its tasks were many and varied, including day and night foot patrols and ambushes, vehicle patrols and small-scale cordon and search operations.

The foot patrols were for the most part sent out without the benefit of specific intelligence and simply served to familiarize participants with the lie of the land, and establish a military presence in the Battalion area. Vehicle operations achieved those same aims and provided constant opportunities to check bridges and culverts for mines and booby-traps and to mount surprise road blocks which, though scarcely ever successful, certainly inhibited the enemy's use of vehicles to move arms, ammunitions, explosives or propaganda literature by road.

On 1 November an additional but fortunately temporary commitment was taken on, with C Company providing the Guard, under 2nd Lieutenant Mermagen, for the Governor's residence in Nicosia.

On 15 November Major-General D.A. Kendrew, CBE, DSO, the

newly appointed District Commander and effectively the Director of Operations, visited the Battalion at Xeros, and at the same time B Company returned to the fold to be replaced at Kakopetria by D Company, who made their way up into the hills equipped with cold-weather clothing ready to face the snows of winter.

B Company's tour in Kakopetria had been very busy with a constant programme of strenuous patrols and ambushes in very rugged terrain. Few concrete successes had been recorded but one patrol did succeed in finding a large cache of some 1,400 sticks of dynamite hidden in a small cave high in the mountains, as a result of considerable determination on the part of the patrol commander. On 19 November the Anti-Tank Platoon, commanded by Lieutenant C.J.N. Trollope, returning in vehicles from Morphou to Xeros, was ambushed by an Eoka group sited high above the road where the rock face thwarted all attempts to scale it and left the Platoon no alternative but to return the enemy's fire as best it could. The ambush was soon over, but three soldiers, Privates Chaplin and Cole of Sp Company and Private Dulton of HQ Company, were wounded. The wounds were fortunately not serious and all recovered quite quickly, though Private Cole was evacuated to the United Kingdom.

November saw a number of other ambushes in Cyprus as Eoka attempted somewhat unsuccessfully to weaken the British efforts involved in mounting the Suez Operation, for which Cyprus was used as one of the assembly areas.

On arrival in Cyprus, the Battalion was operating with four companies in the field, B, C, D and Sp Companies. On 19 December A Company was resuscitated as a Training Company under command of Captain A.L. Willdridge and all cadres and draft training became its responsibility. For some weeks, starting in December, a platoon at a time was withdrawn from operations and joined A Company for a week of intensive retraining.

The winter period witnessed a number of operations at Brigade level in which the Battalion's rifle companies took part. Aimed at swamping with troops large areas of the rocky wooded country on the lower slopes of the Troodos Mountains to the south of the Battalion's area, they produced little tangible result. But in one, Exercise Foxhunter, commanded by Brigadier M.A.H. Butler, DSO, MC, commanding the 16th Independent Parachute Brigade, lately returned from Suez, two small terrorist groups were winkled out of mountain villages.

Because of operational commitments, Christmas, 1956, was

26. The GOC 2nd Infantry Division inspects the 1st Battalion at Wuppertal on Minden Day, 1955. With him is Brigadier R.E. Godwin, CBE, DSO.

27. The Band and Drums of the 1st Battalion decked out with roses on Minden Day, 1955 in Harding Barracks, Wuppertal.

28. A CO's 'O' Group assembles during a BAOR exercise in 1955. Major Dean, Captains Cobbold, Morgan and Willdridge and Lieutentant T.D. Dean have already joined the CO.

29. The Colonel-in-Chief inspects the 1st Battalion at Roman Way Camp, Colchester on Minden Day, 1956.

30. An ambush party from D Company of the 1st Battalion returns to base after
a cold night on the wintry slopes of the Troodos Mountains in Cyprus in
1956.

31. The Officers of the 1st Battalion at Xeros in Cyprus in 1957.

32. The Band and Drums of the 1st Battalion in Cyprus in 1957. The Bandmaster Mr G.A. Holben sits between the CO and Major E.T. Lummis, the Band President.

33. The Company base camp at Kakopetria in Cyprus in 1957.

34. The Commander-in-Chief MELF, General Sir Geoffrey Bourne enjoys a joke with RSM H.J. Gingell and CSM R. Evans, MM, when visiting the Sergeants' Mess at Kykko Camp, Nicosia on 7 November, 1957

35. The Mitsero mine in Cyprus where Private Cornish of B Company
    discovered a large cache of explosives on 24 May, 1958.

36. The explosives found at Miterso mine on 24 May, 1958.

37. The CO, Lieutenant-Colonel W.S. Bevan, receives the 50th Brigade Rifle Championship Bowl from the Brigade Commander in October, 1957. The Battalion went on to win the Cyprus District Rifle Meeting in the same month.

38. Soldiers are searched in front of a monk following a search of Kykko Monastery Annexe in Nicosia during which explosives and EOKA documents were found. Such inspections were routine and avoided false accusations later.

celebrated in a minor key. Families had not been permitted to accompany the Battalion to Cyprus and the large contingent with the Battalion in Germany was scattered throughout the United Kingdom, some being still in Germany. In December District Headquarters approved the Lefka area as one suitable for families, but by Christmas only one family, that of Major Lummis, OC HQ Company, had arrived. The main problem was to find suitable accommodation, which, in such a small town, was very difficult.

The Saturday before Christmas saw a Christmas Fair in Aberdeen Camp with a surprisingly varied selection of side-shows to draw the visitors. The 'Duck the Sergeant Major' stall run by RQMS Calver, BEM, and CSM Jones, proved the most popular, though the latter was forced to retire after his eleventh ducking!

Also in the week before Christmas a revue was produced by 2nd Lieutenant G. Pensotti (his elder brother had served in the Battalion in Malaya), which comprised a number of sketches, interspersed with musical numbers played by the Dance Band Trio of The Band. Captain H.J. Chisnall compered the show in admirable fashion, ably assisted by the Band Master and Colour Sergeant Pratt. In all, there was a cast of sixty.

An excellent Christmas dinner was served to the men by the officers and sergeants, though no other formal celebrations took place on Christmas Day itself. The Battalion Padre, The Reverend T.W. Metcalfe, without a church in Aberdeen Camp, had scrounged the necessary fittings since arrival in Cyprus, and every Sunday converted the cinema into a church with the able assistance of Sergeant Gilbert, the Pioneer Sergeant. He held a full programme of Christmas services with the assistance of the Band. A choir of twenty-four, under the baton of 2nd Lieutenant Isherwood, made a tour of the Cyprus Mining Corporation bungalows and met with a splendid welcome, and on the Sunday before Christmas a service of nine lessons and carols was held with a full congregation.

On Christmas Eve the Padre travelled up to Kakopetria and held a carol service with D Company and returned to Aberdeen Camp for Holy Communion at midnight. Early morning communion on Christmas Day was followed at eleven o'clock with a morning service.

On Boxing Day afternoon an Inter-Company six-a-side knock-out football competition was won by C Company, and this was followed by an extravagant match between the officers and sergeants, armed with all manner of aids to victory, but which as usual, ended in total confusion and uproar, despite attempts by the Intelligence Officer,

Lieutenant North, posing as a UN mediator, to calm things down.

A Combined Services Entertainment Unit show at the end of the week concluded the celebrations and thereafter the full attention of all was directed back towards the operational scene.

For the most part there was little to show during 1956 for the constant round of patrols and ambushes. One of two small caches of explosives and ammunition had been located, but not much else.

Then, on 19 January, 1957, came a major success. D Company in Kakopetria had deployed a set of section patrols high up on the mountain slopes of the Adelphi Forest. The aim was to patrol the area and establish night ambushes on tracks which led down the mountainside out of the pine forests. The guerrilla groups high in the mountains were known to come down to the villages at night to collect food and gather intelligence on the activities of the Security Forces.

One section group of eight men under Corporal King had established their ambush just as darkness was falling. Corporal King had located a track running down a spur out of the trees. An outcrop of rocks on the edge of the spur allowed him to site his ambush using four men who could cover the track effectively.

He found a suitable rest area 150 yards from the ambush position and, leaving Lance-Corporal Fowler and three men there to prepare bivouacs and cook a meal, he returned to establish his four-man ambush.

A biting wind blew up, bringing with it freezing rain, and it was bitterly cold. Corporal King decided that the two groups would change over at two-hourly intervals through the night.

The D Company ambushes were part of a bigger operation involving similar parties from other units further along the mountainside and, as Lance-Corporal Fowler's party came to relieve Corporal King at 1900, the group distinctly heard above the howling wind the sound of several bursts of automatic and rifle fire in the distance. It seemed that someone else might have been successful.

The ambush groups changed at 2100 and Lance-Corporal Fowler's group was just taking over again at 2300 when one of the men, Private Woods, became aware of the lone figure of a man on the track seven or eight yards from him. He fired at him instantly and the terrorist returned his fire just as quickly. The remainder of the section brought fire to bear as well, on seeing the flashes from the enemy's gun. He fell to the ground. During the firing a second man was heard to cry out but he was never seen.

The ambush was sustained throughout the night without further incident and the next morning the terrorist's body was located and carried down the mountainside to the track where a vehicle waited to collect the patrol to return to Kakopetria.

The dead terrorist was later identified as Markos Drakos, second-in-command of Grivas's Eoka organization. Contact with the enemy had been long in coming but, when it did, it was a very real success. Messages of congratulation flowed in to the Battalion and the next day His Excellency the Governor flew in to D Company's base by helicopter to congratulate the Ambush Party. Corporal King, Lance-Corporal Fowler and Private Woods were later to be Mentioned in Despatches for their part in the operation.

In January it was found possible to reduce the guards and escort duties sufficiently to be covered by one company, thus freeing two companies in Aberdeen Camp for general operational duties.

At this time, also, an RAF Squadron of Sycamore helicopters became available for the movement of troops on operations. The Battalion was quickly trained in the use of these helicopters at Aberdeen Camp, and thereafter companies were frequently deployed in them up into the rugged territory in the south of the Battalion's area.

Using these machines was something of a novel experience for soldiers in the mid-fifties. Abseiling techniques had yet to be perfected and, where it was not possible for the helicopter to land its cargo of men, they would simply climb down a rope to the ground. If, as so often happened, it was necessary to descend the rope on to a steep-sided spur, it only needed the helicopter to drift slightly for the men descending to run out of rope! Not a few injuries were suffered dropping several feet on to rocks.

The new Commander of 50th Infantry Brigade, Brigadier F.R. St P. Bunbury, DSO, paid his first visit to the Battalion in January, and on 10 January the Right Honorable John Hare, OBE, MP, Secretary of State for War, arriving by helicopter, made a comprehensive tour of Aberdeen Camp and was briefed by the Commanding Officer and the OCPD at the Combined Operations room in Lefka Police Headquarters.

Throughout the winter heavy operational duties curtailed opportunities for sport, but the Battalion managed to enter, if sometimes only a scratch team, in the Nicosia Garrison Major Units football league, achieving some moderate success.

As the Cyprus winter came to an end, the tempo of operations increased. Following up an intelligence lead, 8 Platoon of C

Company succeeded in late February in locating a man from the Police 'wanted' list hidden under the floor of a village house.

Then in early March the Company took its turn of duty up in the mountains of Kakopetria. Although detached and under command of 40 Commando, Royal Marines, in the Troodos Mountains area, the Company helped out the Battalion in two major operations aimed at coming to grips with a particular mountain gang of terrorists, operating in the Battalion area. The first, Operation Blackbird, started in early March and continued till the end of the month. Counting C Company, three companies were involved in the widespread patrols and ambushes in the hills and on the mountain slopes in the southern part of the Battalion area.

In early April there came a brief lull in operations and then Operation Bullfinch went ahead, following the pattern of its predecessor. On Good Friday, 19 April, after weeks of persistent effort, the reward came. A routine patrol from the MMG Platoon of Sp Company under a National Service officer, 2nd Lieutenant B. Marriott, succeeded in capturing a mountain gang of seven men, including their leader, Georghios Demetriou.

The success was one of those lucky breaks. The patrol was moving through low hills at the foot of the mountains and literally walked into the group resting under the shade of some trees. Totally surprised, they surrendered without a fight.

The capture of Demetriou was a grave setback to Eoka, coming, as it did, at the end of a two-month period in which the movement had suffered similar losses throughout the island.

At least temporarily, Grivas had lost the initiative and one of the results was an official reduction in the restrictions imposed on the movement of off-duty Army personnel.

The Easter weekend was thus, for the Battalion, a brief if unexpected opportunity to relax. With the capture of Demetriou and his gang, Operation Bullfinch, which had been designed to flush him out, was concluded and companies enjoyed the chance to laze in the sun on the Battalion swimming beach on Morphou Bay.

The relaxation of personal security regulations also meant that more families were able to join the Battalion and by 5 April four had arrived to join Mrs Lummis who had been the pathfinder earlier in the year.

In early April the Battalion was warned of an impending move to Nicosia, probably in May, and preparations went ahead. The move was greeted with mixed feelings. No one relished the prospect of internal security duties in an urban setting, preferring the freedom of operations in the hills, and yet there were clearly some attractions of a different sort to be found in the capital city.

One member of the Battalion may well have been pleased at the prospect of a move. Corporal Wiffen, the Battalion Post Corporal, had driven the road from Xeros to Nicosia every day since arrival in Cyprus, collecting and delivering mail. His was not an enviable task. There was only one road and there was little he could do to vary the times that he used it. He was effectively a 'sitting duck' for any ambusher, and sure enough in early April an attempt was made. A remotely detonated bomb suspended in a tree above the road exploded as his vehicle drove under it. By good fortune neither he nor his driver were hurt. Little could be done to prevent a repetition of the incident, but all the trees in the area that overhung the road and could have been used for a similar purpose in future were felled. The whole Battalion was delighted when in February, 1958, Corporal Wiffen was awarded the BEM for devotion to duty and courage displayed since arrival on the island.

April, too, saw an opportunity for the Band and Drums, which for months had been starved of engagements, to play a part in winning the hearts and minds of the local people. Throughout the month a series of Band Concerts and Retreats was staged in the villages within the Battalion area.

The Advance Party of the 1st Battalion, the Royal Ulster Rifles, who were to take over from the Battalion at Xeros, arrived from BAOR in early May, and last-minute preparations for the move to Nicosia went ahead. Planning was difficult, as it was not known until the last moment to which camp the Battalion would be transferring. Eventually it was learned that it would be to Kykko East Camp, which was to be vacated by Cyprus District HQ on its move to Wolseley Barracks in Nicosia.

The Camp was, naturally enough, well furbished and all looked forward to moving into good accommodation. The Advance Party moved on 15 May, to be followed on the 25th by the main body of the Battalion.

Just before the move, on 13 May, His Excellency the Governor paid an informal visit to Aberdeen Camp. Accompanied by the CO, he walked round the camp talking to the men at their work. He wanted particularly to speak to the men of 2nd Lieutenant Marriott's patrol which had captured Georghios Demetriou and his group.

The Battalion's arrival in Nicosia coincided with an island-wide lull in the intensity of operations. Attempts were being made by the

British Government, fruitless as it was to turn out, to seek some form of political settlement. As a result the Battalion's commitment centred on a number of guard duties which included Camp K where over 700 detainees were housed, the Central Prison in Nicosia which contained the hardcore terrorists, serving prison sentences or awaiting trial, and two mining complexes of the Hellenic Mining Company in the villages of Mitsero and Kambia, some twenty miles from Nicosia.

To compensate for these rather tedious duties, restrictions on off-duty movements remained minimal and there were plenty of opportunities for relaxation and the frequent chance to enjoy the marvellous beaches which abound in Cyprus. Local leave facilities in Kyrenia and Famagusta were excellent and fully taken advantage of at this time, and many more families joined the Battalion after its arrival in Nicosia. By the height of summer they numbered forty-two.

The parade in honour of the Queen's birthday took place in the moat below the walls of Old Nicosia on 13 June. His Excellency the Governor took the salute at a large ceremonial parade, for which the Battalion had the headache of being responsible for security. Fortunately all went well and without incident.

For some months rumour had abounded regarding impending changes in the organization of the Army. In April the end of National Service and a consequent reduction in the size of the armed forces was announced in Parliament and it seemed certain that some Regiments would either disappear or suffer amalgamation.

On 25 July all members of the Battalion not on duty were assembled in Kykko East Camp for an announcement by the Commanding Officer. In his address the CO confirmed that the Regiment was, in 1959, to be amalgamated with the Royal Norfolk Regiment. He read out messages from the Commander-in-Chief Middle East Land Forces and the GOC Cyprus District and also from Brigadier R.H. Maxwell, CB, Colonel of the Regiment since 10 June, following Brigadier Backhouse's retirement. At one fell swoop the rumours were quelled, but it was a day of great sadness in the Battalion as the full meaning of the announcement slowly sank in.

But life went on, and four days later, on 1 August, Minden Day was celebrated with the usual enthusiasm. In the morning a parade was held at which the salute was taken by the GOC Cyprus District and Director of Operations, Major-General D.A. Kendrew, CBE, DSO. The Escort to the Colours was provided by C Company under Major G.T.O. Springfield and three other companies were also on parade.

After the ceremonial the whole Battalion, complete with families, travelled to a beautiful sandy beach some four miles long on Morphou Bay, where a working party under the 2ic, Major Eliot and CSM Richardson, had set up, as it was described in the *Regimental Gazette*, a 'miniature Southend-on-Sea' complete with side-shows, stalls, railway rides, donkey rides, a skiffle group, boats, floats and rafts. Ice-cream, a picnic lunch and plenty of beer, made the occasion go with bang and, returning to camp in the evening, a special supper was served in the men's dining hall to bring a successful day to a close.

Later in August the Battalion Rifle Meeting was held at Athalassa Range, Nicosia. It was a rather extended affair lasting a week to allow all duty companies to participate. Major Willdridge was Champion Shot, with C Company carrying off the Inter-Company Trophy, which was decided at the last moment by the falling plate competition.

The Battalion went on to win the Inter-Unit Championship at the Brigade Meeting in September and the Cyprus District Unit Championship in October.

A taste of what was to come in 1958 was provided on Okhi Day, 28 October, in Nicosia. The day is celebrated throughout the Greek world, remembering the day in 1940 when the Greek people rejected Mussolini's ultimatum to accept his authority or take the consequences of invasion (Okhi is the Greek word for no).

In Cyprus Okhi Day provided the excuse for school children and students to form processions on leaving churches and voice support for Eoka. The main procession in Metaxa Square was broken up by B Company under Major Ingle, together with the Corps of Drums.

The Governor, Field-Marshal Sir John Harding, ended his tour of duty early in November. A farewell parade took place at RAF Nicosia on 31 October, at which the Battalion was represented by the Commanding Officer, five officers and twenty-four men. Then, on the day of his departure, 3 November, the Battalion was responsible for securing the route he took from Government House to the airport.

The Commander-in-Chief Middle East Land Forces, Lieutenant-General Sir Geoffrey K. Bourne, KCB, KBE, CMG, visited the Battalion on 7 November, making a tour of the camp and watching training in progress.

Remembrance Sunday was celebrated by a Drumhead Service at which the Battalion was joined by the Cyprus District Signals Regiment based in the adjacent camp. The opportunity was taken to present Sergeant Gilbert, the Pioneer Sergeant, with the MSM. The award paid tribute to Sergeant Gilbert's thirty-one years' service to the Regiment (he enlisted at the Depot in August, 1926), during which he had served extensively with the 1st Battalion, but also the 2nd Battalion, the 8th Battalion, the 70th Battalion and at the Depot.

12 November saw B Company move to Dhavlos, on the coast to the east of Kyrenia, on detachment. The camp was attractive and provided a pleasant change from the somewhat drab plains around Nicosia. The country inland from the camp was hilly and, on the upper slopes, very rugged and the opportunity was seized to move the whole Battalion into the area for a fortnight's intensive training from 23 November to 6 December.

Back in Nicosia, December saw an upsurge of petty nuisance attacks against the Security Forces and the Battalion had its fair share. The UN were debating the Cyprus issue and Grivas ordered his more youthful supporters in towns and villages to stone military vehicles and erect road blocks in an attempt to keep his movement in the public eye during the debate.

Several foot patrols and vehicles from the Battalion were confronted by these irritating but rarely harmful escapades. There were no serious casualties, however, with only one NCO suffering a broken thumb when hit by a flying stone.

In December, also, Lieutenant B.G.H. Mills and two men of B Company caught the leader of Eoka in Dhavlos and one of his henchmen red-handed as they were haranguing the people of the village and distributing leaflets. Both were later sentenced to two years' imprisonment.

HQ (2) Company, as Sp Company had been renamed, relieved B Company on detachment at Dhavlos on 16 December. Then on 19 December the C-in-C Middle East Land Forces attended a joint farewell parade by units in the Kykko Garrison on relinquishing his command.

Christmas was celebrated with the usual gusto, companies on duty being relieved from guards for sufficient time for their share of the festivities. 'Camp Follies', a revue organized by Captain H.J. Chisnall, the PRI, was a great success as was the choir, which, with the assistance of members of the Band, sang carols at a number of residences in Nicosia, including Government House where the new Governor, Sir Hugh Foot, had recently been installed.

On 10 January, 1958, a Guard of Honour was provided at Wolseley Barracks to mark the arrival of the new C-in-C Middle

East Land Forces, Lieutenant-General Sir Roger Bower, KBE, CB. The Guard was commanded by Major E.T Lummis, OC HQ (1) Company and the Regimental Colour was carried by Lieutenant Mills.

In their turn, HQ (2) Company was relieved at Dhavlos by C Company on 18 January and the former had scarcely returned to the fold when a new source of trouble manifested itself in Nicosia.

Fearful that the Government was about to make concessions to Greece and the Greek Cypriots, the Turkish Cypriot population in the Old City of Nicosia suddenly exploded in an outburst of violent protest in which the demands for partition of the island were heard for the first time. Serious rioting broke out on 28 and 29 January, 1958, and the Battalion, together with other units, was heavily engaged in restoring order.

Two stand-by companies for riot dispersal were based at Nicosia Central Police Station, with their vehicles packed into the small compound at the rear of the building. At this stage liaison with the Police and Civil Authorities was very close and cooperation was easily effected. Platoons were frequently turned out to face a barrage of stones as Turkish Cypriots went on the rampage. Many vehicles were burnt and thousands of pounds worth of damage was done before order was restored. The Battalion suffered no serious casualties, but a few men were cut and bruised by stones hurled at them as they made repeated baton charges to disperse the mob.

By the New Year a number of changes had taken place among senior personnel in the Battalion, and, in January, 1958, main appointments were held as follows:

CO:	Lieutenant-Colonel W.S. Bevan
2ic:	Major K.M.J. Dewar, OBE
Adjt:	Captain R.M. Holman
QM:	Captain T.C. Warren
RSM:	RSM Gingell
OC A Company:	(Training Organization)
	Major A.L. Willdridge
CSM:	CSM Lyon
OC B Company:	Major F.D. Ingle
CSM:	CSM Drew
OC C Company:	Major P.D.F. Thursby
CSM:	CSM Evans MM
OC D Company:	Captain H.J. Chisnall
CSM:	CSM Richardson
OC HQ (1) Coy:	Major E.T. Lummis

CSM: CSM Jones
OC HQ (2) Coy: Major W.J. Calder
CSM: CSM Bates

After the January riots a brief period of comparative calm prevailed. The Battalion continued to provide its share of the ever-monotonous static guards, mobile patrols both in Nicosia and the surrounding countryside and a constant repetition of temporary road blocks. These tasks rarely bore fruit and, what is more, came round ever more frequently for the men involved as drafts of new recruits from England failed to match the numbers of National Servicemen returning home at the end of their service (a prelude to the end of National Service and the forthcoming amalgamation).

The Company Detachment at Dhavlos came to an end on 4 February and C Company returned to Kykko East Camp and this helped relieve the strain of duties on the other companies.

Continued vigilance by officers and men was sustained and occasionally it paid off, as when on 17 March a Platoon road block under 2nd Lieutenant Orr arrested two Eoka couriers, one of whom had been observed attempting to hide something in the car in which they were travelling.

In March the general routine was enlivened by the visit for a few days of the destroyer HMS *Alamein*. The Battalion was affiliated to the ship and a number of men from the rifle companies enjoyed a brief cruise aboard her while sailors filled their places in platoons on various IS duties.

On 22 March the Battalion joined other units in ringing Nicosia for twenty-four hours with a comprehensive system of road blocks. Diligent searching of all vehicles revealed little, though three men were arrested by a Battalion road block for carrying Eoka leaflets.

A major operation of this sort resulted in a shortage of female police, both military and civil, who were needed to search women in cars which were stopped. To alleviate this problem, several wives with the Battalion were enrolled as Special Constables and went out on duty with the road block parties.

Freed from all IS duties from 27 to 29 March, the CO ran an exercise in the area of the Adelphi Forest on the slopes of the Troodos Mountains. D Company provided a very realistic guerrilla gang which was, after much effort, finally brought to bay by the other companies.

In the last two days of the month a heavy deployment of rural vehicle patrols and snap road blocks led to a B Company group capturing another Eoka courier.

On 10 April C Company was turned out to deal with detainees rioting in Camp K. The Company Commander, Major P.D.F Thursby, took over briefly as Commandant of the camp and his men quickly restored order over the next forty-eight hours. D Company helped on the second day, and the camp was then handed over to the 1st Battalion, the Lancashire Fusiliers.

Throughout the remainder of the month normal duties continued. On 17 April D Company conducted a cordon and search operation at the village of Ayia Varvara. A shotgun, a sten gun magazine and seventeen shotgun cartridges were recovered.

The whole Battalion was deployed in Riverside Camp, Nicosia at immediate notice to move, on 23 April, Turkish Independence Day, but the day passed uneventfully.

Then, on 26 April a routine night patrol from D Company, commanded by 2nd Lieutenant Catchpole, noticed newly posted Eoka leaflets on walls in the village of Dhenia. The paste was still wet. Every house was thoroughly searched and two youths with paste still on their hands were detained.

Eoka threatened a new campaign of violence on 28 April and immediately a higher state of alert within the Battalion was introduced. The next day a patrol commanded by Captain Mills raided a coffee shop in the village of Meniko. Three men attempted to hide and were arrested. One of them proved to be the leader of the Eoka village group.

The Brigade Commander carried out the annual administrative inspection of the Battalion on 8 May, and the following day the Band and Drums beat retreat. It was the first such ceremonial occasion since the arrival from the Grenadier Guards of Drum Major Hitchen. He had in the previous two months built the Drums up from a very low ebb and they performed very effectively on this first public occasion for almost a year. The Drummers were resplendent in their newly acquired tiger skins which had been given to the Regiment following a request from Major Thursby, when Adjutant, published in the *Regimental Gazette*, and later taken up by the National Press, which publicized the story and led to the donation of many skins.

The winter had seen limited successes for the Battalion on the sporting field, but football, rugby and hockey teams had been active in local leagues. With the advent of warmer weather an athletics team was selected and trained with vigour and discipline by the PTI, SSI Macdonald, APTC. The training paid off and successes were achieved. In particular, the 4 × 110 yards relay team won great distinction. In April and May they ran undefeated through four meetings and achieved a time only point nine of a second outside the Army record.

Hopes were high also for a good cricket season. A full fixture list had been arranged, but then in June, after only the second match, the security situation deteriorated dramatically and there was time only for operations throughout the remainder of the summer.

From 14 May the Battalion took its turn of guard duties for two weeks at Camp K, the Central Prison and the Mitsero mine.

On 21 May the GOC Cyprus District completed a lightning tour of inspection of all guards and the Battalion accommodation at Kykko East Camp. On the 24th B Company, under Captain H.J. Chisnall, was on duty at the Mitsero mine. The need for this guard was two-fold: to ensure its workings were not sabotaged and to prevent the loss of explosives used in the mining operation to the terrorists. During a routine search of the mine shaft Private Cornish of B Company uncovered a secret store of 435 sticks of dynamite and the mine was closed. During the next five days the Company carried out a thorough search of the whole site and located a further sixty-five sticks of dynamite and a considerable quantity of safety fuse and detonators.

In the first week of June the Battalion carried out patrols in its rural area and then the long-awaited storm broke. 7 June and the days that followed witnessed ferocious inter-communal fighting between Greek and Turkish Cypriots.

Leaving D Company to guard Mitsero mine, the Battalion called off its rural patrolling and concentrated in Kykko East Camp. One company was already deployed in the walled city on IS duties by nightfall. The next day C Company was put under command of 43rd LAA Regiment, RA, in the walled city to assist in maintaining the curfew, which had by then been imposed.

On 9 June HQ (1) Company was also committed to curfew duties.

The remainder of June and July followed much the same pattern. The Battalion took it in turn with the 43rd LAA Regiment, RA, the 1st Battalion, the Lancashire Fusiliers and the 1st Battalion, the Royal Berkshire Regiment to provide the Duty Battalion within the walled city, twenty-four hours at a time. The rota was so organized that in the days following the duty the Battalion's notice to move would be gradually increased from half an hour's notice to move to one hour's notice to two hours' and then, finally, to four hours' notice to move. As soon as the four-hour notice came into effect it allowed the Battalion to get to a beach for rest and recreation. The cycle was inexorable.

On 10 June D Company unearthed a further forty-five sticks of dynamite in the Mitsero mine and a team of five blasters on the mine staff was arrested. The following day 2nd Lieutenant Catchpole, with his Platoon, broke up a fight between Greeks and Turks in the village of Pyroi.

On 22 July the Battalion took part in an island-wide operation called Operation Matchbox. In all over 1200 Greek and fifty Turkish Cypriots were arrested and detained, of which the Battalion accounted for fifty.

With little let-up from operations, Minden Day, 1958, was once again celebrated less actively than the Battalion would have liked. 1 August itself was a holiday free from operations, but the Battalion was Duty Battalion in Nicosia the day before and at two hours' notice to move the day after. Despite such curtailment to preparation, there was a parade. It took place very early in the morning and was inspected by the Governor, Sir Hugh Foot, accompanied by Lady Foot and the C-in-C Middle East Land Forces, Lieutenant-General Sir Roger Bower, KBE, CB. Five companies were formed to participate in the parade and, despite the lack of opportunity to practise and a few sleepless nights for the RSM in consequence, it went very well. RSM Hazelwood had by then taken over from RSM Gingell on the latter's posting to the Depot.

After the parade the Governor visited the Officers' and Sergeants' Messes and sat for group photographs with both. He then joined a reception in the Officers' Mess attended by over a hundred guests, including the C-in-C.

The remainder of the morning was given over to a Minden Fair which had been planned to be by the sea, but had to be in camp owing to the security situation. Dinner was served to the men by the officers and sergeants and then total quiet descended on the camp in the sweltering heat of the afternoon sun. In the evening there was a full house at the Minden theatre for a CSEU Show starring Harold Berens.

As a footnote to Minden Day, great difficulties had to be overcome to deliver the customary bouquet of Minden Roses to Her Royal Highness the Princess Margaret, Colonel-in-Chief. She was on an official tour of Canada at the time and at Niagara Falls on 1 August she was presented with the roses by an Officer of the Canadian Army!

5 August saw HQ (2) Company providing the Guard at Government House and then, with not a little relief, the whole Battalion moved out of the Nicosia plains to the area of the Makhaeras Forest

for seven days of operations from 7 to 14 August. Battalion HQ was established at Makhaeras Monastery and the Battalion was commanded during these operations by Brevet Lieutenant-Colonel A.F. Campbell, MC. Through a combination of patrols, observations posts and night ambushes, the allotted area was covered very effectively and six men on the wanted list were arrested.

16 August saw the Battalion back in Nicosia on IS duties and then from 17 to 21 August, with no stand-by commitment, a brief programme of company training was put into effect.

August came to an end with C Company guarding Peristerona and Dheftera Police Stations and the Orounda Mine from 21 to 30 August, and with the remainder of the Battalion once more on IS duties in the Old City from 22 to 30 August.

On 1 September a Signal Platoon vehicle party under Corporal King was ambushed in the village of Dheftera, five miles outside Nicosia. The village Eoka group carried out the attack and one member of the Platoon was slightly wounded in the leg by an automatic weapon.

On 3 and 4 September, following the murder of an RAF Warrant Officer, the Battalion carried out a cordon and search operation in the village of Eylenja. The search unfortuntely drew a blank.

On 6 September a major cordon and search operation was conducted at Kykko Monastery Annexe in Nicosia. The Monastery was frequently used by Eoka groups to obtain sustenance and intelligence on security forces activities. On this occasion a quantity of Eoka leaflets and other propaganda material was found.

The next week, 7 to 13 September, saw a return to IS duties in the capital where little of interest occurred. Such standby duty in Nicosia, if uneventful, was tedious in the extreme and it was with great relief that plans were made for a further brief period of operations in the foothills and lower slopes of the Troodos Mountains.

Harbour parties from Battalion HQ and the companies moved out to the Makhaeras Forest on 14 September and from the 15th to the 23rd the Battalion conducted a series of intensive operations in the vicinity of the villages of Kythrea and Lythrodhonda. A combination of patrols and ambushes, together with surveillance of the area from continuously manned OPs, produced reasonable results, and a .38 pistol, five home-made pipe bombs and seven 36 grenades were recovered. These operations concluded with a cordon and search of Kykko Monastery in the mountains on 24 September.

An attempt on the life of Major-General Kendrew occurred on 26 September. He was travelling by car into Nicosia to a meeting at Government House with the Governor when a mine was exploded just behind his car. He was unhurt, but a Military Policeman in the following escort vehicle was killed. The Battalion mounted an immediate cordon and search operation in the Strovolos area where the incident happened, but, as was so frequently the case, no trace of the culprits was found.

At this time intensive negotiations were in hand at an international level to resolve the Cyprus problem, with the British Government now acknowledging that some form of independence might be offered to the Cypriots. To keep the Army in the picture, Sir Hugh Foot, the Governor, visited units to brief officers on the political situation at the end of September. He talked informally to officers of the Battalion on the 28th and confirmed their feelings that a political solution was the only answer and that military operations, at best, could only serve to strengthen the politicians' hand in negotiations.

Late in September the Battalion learnt with great pleasure that the Commanding Officer, Lieutenant-Colonel W.S. Bevan, had ben awarded an OBE in recognition of distinguished services in Cyprus.

With tension rising, the whole Battalion spent 1 October deployed at Riverside Camp in Nicosia at immediate notice to move. The situation remained calm, however, and the routine chore of IS duties in Nicosia was resumed the next day and sustained until 10 October. Two incidents occurred during this period. On one occasion two grenades were thrown at a landrover patrol. Fortunately both failed to explode. In the second, a D Company vehicle was blown up by an electrically detonated mine. One man was slightly wounded and the vehicle suffered moderate damage.

From 15 to 18 October the Battalion once more found itself on rural operations, this time under temporary command of the 1st Guards Brigade. The Brigade was conducting a major cordon and search operation in the Kythrea area and the Battalion's role was in part to maintain the curfew, and also to provide an element of the cordoning troops.

Following this operation, which was disappointing in its result, OPs overlooking the village were established for a number of days in the hope of observing Eoka groups returning there. C Company provided these OPs for six days from 23 October, but nothing came of the surveillance.

A vehicle party under the command of Sergeant Jones was blown up near Akaki village by an electrically detonated mine on 23 October. Fortunately there were no casualties. An immediate search of the area failed to locate the culprits.

D Company, back on mine guard duties on 26 October, found a cache of forty-nine sticks of dynamite hidden away at Mitsero mine.

Okhi Day, 28 October, saw the Battalion in Nicosia once more, at immediate notice to move, but the day passed quietly enough. The next day, however, two grenades were thrown at a C Company convoy returning after dark from Dheftera Range. There were no casualties, nor unfortunately were the culprits caught.

On one of the rare days in October when the Battalion was in camp, it was visited by the new Director of Operations and GOC Cyprus District, Major-General K.T. Darling, CBE, DSO. He addressed the whole Battalion and then met the officers and sergeants informally in their respective messes.

All companies mounted mobile 'snap' roadblocks in the Nicosia area from 1 to 3 November, and then from the 4th to the 11th the Battalion took over IS duties once again in Nicosia. At this time there was a spate of car burnings by youths in the city. The fire alarm would sound, a column of smoke would be seen and a vehicle would immediately race to the spot to catch the culprits. Almost invariably a blank was drawn.

During this period Sergeant Harris with the Mortar Platoon was lucky not to have been hurt when the Ferret scout car in which he was travelling was blown up by a mine when returning to camp from training on a range outside Nicosia.

From 12 to 20 November the Battalion was on half-an-hour's standby at Kykko Camp. There were no call-outs and the period was profitably devoted to training and administration.

Another stint of duty as Rural Battalion followed from 20 to 28 November. Platoon bases were established at various Police Stations including Kythrea, Dheftera, Perachorio, Pyroi and Mitsero, and sections were deployed to Peristerona, Orounda and Strovolos. OPs were established elsewhere in the area and patrols and ambushes were also sent out. A further six sticks of dynamite were uncovered during a diligent search of Mitsero mine.

The period 28 November to 6 December saw the Battalion acting as the Reserve for 50th Brigade. D Company spent five days of this period in the Kythrea area while C Company provided all routine guards and escorts.

Time was taken off from operations on Sunday, 30 November for a brief ceremonial parade marking another step towards amalgamation. The occasion commenced with a Drum Head service conducted by the Padre, the Reverend T.W. Metcalfe, during which the new cap badge of the 1st East Anglian Regiment was blessed. There then followed a beating of retreat by the Band and Drums. The next day, 1 December, the new cap badge was taken into use in the Battalion and the old Suffolk Regiment badges were removed for the last time to be kept as treasured souvenirs.

At this time main appointments in the Battalion were held as follows:

CO:	Lieutenant-Colonel W.S. Bevan, OBE
2ic:	Major K.M.J. Dewar, OBE
Adjt:	Captain P.D.L. Hopper
QM:	Major L.B. Day (Bedford and Hertfordshire Regiment)
RSM:	RSM Hazelwood
OC A Company:	(Training Organization) Major P.B. Forrest, MC
CSM:	CSM Lyon
OC B Company:	Major W.D.G. Fairholme
CSM:	CSM Loveday
OC C Company:	Captain R.M. Holman
CSM:	CSM Evans, MM
OC D Company:	Major A.L. Willdridge
CSM:	CSM Kerridge
OC HQ (1) Coy:	Major C.J.V. Fisher-Hoch
CSM:	CSM Jones
OC HQ (2) Coy:	Captain A.G.B. Cobbold
CSM:	CSM Moyes

The remainder of December saw the Battalion alternating between duties as IS Battalion in Nicosia and Rural Battalion of the Brigade. The Director of Operations visited the guards at Kambia and Mitsero mines on 14 December.

The month passed fairly peacefully except for the occasional burning of British-made cars in the Old City. The lull was largely as a result of the knowledge that important decisions regarding the future of Cyprus were about to be announced. They came, in fact, on 18 December, when, after meeting the Greek and Turkish Foreign Ministers in Paris, the British Foreign Secretary, Mr Selwyn Lloyd, announced the decision to grant independence to Cyprus in exchange for the retention of two areas, Episkopi and Dhekalia, which were to remain as British Strategic Bases and British Sovereign Territories.

The year thus ended on a hopeful note. The preceeding twelve months had been hectic in the extreme as the Battalion grappled with its various IS responsibilities. Hectic, that is, in the sense that its role was forever changing. While in general there had been few concrete successes, it had maintained an active and forceful presence which had deterred the Eoka enemy from attempting any major move to breach the security situation in those areas for which it had been responsible.

Frequent and extended periods of standby had brought sporting and recreational activities almost totally to a standstill in the summer and autumn. The Battalion cricket team played a game on 7 June and thereafter there were never eleven players free from operational duties to field a team again. The Officer in Charge of hockey thought he could get a side together in the autumn to play a Royal Engineer team. On the day of the game all eleven members of the Battalion team were whisked away for operations and the Band found a scratch eleven which won 3–2!

The Padre's contribution to the autumn number of the *Regimental Gazette* somehow expresses it all: 'The Summer months have been quiet for the Church owing to the Battalion being constantly out on IS duties and the overpowering heat in the Church'. He went on, plaintively, 'Now that most of the heat is over, we have had six fans installed' then, optimistically 'at any rate we've got them for next year'!

Despite the slackening pace of operations, Christmas, 1958, was an extended affair as guard duties and stand-by arrangements continued unabated. A, B, C and HQ (1) Companies took Christmas Day itself off, then changed over to allow D Company and HQ (2) Company their Christmas break on 27 December.

As in previous years, a large group of singers with a quintet from the Band, under the Reverend T.W. Metcalfe and Band Master Holben, sang carols on 20 December at the British Military Hospital, Nicosia, Government House and the Brigade Commander's home, and on 23 December at the home of the Government Attorney-General and the Director of Operations.

A pantomine 'Babes in Cyprus', produced by OC HQ (1) Company Major Fisher-Hoch, with musical help from the Band Master and members of the Band and a large cast of members of the Battalion and their wives, was a great success, packing the house on the night it was performed. Children of the Battalion put on a Nativity Play on 21 December and the Padre had a full house for the service of nine lessons and carols on Christmas Eve. A large congregation also attended Midnight Mass a few hours later.

On 4 January, 1959, the Battalion returned to the Old City for a week of IS duties which were again without incident. Then from 12 to 19 January it was back to rural operations, which now consisted of guard commitments as before, plus periodic vehicle patrols. At this time C Company was attached to the 1st Battalion, the Lancashire Fusiliers for an operation in the Kambos area of the Troodos Mountains.

Brigadier Bunbury, 50th Brigade Commander, paid a farewell visit to the Battalion on 14 January and six days later his successor, Brigadier D. Lister, DSO, MC, visited the Battalion's guards and rural patrols. The next day he went to Kykko Camp where he addressed the Battalion, met the WOs and Sergeants and had lunch in the Officers' Mess.

In the latter half of January intelligence pointed to a gang of Eoka terrorists active in the Adelphi Forest near Mitsero. Over the next four weeks a succession of operations was mounted to eliminate the gang.

On 23 January the Battalion, working with the 1st Battalion, the Royal Welch Fusiliers, conducted a cordon and search operation at the village of Ayia Marina, on the edge of the forest, but without success. Then, when acting as Rural Battalion, a programme of patrols and ambushes, supported by OPs was organized from 24 January to the end of the month in the Nicosia rural area.

The Battalion assumed command of the Patrol Bases at Peristerona, Mitsero and Kambia on 2 February and for the next week maintained a programme of patrolling and ambushing out of these bases.

Information from Police sources continued to confirm the presence of the Eoka gang in the Adelphi Forest and on 12 February the Battalion, with a Company of the 1st Battalion, the Lancashire Fusiliers under command, was released from all other commitments to mount a major operation to gain information on the pattern of movement of the gang. Battalion Tac HQ was established at the Mitsero mine and for the next five days six small parties were sent out in the Mitsero and Ayia Marina areas of the Adelphi Forest, with the aim of lying up in hides by day and mounting ambushes at night. On the night of 16 February two of the parties, under the command of Lieutenant Peat and 2nd Lieutenant Chapman, clearly observed the flickering light of a hurricane lamp in the forest. The sightings were reported back to Battalion Tac HQ and all parties were withdrawn from the area to allow for an operation to be mounted to attack the Eoka camp which had clearly been pin-pointed.

The operation was planned for 19 February but was called off at the last minute, when all operations were cancelled, consequent upon the signing on that day of a formal agreement between the British, Greek and Turkish Governments in consultation with Archbishop Makarios and Dr Kutchuk (the Turkish Cypriot Leader), which granted independence to Cyprus and provided for the retention of the British Sovereign Base areas of Dhekalia and Episkopi.

Over the next three days the Battalion was required to send out a series of small patrols in the Nicosia rural area to observe and report on Greek and Turkish Cypriot reactions to the agreement.

On 24 February Colonel W.A. Heal, OBE, Brigade Colonel, East Anglian Brigade, arrived for a brief visit to the Battalion. During his stay Colonel Heal visited various activities and renewed acquaintances in both the Officers' and Sergeants' Messes.

While active operations had now come to an end, it was still necessary to retain a military presence throughout the island and, of course, guard duties continued unabated. C Company took over the guard at the Kambia and Mitsero mines from 3 to 9 March and B Company was lucky enough to go on a six-week detachment to Kakopetria, also starting on 3 March.

Brigadier R.H. Maxwell, CB, Colonel of the Regiment, arrived on an official visit to the Battalion on 10 March. His six-day programme was very full. The day after he arrived he inspected the Battalion and took the salute at a ceremonial parade. On 12 March he was whisked off to Kakopetria, Kambia and Mitsero to visit B and C Companies and, finally, on 14 March he received the guests at a beating of retreat by the Band and Drums, which was attended by a number of senior political and military figures in Cyprus, including the Governor and Lady Foot.

No sooner had Brigadier Maxwell left for the United Kingdom than the Battalion was visited by the Quartermaster-General on 17 March and on the next day the Brigade Commander inspected various training activities in progress in Kykko Camp.

The last half of March saw the Battalion back on duty in Nicosia. There was no call on it for IS duties, but it did now have to provide, with other units in turn, a company to patrol the city streets to prevent disturbances between off-duty soldiers who were no longer armed and Cypriots who were jubilant and decidedly high-spirited following the agreement on Independence.

On 2 April command of the Battalion was handed over by Lieutenant-Colonel W.S. Bevan, OBE, on completion of his tenure, to Lieutenant-Colonel K.M.J. Dewar, OBE, who was to have the sad honour of leading the Battalion into amalgamation.

Lieutenant-Colonel Bevan had commanded the Battalion throughout its tour of duty in Cyprus and thus held the distinction of being the last CO of a Battalion of the Suffolk Regiment on active service.

After a summer virtually unable to participate in sports because of IS commitments, the winter and spring of 1959 brought more opportunities. The Battalion Hockey Team achieved excellent results, winning twenty-six of thirty-six games played, winning the 50th Independent Infantry Brigade Cup and the Cyprus Six-a-side tournament and finishing as runners-up in the Cyprus Major Units Cup.

The Football Team also played well and won twelve of seventeen matches played in the Nicosia Area League.

Due to leave Cyprus in May, by the middle of April preparations were in hand for the journey. Heavy baggage was packed and farewell parties were organized.

On 15 April the C-in-C Middle East Land Forces, Lieutenant-General Sir Roger Bower, KBE, CB, paid a farewell visit to the Battalion and lunched with the officers. The Director of Operations and GOC Cyprus District, together with the Brigade Commander, 50th Independent Infantry Brigade, paid a farewell visit to Kykko Camp on 8 May, and that evening the Governor, Sir Hugh Foot, and his wife paid an informal visit to the Officers' Mess on the eve of departure.

Reveille on 9 May was at 0330 but the whole Battalion was awake long before, and everyone made the trip successfully to Limassol to board the *Dilwara* which sailed that evening.

There was one stop over en route for the UK at Gibraltar where a few hours' shore leave was granted.

The voyage passed uneventfully on a calm sea and the *Dilwara* docked at Southampton at 1630 on 19 May, 1959, bringing an eventful overseas tour of duty to an end. The last one for a Battalion of the Suffolk Regiment.

CHAPTER VIII

THE DEPOT: 1946–1959

'A Happy Home Posting'

Part I

It is difficult to know where to begin the story of the Depot in the post-Second World War years.

A glance through the pages of the *Regimental Gazette* published in 1945 and 1946 leaves one with the impression that during the War the Depot had virtually ceased to exist, swamped as it was by the Infantry Training Centre which had been established for recruit training in both Gibraltar Barracks and Blenheim Camp. And yet it did continue to live, even in those turbulent times. It was almost as if it was forced to remain alive at the insistence of a steady trickle of officers and men who, on returning to the United Kingdom from war service overseas, made it their business to visit the place where they had at one time or another first joined the Regiment and come to feel a sense of belonging to it.

But sentiment would scarcely have sufficed and if one is to look for one man who brought the Depot, alive and safe, into the post-War world, that one man must surely be Major F.V.C. Pereira. He took over command in 1936 and remained at the helm until he retired from regular service in 1948. Even then, he did not leave the Depot, but as a retired Officer became its Administrative Officer until 1950. In these two capacities, he not only served the Depot, but on a broader scale the Regiment as well. He managed to publish the *Regimental Gazette*, nurture the Old Comrades Association, look into the problems of former men of the Regiment on hard times and, after the War, to resuscitate the Officers' Dinner Club, the Annual Old

Comrades' Association Reunions and help to build up the Sergeants' Dinner Club.

In 1946, despite a threatened closure of Regimental Depots consequent upon a reorganization of the Infantry, a new establishment for the Depot was announced. It was to comprise a Commanding Officer plus fourteen all ranks! Its responsibilities were inevitably limited and it shared its barracks with a much larger training organization, now renamed the 12th Primary Training Centre (PTC).

This organization was to continue for two years only in this form. In 1948 the 12th PTC ceased to exist and its training function was assumed by an East Anglian Brigade Training Centre in Colchester. This left the Depot party of fifteen alone in Gibraltar Barracks.

The establishment was slightly enhanced later in the year and remained at thirty (including civilian staff) until 1951, when the War Office decided that recruit training should once more be conducted at Regimental Depots. Joy in the Regiment was unconfined when it was learned that recruits to the Regiment were once more to be trained at Bury St Edmunds.

The Depot was from then onwards to have an East Anglian Brigade function as well and the establishment allowed for continuation training to be given to soldiers from all the East Anglian Regiments if they were destined for overseas service with a Battalion. There was also a small headquarters established under the East Anglian Brigade Colonel, which watched over the training and administration of all the depots in the Brigade and which played a major part in the postings of officers and senior ranks within the Brigade.

Although the organization and responsibilities of the Depot were occasionally modified over the years, it continued to train recruits for the Regiment, to organize Regimental functions and to foster the good name of the Regiment in its home town and county until amalgamation in 1959.

The impression created by Gibraltar Barracks on approaching it was never one of grandeur. Indeed, the high red brick walls and starkly rising keep were rather a severe sight as one approached. Inside the gate one saw the square and the barrack blocks and to the left the headquarters buildings and, beyond trees and grass, the gardens leading to the Officers' Mess. Nothing too presumptious about the place, but it did undoubtedly really feel like a regimental home.

Young officers posted back to the Depot as training subalterns or later as Adjutant or Company Commander, or even to command, might well have sighed for the excitement of a foreign posting, perhaps on active service, or for a warmer more exotic climate, but within a few months the compensations made themselves felt. The job of training recruits for the Regiment was rewarding and life in the Officers' Mess was very civilized. Mr Percy Watts, the Mess Steward, had been in the Mess in that capacity since 1928. He had known practically every officer of the Regiment as a subaltern and he and his wife, who had been Officers' Mess Cook since their marriage in 1929, treated all Mess members as though they were part of one family.

For the warrant officers and sergeants, the Depot was home as well. Scarcely a night and certainly not a week passed without a former member of the Sergeants' Mess looking in to see how things were. Whether from Suffolk or not, practically all members of the Mess found work in the County after leaving the Regiment, so strong was the pull.

Gibraltar Barracks was blessed with good sporting facilities and games were played with great enthusiasm throughout the year. East Anglian District competitions were sometimes won, even against major units, in shooting, football and hockey, and that, on occasion, when the Depot could number but thirty officers and men. Local County Leagues were entered and every season was packed with friendly matches against civilian, Police and RAF teams.

Tennis was played particularly by the officers and some of them kept horses too, in the stables behind the Mess.

And then there were the annual Regimental occasions which the Depot staff inevitably found themselves organizing. The Sergeants' Mess (Past and Present) Dinner was one such event which continued to grow in popularity as the years went by. Usually chaired by the Colonel of the Regiment and supported by a sprinkling of senior officers, it came to provide an opportunity each year for the Colonel of the Regiment in his after-dinner speech to make as it were a report on 'the State of the Regiment'. It was the proper place to do it, for no one knew better than the Colonel of the Regiment that its quality rested in the hands of its warrant officers and sergeants.

Daffodil Sunday was another such annual occasion. The choice of the day when the daffodils were likely to be at their best was not easy. One Depot Commander whose task it was to make this choice reckoned it to be by far and away his most difficult decision of the year! But, joking apart, it was important, for when the daffodils bloomed the Depot looked at its most gentle and beautiful best, and visitors always flocked into the Barracks in their thousands on that day, either simply to stroll along the paths through the trees or be entertained by whatever displays were provided.

Each year, too, came the dinner of the Past and Present Officers of the (XIIth) Suffolk Regiment. Held in London, most frequently at the Trocadero Restaurant, but once or twice at the Army and Navy Club, these dinners provided officers of the Regiment with the opportunity to meet and renew old friendships. It gave newly joined officers the chance to learn something more about the Regiment, and the older retired officers were able to talk to those still serving and get a feeling from them of how things were in the Battalions and at the Depot. Normally between sixty and eighty officers dined, except in 1953 when, with the 1st Battalion in England on return from Malaya, a total of ninety-seven attended the dinner.

The Old Comrades Association, which had been formed in 1908, continued to flourish during these years. It was administered by staff at the Depot and annually held its reunion at Gibraltar Barracks. In the early post-Second World War years attendance was comparatively small, due largely to problems with public transport, but over the years it increased as more and more men were able to make the annual pilgrimage to the home of the Regiment.

Each year the programme varied but the reunion always began with a Drumhead Service followed by a brief address by the Colonel of the Regiment in which he summarized the year's activities of the Battalions and the Depot. Afterwards there would be a Band Concert or a PT display and often a concert party would offer entertainment in the Rock Theatre.

These occasions were full of warmth and happiness: rank and status were forgotten as old friendships, often made in difficult and dangerous circumstances, were renewed.

The most significant reunion took place in 1954, when Her Royal Highness the Princess Margaret was present. The Depot provided a Guard of Honour and a Detachment from the 4th Battalion and over 550 Old Comrades were also on parade.

It was on this occasion that the Regimental Brooch was presented to the new Colonel-in-Chief and, despite attempts by the weather to mar the day (it rained almost nonstop), it was undoubtedly the most important single event in the post-War history of the Depot, one thoroughly enjoyed and long remembered by those who participated in or witnessed it.

But none of this could slow the remorseless pace of change which was to bring an end to the Depot of the Suffolk Regiment, as countless generations had known it, and, with amalgamation on 29 August, 1959, the Regimental Flag was lowered for the last time.

Part II

Daffodil Sunday was celebrated in early April, 1946, at Gibraltar Barracks. It was organized by the Staff of No 3 ITC for the last time. There was a parade on the square and afterwards the Band of the 1st Battalion played a concert. The sun shone and the daffodils flowered in profusion in the Officers' Mess gardens between the Mess and the square. A considerable crowd of spectators from the town attended.

In August No 3 ITC celebrated a combined Minden and Blenheim anniversary on 3 and 4 August. The occasion began with a parade of over 2,000 men, commanded by Lieutenant-Colonel G.A. Anstee, MC, of the Bedfordshire and Hertfordshire Regiment, at which the following Colonels of Regiments and other Senior Officers were present: Colonel W.N. Nicholson, CMG, DSO, Colonel of the Suffolk Regiment; General Sir Henry C. Jackson, KCB, CMG, DSO, DL, Colonel of the Bedfordshire and Hertfordshire Regiment; Major-General R.M. Luckock, CB, CMG, DSO, Honorary Colonel of the Cambridgeshire Regiment; Brigadier J.A. Longmore, CBE, TD, DL, and Brigadier-General the Viscount Hampden, GCVO, KCB, CMG, Honorary Colonel the Hertfordshire Regiment.

The remainder of the celebration included cricket matches, displays, an all-ranks ball, the Old Comrades Association Reunion and a Drumhead Service.

The editorial of the *Regimental Gazette* for November and December, 1946, recorded with dismay the proposed War Office reorganization of the Infantry Regiments of the Line, which meant that the Depot would cease to exist! With a show of some determination, it went on in the following vein, 'We trust that all past and present members of the Regiment, who pay a visit to Gibraltar Barracks, shall be greeted by the Suffolk Regiment Flag and be accommodated in rooms set aside for their convenience and comfort.' It seemed that it was likely that it would take more than a War Office decision to 'kill off' the Depot!

In the same *Gazette* it was recorded that No 3 ITC would be disbanded and replaced by No 12 PTC and the Depot, the Suffolk Regiment and that the latter would consist of a party of fifteen all ranks commanded by Major F.V.C. Pereira. The function of No 12

PTC would be to receive recruits and give them six weeks' basic training. If they were destined for the Regiment or any other regiment of the East Anglian Brigade Group, they would continue their training at Colchester at the East Anglian Brigade Training Centre. If selected for any other corps, their continuation training would be at their corps depot or training regiments. No 12 PTC was not an integral part of the Suffolk Regiment but it was completely staffed by the Regiment.

The responsibilities of the Regimental Depot Party would be to take into custody the Colours and property of the 2nd Battalion on going into suspended animation, to maintain the Regimental links with the Territorial Army and to administer officers and men of the Regiment on postings to Extra-Regimental Employment.

The new organization came into effect on 19 December, 1946, when Lieutenant-Colonel F.A. Milnes returned from the 1st Battalion to take command of No 12 PTC.

On 10 June, 1947, Colonel Nicholson retired as Colonel of the Regiment following the appointment of Brigadier E.H.W. Backhouse to succeed him. Colonel Nicholson had assumed the Colonelcy in February, 1939, and his active and enthusiastic tour of duty, embracing the War years, culminated in his writing of the Third Volume of *The Regimental History*, which was published in 1948.

The sixty-third Annual Dinner of the Suffolk Regiment Officers' Dinner Club was held at the Trocadero Restaurant in London on 27 June. Seventy-four members of the Club were present.

Minden Day, 1 August, was a sad day for those present at the Depot. No 12 PTC was on parade under the Commanding Officer and music was provided by the Band of the 2nd Battalion, the Northamptonshire Regiment. The Colours of the 2nd Battalion, recently returned to England from India, were handed over during a somewhat subdued ceremony to the Officer Commanding the Depot, Major Pereira, for safekeeping, while the Battalion remained in suspended animation.

On Sunday, 3 August, the Suffolk Regiment Old Comrades Association Annual Reunion took place in Gibraltar Barracks. The first proper reunion since the War, it was a great success, with a large gathering present, despite the difficulties connected with travel in those early post-War years.

On 21 April, 1948, Major J.W. Josselyn assumed command of the Depot from Major Pereira, who retired from full-time service and took over the appointment of Administrative Officer of the Depot.

Major Pereira first took over at the Depot in 1936 and had thus been a key figure in Regimental affairs for twelve years.

Senior appointments at the Depot at this time were as follows:

OC:	Major J.W. Josselyn
Adjt:	Captain F.J. Lockett
Amin Officer:	Major F.V.C. Pereira
QM:	Captain H.R. Cotton
RSM:	RSM Jasper

On 21 April, also, No 12 PTC ceased to exist, transferring its training function to the East Anglian Brigade Training Centre at Colchester, which also ceased to exist on 13 May, when its training functions were assumed in Colchester by the 1st Battalion, the Essex Regiment based in Meanee Barracks.

On 5 June the Regiment was granted the Freedom of the Borough of Ipswich. The ceremony took place at Christchurch Park and the Colours of the 4th Battalion were on parade. The Colonel of the Regiment received the illuminated scroll on behalf of the Regiment.

The annual Officers' Club Dinner took place at the Trocadero Restaurant on Friday, 25 June. Seventy-two officers under the chairmanship of the Colonel of the Regiment, were present. The Sergeants' Dinner Club (Past and Present) held their first annual dinner since the War in the Rock Theatre at Gibraltar Barracks on 11 September. The occasion was an immense success with 110 members at table. The Colonel of the Regiment took the Chair as Club President and the Mayor of Bury St Edmunds was the Guest of Honour. The Club had been in existence since 1908 and, except during the two World Wars, had met annually since then.

On 10 April Daffodil Sunday was celebrated once more, when the gates of the Depot were opened to the public to make this annual visit. Added interest was attached to the occasion, as it provided an opportunity to bring to an end a somewhat unusual historical incident.

When the Colours, still carried by the 1st Battalion, were presented at Weedon in 1849, it was sought to have the old Colours laid up in Ipswich Parish Church. Following intervention by a church warden, supported by the Archdeacon, this was not allowed and they were as a result retained by the then Colonel of the Regiment, General the Honorable R. Meade. They remained with the Meade family until returned to the Regiment by his descendant, Major Wyndham Meade, of Earsham Hall in Suffolk.

Major Meade presented the Colours to the Colonel of the Regiment at Earsham Hall and they were taken to Gibraltar

Barracks where, during a parade, the highlight of Daffodil Sunday, they were handed to the OC the Depot, Major Josselyn, for safekeeping.

Seventy-nine officers attended the Past and Present Officers' Dinner at the Trocadero Restaurant on 24 June.

Minden celebrations began on 28 July with a Minden Ball organized by the Depot's Families Club. Then on the 29th and 30th the annual cricket match between the Gentlemen of Suffolk and the Officers of the Regiment, was played, though bad weather caused the match to be drawn. The annual reunion of the Old Comrades' Association took place on Sunday, 31 July. The day began with a memorial service in St Mary's Church, when the casket containing the Roll of Honour for the 1939–45 War was unveiled by Field-Marshal Lord Wilson of Libya and Stowlangtoft.

After an address by the Field-Marshal, the casket was dedicated by the Bishop of Ipswich and St Edmundsbury. The Colonel of the Regiment gave an address to conclude the service and then over 700 Old Comrades, headed by the Drums of the 5th (Cadet) Battalion, the Suffolk Regiment, marched to Gibraltar Barracks where the remainder of the celebrations took place, attended by some two thousand people who renewed acquaintances, took part in sports and enjoyed the concert played by the Band of the 1st Battalion, the Essex Regiment.

Life at the Depot continued in the usual way through the year. Its role did not change and its key functions were to look after officers and men of the Regiment in between postings. There were occasional training days run jointly with other Depots of the East Anglian Brigade and the annual range course was fired at Barton Mills Ranges. Training assistance was also provided for Home Guard and Army Cadet Force Units, but most time-consuming of all duties was the up-keep and maintenance of the Depot grounds and the preparation and organization of the Regimental functions throughout the year.

The annual Past and Present Sergeants' Dinner took place in the Rock Theatre on 17 September, when 163 members sat down. Lieutenant-Colonel H.B. Monier-Williams, OBE, MC, was in the Chair, and there were two guests of honour, His Worship the Mayor of Bury St Edmunds and Lieutenant-Colonel G.A. Anstee, OBE, MC, former Commanding Officer of No 3 ITC from 1944 to 1946.

The Depot Rifle Team, chosen from the thirty officers and men on the staff, achieved considerable success at the East Anglian District Rifle Meeting at Colchester on 2 September. They won the Minor

Units competition and came third in the Major Units event. Captain Lockett, RSM Jasper, Sergeant Barrett and Private Facey made up the team.

The Deputy Commander, East Anglian District, Brigadier H.D.W. Sitwell, CB, MC, carried out the annual administrative inspection of the Depot on 14 October.

The Adjutant and RSM, Captain Lockett and RSM Jasper, took part in Exercise Victor on 20 November. The exercise was held on Stanford Battle Area and involved activities at Brigade level.

The Depot was very quiet over the Christmas period, though a very successful children's party was held by the Married Families Club in the Rock Theatre. Funds for this party had been raised by a Christmas bazaar held in early December, at which items made by members of the Depot and their families were sold.

Sunday 2 April, 1950, saw the Depot throw open its gates to the general public for Daffodil Sunday. Despite an extremely cold day, accompanied by a biting east wind, many citizens of Bury St Edmunds and Old Comrades of the Regiment attended and were able to watch the Drums of the 5th Cadet Battalion, the Suffolk Regiment beating retreat on the square and listen to a concert by the Band of the 1st Battalion, the Bedfordshire and Hertfordshire Regiment in the Rock Theatre (the Battalion had been resident over the road at Blenheim Camp since early in the new year).

The East Anglian District Rifle Meeting took place on 13 and 14 May and, once more, the Depot four-man team, comprising this year Captain Lockett, RSM Jasper, WOII Peck and CSM Newman achieved great distinction by being runners-up to the 1st Battalion, the Essex Regiment in the Unit Open Team match and winning the Minor Units Open match for the second year running, a remarkable success from a Unit still with an establishment of only thirty all ranks. The sixty-sixth annual dinner of the Past and Present Officers' Dinner Club took place at the Trocadero Restaurant on Friday 23 June. The Colonel of the Regiment presided and the Guest of Honour was Colonel C.F. Seaward, DSO, MC, ED, Colonel of one of the affiliated Regiments, the Auckland Regiment of New Zealand. Seventy-five officers dined. The Adjutant, Captain Lockett, completed his tour of duty at the end of June and, after attending a course, he was posted to the 1st Battalion. Captain Lockett had, during his two years at the Depot, done much to foster the corporate spirit of the Depot through the creation of a thriving Families Club. He was much helped in this by his wife who had also always kept a close eye on the Regimental Chapel in the Cathedral Church of St Mary.

Captain Lockett's post was filled briefly by Captain N.A.M. Balders who then volunteered for service in Korea and joined the 1st Battalion, the Royal Ulster Rifles there in October, 1950, leaving the Adjutant's chair vacant (on 20 February, 1951, he was killed while commanding the Royal Ulster Rifles Battle Patrol in action on the Han River).

The annual Minden Reunion of Old Comrades took place on 30 July when over 1,000 Old Comrades and their families came together to celebrate at Gibraltar Barracks. The programme began with an open-air church service on the Barracks Square and the rest of the day was spent in the usual manner, with a sports competition and a PT display by a team from the 1st Battalion, the Bedfordshire and Hertfordshire Regiment, whose Band also played throughout the day.

4 August saw an all ranks Minden Ball in the Rock Theatre attended by over 300.

The annual Past and Present Sergeants' Dinner was held in the Rock Theatre on 16 September when Lieutenant-Colonel H.W. Dean took the chair and 140 members sat down to dinner. The Colonel of the Regiment attended and the Guest of Honour was once more the Mayor of Bury St Edmunds.

On 15 October Major Pereira retired as Administrative Officer at the Depot and his place was taken by Lieutenant-Colonel H.R. Hopking, OBE.

With the arrival of autumn, the Depot took on an additional role, that of processing National Servicemen returning to the Depot for release and arranging for their service with a TA Unit for three years, which had become a requirement for them.

On 15 December Captain Wiggington arrived to take up the appointment of Adjutant and at the end of 1950 senior appointments at the Depot were held as follows:

OC: Major J.W. Josselyn
Adjt: Captain H.E.W. Wiggington
QM: Major J. Longstaff
RSM: RSM Jasper

Daffodil Sunday was delayed in 1951 owing to the severe spring weather. It finally took place on the last Sunday of April, by which time the weather had markedly improved. Large crowds attended as usual and the Band of the 4th Battalion entertained visitors with a concert.

The War Office decision that Group Training Centres should be abolished, and that recruits for the Infantry should once more be trained at Regimental Depots, was greeted with delight by the Regiment. Once more the Depot would actually prepare recruits for service with the 1st Battalion. The Suffolk Regiment Depot had also been chosen as the Brigade Depot with additional responsibilities as a result. This extra commitment was two-fold. On the one hand the Depot would be responsible for continuation training for all recruits to Regiments of the East Anglian Brigade, whose Battalions were engaged on active service, and on the other, it would be responsible for holding all soldiers of the Brigade on postings to or from battalions, courses and extra-regimental employment. To co-ordinate these latter activities and also assume responsibility for officers' postings, a small Headquarters East Anglian Brigade was also established and the first Brigade Colonel was Colonel R.P. Freeman-Taylor (late of the Royal Norfolk Regiment).

The new tasks commenced in May and from then the small establishment of the Depot was greatly enhanced with new arrivals, including officers and senior ranks from other Regiments of the Brigade, to share in the Brigade Depot responsibilities.

The new organization of the Depot comprised A Company, located in Gibraltar Barracks and responsible for the Suffolk Regiment recruit training, and B and C Companies located in Blenheim Camp and responsible respectively for the holding and the continuation training functions.

The sixty-seventh dinner of the Officers' Dinner Club took place at the Trocadero Restaurant on 22 June under the chairmanship of the Colonel of the Regiment. Sixty-six officers sat down to dinner with two guests, Major H. Fowler, RA, and Major W.F. Page, MC, the Cambridgeshire Regiment.

The East Anglian District Small Arms Meeting took place from 21 to 24 June. The Depot team was not as successful as in the previous two years, but did win the Young Soldiers' Cup.

The East Anglian Brigade Group Regimental Colonels visited the Depot on 28 June. They included Major-General E.C. Hayes, CB, Colonel, the Royal Norfolk Regiment, Brigadier E.H.W. Backhouse, Colonel, the Suffolk Regiment, Lieutenant-General Sir Reginald Denning, KBE, CB, Colonel the Bedfordshire and Hertfordshire Regiment, Brigadier C.M. Paton, CVO, CBE, Colonel the Essex Regiment, and Major General G. St G. Robinson, CB, DSO, MC, Colonel the Northamptonshire Regiment.

The visit was designed to allow the Colonels to see the newly functioning Depot system at work. They visited all three companies and met and spoke to warrant officers, sergeants and men of their own Regiments. A meeting of the newly formed Council of Colonels was also held and in the evening the Colonels dined in the Officers' Mess and later attended a dance in the Sergeants' Mess.

Command of the Depot was handed over by Major Josselyn on his retirement from the Army to Major J.C.R. Eley, in July.

Minden Day was celebrated by a parade on Gibraltar Barracks square when the salute was taken by the Colonel of the Regiment. There was a small cocktail party in the Officers' Mess early in the evening and also an all-ranks dance which was held in the Rock Theatre.

The annual Old Comrades Association Minden reunion took place on Sunday 5 August and was attended by just over 1,000 members of the OCA and their families. The Drumhead Service was conducted by the Vicar of Fornham St Martin, a former Royal Naval Chaplain, assisted by the Reverend W.M. Lummis, MC, a former Officer of the Regiment. Lunch followed the service and the afternoon's entertainments included a Band Concert by the Band of the 4th Battalion, a PT display and a performance by a concert party in the Rock Theatre.

The GOC-in-C Eastern Command, General Sir Gerald Templer, KCB, KBE, CMG, DSO, ADC, inspected the Depot on 3 September and had lunch in the Officers' Mess after his inspection. (General Templer was to learn more of the Suffolk Regiment some five months later when he became High Commissioner in Malaya, where he visited the 1st Battalion on several occasions.)

The Past and Present Sergeants' Dinner Club held its annual dinner on the 6th October under the chairmanship of Lieutenant-Colonel J.W. Josselyn. Guests of Honour included the Mayor of Bury St Edmunds, Brigadier Backhouse, the Colonel of the Regiment, Colonel Nicholson, (former Colonel of the Regiment) and the East Anglian Brigade Colonel, Colonel Freeman-Taylor. 165 members and guests sat down at table in the Rock Theatre and the Band of the 4th Battalion played during the dinner.

Major H.R. Cotton took over as QM at the Depot from Major J. Longstaff at the end of November.

The annual administrative inspection was carried out by the GOC East Anglian District on 31 January, 1952.

Daffodil Sunday was celebrated on 20 April and visitors flocked into the Depot to visit the museum and the barrack room set out for an inspection. A PT display was watched with enthusiasm, and the

Band Concert gave great pleasure. This year the concert was performed by the Band of the 1st Battalion under Band Master A. Mitchenall. The Band had returned from Malaya in the autumn and, besides playing at numerous functions throughout East Anglia, had already added much to the various social occasions at the Depot since being posted there.

On 13 May the Depot played host to a group of some twenty foreign Military Attachés who visited training in progress and had lunch in the Officers' Mess. The *Regimental Gazette* correspondent described the visit as 'one of the most colourful military occasions we have had in the Mess'.

The Colonel of the Regiment, Brigadier Backhouse, carried out a tour of inspection of the Depot, Gibraltar Barracks and Blenheim Camp on 23 May.

The Regimental Museum provided an interesting display at Colchester on 6 and 7 June as part of the East Anglian District Summer Show.

A former Colonel of the Regiment, Major-General Sir John Ponsonby, KCB, CMG, DSO, died on 2 June and a Memorial Service was held on 13 June in the Suffolk Regiment Chapel at St Mary's in Bury St Edmunds. Representatives of the Regiment led by the Colonel of the Regiment included a number of officers, serving and retired, and a detachment thirty strong from the Depot. The Band of the 1st Battalion provided the music for the service. General Ponsonby was Colonel of the Regiment from 1925 until 1939.

The annual Minden reunion of the Old Comrades' Association was held on 6 July, rather earlier in the year than usual, owing to heavy commitments at the Depot in early August. Well over a thousand people attended and the weather was warm and sunny. The day began with a Drumhead Service conducted by the Venerable H.R. Norton, Archdeacon of Sudbury, assisted by the Reverend W.M. Lummis. At the end of the service the Colonel of the Regiment addressed the gathering. Lunch followed and the remainder of the day took the usual form, including performances by the 1st Battalion Band, a PT display by the Depot PT staff and a concert party. Sudden heavy rain brought the day to a close at 7.30 pm.

The annual cricket match between the Regiment and the Gentlemen of Suffolk was played on 19 and 20 July and resulted in a win for the Regiment.

The GOC-in-C Eastern Command, Lieutenant-General Sir George Erskine, KCB, KBE, DSO, visited the Depot on 24 July.

A recruit passing-out parade was held by A Company on 29 July. The salute was taken by the Mayor of Ipswich. Two platoons of recruits took part.

An all-ranks Minden Ball was held in the Regimental Institute in Blenheim Camp on 31 July. The Dance Band of the 1st Battalion Band provided the music and some 600 people attended the function.

The next day, 1 August, the whole Depot paraded to celebrate Minden Day under the command of the Depot Commander, Major Eley. The Colours of the former 3rd Battalion were on parade bedecked with wreaths of Minden Roses and all members of the Suffolk Regiment on the parade wore red and yellow roses. The Colours were carried by Lieutenant W.D.G. Fairholme and Lieutenant J.G. Starling, MC. Brigadier Backhouse, Colonel of the Regiment, inspected the Parade and took the salute at the march past. Music for the parade was played by the 1st Battalion Band.

On 15 September a delegation of three officers from the Burmese Military Mission spent the day at the Depot, visiting training in progress and two days later, on 17 September, a recruit passing out parade was held at which the salute was taken by the Mayor of Sudbury.

In October the function of the Depot was once again reorganized. C Company was abolished and A Company took on the responsibility for all training. Instead of the recruit course of six weeks' duration, which had previously been run, there would now be a course ten weeks long, after which recruits would go straight to whichever Battalion of the Brigade Group they had been allotted. The full title of the Depot remained The Depot, the Suffolk Regiment (East Anglian Brigade Depot) and the headquarters of the East Anglian Brigade remained located in Blenheim Camp.

In October also, Captain Howgego arrived to take over command of A Company from Captain E.E. Mayes (Royal Norfolk Regiment).

Senior appointments on the Depot staff at this time were held as follows:

OC:	Major J.C.R. Eley
Adjt:	Captain H.J. Chisnall
QM:	Major H.R. Cotton
RSM:	RSM Gingell
OC A Company:	Captain G.C. Howgego
OC B Company:	Captain Nichols (Bedfordshire and Hertfordshire Regiment)

The sixty-eighth annual Officers' Dinner took place at the

Trocadero Restaurant, Piccadilly on 3 October. The Colonel of the Regiment was in the chair and sixty-five officers were present. The Past and Present Sergeants' Dinner was held in the Rock Theatre at the Depot on 11 October. Colonel A.M. Cutbill, MC, was Chairman. The 1st Battalion Band played during the dinner, adding greatly to the occasion.

The last six-week recruit course passed out on 28 October, when the salute was taken by the Colonel of the Regiment. The Colonel also presented Long Service and Good Conduct Medals to Colour Sergeant Ogg, Sergeant Ling and Sergeant Garwood.

During the first week of November the Potential Leaders Platoon (for all Regiments of the Brigade), under Lieutenant L.A. Palmer, transferred from C Company to A Company as C Company was disbanded. On arrival with A Company the Platoon was renamed the Viking Platoon.

On 19 November the CIGS, Field-Marshal Sir John Harding, KCB, CBE, DSO, MC, visited the Depot. He was accompanied by the GOC-in-C Eastern Command, the District Commander and the District Home Guard Commander.

1953 brought with it a thrill of anticipation for the arrival home of the 1st Battalion from Malaya, tempered with the knowledge that much of what would happen by way of celebrations would fall to the Depot to organize.

The first passing out parade of 1953 took place on 13 March. Lieutenant-Colonel K.J.K. Pye, CO of the 4th Battalion, inspected the parade, took the salute at the march past and presented trophies and medals.

Daffodil Sunday was celebrated in April. Unfortunately, the weather was atrocious, both bitterly cold and very wet. Only about 200 visitors came to Gibraltar Barracks compared with the usual large crowd. The Band of the 1st Battalion at least provided the few who braved the day with an exciting concert in the old gymnasium.

The sixty-ninth annual dinner of the Officers of the Regiment was held at the Trocadero Restaurant on 16 April. Held early in the year, while the 1st Battalion was still in the United Kingdom, it was a great success, with ninety-seven officers sitting down to dinner. The Colonel of the Regiment, Brigadier Backhouse, presided and the East Anglian Brigade Colonel, Colonel Freeman-Taylor, was the guest of honour.

On 25 April A Company provided a contingent of seventy-five officers and men to witness the ceremony granting the Freedom of the Borough of Sudbury to the 1st Battalion.

The Sudbury parade was held in perfect spring weather, but when A Company again paraded, as spectators, after the welcome home ceremony for the 1st Battalion at Bury St Edmunds, the weather was extremely unkind: rain fell steadily throughout the day.

In the evening an all ranks welcome home dance was held in the Regimental Institute in Blenheim Camp. The whole affair was organized by the Depot staff, including decorations, catering and the bar, as well as the sale of tickets and advertising beforehand. Over 800 people attended the dance for which music was played by the 1st Battalion Dance Band.

On Friday 1 May, an Officers' Regimental Ball was held in the Athenaeum on Angel Hill at Bury St Edmunds. Once again the Depot staff played the major role in organizing the event, with Lieutenant-Colonel Hopking and Captain Howgego bearing the brunt of the work. The occasion was a great success, achieving its dual aim of welcoming home the 1st Battalion and repaying the County for its hospitality. The Lord-Lieutenant of Suffolk, Commander The Earl of Stradbroke, and the High Sheriff of Suffolk, Lieutenant-General Sir R. Harold Carrington, KCB, DSO, were among the guests.

4 May saw another recruit passing out parade at which the salute was taken by Colonel Freeman-Taylor, Colonel East Anglian Brigade.

On 1 June the Regiment learned with great pride that Her Majesty the Queen had, on the occasion of Her Coronation, appointed Her Royal Highness The Princess Margaret, CI, GCVO, as Colonel-in-Chief, the Suffolk Regiment.

Brigadier Backhouse, as Colonel of the Suffolk Regiment, attended the Coronation of Her Majesty the Queen at Westminster Abbey on 2 June and a small party from the Depot under Lieutenant L.A. Palmer also journeyed to London to help line the route of the Coronation procession. A Company provided a contingent which participated in the celebrations in Bury St Edmunds.

The Depot Rifle Meeting was held on 12 and 13 June and a successful team was selected to represent the Depot at the East Anglian District Rifle Meeting. QMSI Connolly (SASC) won the Individual Rifle Championship and Sergeant Hazelwood came a close third. The young soldiers rifle team won their event, and Lance-Corporal Farrow came second in the young soldiers individual competition. QMSI Connolly and Sergeant Hazelwood won the LMG Pairs competition and Lieutenant Starling, MC, and Lance-Corporal Farrow came second. The Depot team was captained by Lieutenant Starling.

The Depot Athletics team virtually swept the board at the East Anglian District Athletics Meeting at Colchester on 1 July, winning eleven out of fourteen events. The team was coached and managed by the Adjutant, Captain H.J. Chisnall.

In the Eastern Command Athletics Meeting held at Chatham on 10 July, the team faced stiffer opposition from much larger units and acquitted itself well by coming third, losing only to the School of Military Engineering and the Guards Depot.

The Depot played host to two Regimental cricket matches in July. On the 17th the Regiment played the Royal Norfolk Regiment and on the 18th and 19th the Gentlemen of Suffolk.

In July also the quarterly conference of East Anglian Brigade Depot Commanders was held in Gibraltar Barracks.

3 October saw the annual dinner of the Sergeants' Dinner Club. Brigadier R.E. Goodwin, DSO took the chair and 130 members and guests sat down to dinner in the Rock Theatre. The Colonel of the Regiment was also present and the Mayor of Bury St Edmunds was, as usual, the guest of honour.

In November the Colonel of the Regiment established a fund to give all ranks of the Regiment, past and present, an opportunity to contribute to the purchase of a Regimental Brooch, to be presented to Her Royal Highness the Princess Margaret, the new Colonel-in-Chief. Within two months one thousand two hundred and seventy-two members of the Regiment had made donations to the fund and the brooch had been ordered. It had also been announced that it would be presented to the Colonel-in-Chief when, on her first visit to the Regiment, she attended the annual reunion of the Old Comrades' Association at Gibraltar Barracks on 25 July, 1954. At the beginning of 1954 senior appointments at the Depot were held as follows:

OC:	Major J.C.R. Eley
Adjt:	Captain H.J. Chisnall
QM:	Major H.R. Cotton
RSM:	RSM Gingell
OC A Company:	Captain J.G. Starling, MC
CSM:	CSM Ramplin
OC B Company:	Captain P. Wakefield
	(The Royal Norfolk Regiment)

The first recruit passing out parade of 1954 took place on 29 January, when the salute was taken by His Worship the Mayor of Sudbury.

A further activity involving A Company comprised a series of weekend courses, organized for members of the Suffolk Home Guard during January and February.

A passing out parade was held on 3 April at which Colonel Freeman-Taylor took the salute for the last time, his successor as East Anglian Brigade Colonel, Colonel R.E. Osborne-Smith, DSO, OBE, having already been nominated to take over at the end of the month.

Daffodil Sunday on 18 April coincided with Easter in 1954. The weather was much kinder than in the previous year and an enormous crowd of visitors, over 4,000, flocked into Gibraltar Barracks to enjoy the fine show of daffodils. The museum was open to visitors all day and in the afternoon the Band of the 4th Battalion gave a concert on the square.

Ideal weather also prospered the Depot Rifle Meeting on Thetford Range on 22 and 23 April. Lieutenant R.M. Holman won the Individual Rifle competition and Privates Amies and Greenwood the LMG Pairs. The Sergeants won a falling plate competition against the Officers. The prizes were presented by Colonel Freeman-Taylor.

A recruit passing out parade was held on 14 May at which the salute was taken by Colonel Osborne-Smith.

The District Three-Day Rifle Meeting began on 14 May and the Depot assembled a very strong team for it. The team began well, beating all other units to win the Regular Army Rifle Team Match. It also won the Minor Units LMG Pairs and the Sten Machine Carbine Competition. The Depot was represented in the various matches by Lieutenant R.M. Holman, Lieutenant A.K. Catchpole, RSM Duffy, QMSI Carey, Sergeant Rinder, BEM, Sergeant Carpenter, Corporal Kelly, Corporal Myhill and Private White.

On 3 June Major Eley relinquished command of the Depot on leaving the Army and handed over to Major C.A. Boycott, MBE. Major Eley's three years in command had seen the Depot prosper, both as a training centre and as the home of the Regiment and the hub of all its functions. Dedicated to making the Depot effective in these tasks, Major Eley also personally instituted a number of physical changes within the walls of Gibraltar Barracks, thereby much enhancing its appearance. Many flourishing trees and new flower gardens bore witness to his enthusiasm.

On 4 and 5 June the Depot accepted the invitation of the Borough of Bury St Edmunds to share its stand at the Suffolk County Show at Cavenham. The Depot's part of the display comprised a selection of weapons, both modern and from the past, and they attracted considerable interest among the crowds of visitors.

On 15 June Mr Percy Watts, the Officers' Mess Superintendant and Mrs Watts, the Officers' Mess Cook, celebrated their Silver Wedding and also twenty-five years joint service in the Officers' Mess. Mr Watts first joined the Mess staff in 1928, marrying shortly afterwards. On the evening of their celebration, the Colonel of the Regiment, on behalf of all the Officers, presented Mr and Mrs Watts with a pair of Sheffield Plate candlesticks. In a brief speech, he thanked them for making the Officers' Mess a real home to every officer of the Regiment and for maintaining such a high standard.

The seventieth dinner of the Past and Present Officers was held at the United Service Club in London on 22 June. The Colonel of the Regiment took the chair and sixty members were present.

The Colonel of the Regiment took a recruit passing out parade on 2 July, at which Gaza Platoon was awarded the Efficiency Shield and Minden Platoon the Shooting Shield.

The annual cricket match between the Regiment and the Gentlemen of Suffolk, on 17 and 18 July, was dogged by heavy rain. The match was played in between heavy showers on both days and finally, when time ran out, had to be abandoned drawn.

A week later, on 25 July, came the Old Comrades' Association Minden Reunion, which was graced by the Colonel-in-Chief Her Royal Highness, the Princess Margaret, CI, GCVO, on her first visit to the Depot.

Sadly rain fell throughout the day, but for an occasional brighter interlude, and as a result it was decided to cut out parts of the programme. The Princess arrived at 1220 and was received by the Lord-Lieutenant and the Colonel of the Regiment outside the Officers' Mess, where a number of presentations were made. The Princess then drove to the square and mounted the dais to receive a Royal Salute from the Parade, commanded by OC the Depot, Major Boycott.

The Parade comprised a Guard of Honour from the Depot, commanded by Captain Starling, a detachment of the 4th Battalion under Major J.S.H. Smitherman, ERD, and a body of some 550 Old Comrades. The Band of the 4th Battalion provided the music.

Her Royal Highness carried out an inspection of the whole Parade and this was followed by a Drumhead Service conducted by the Venerable Hugh R. Norton, Archdeacon of Sudbury, assisted by the Depot Chaplain the Reverend K.W. Brassell and the Reverend W.M. Lummis, Rector of Bungay. The Clergy were presented to the Princess at the conclusion of the service.

At this point Sergeant C.A. Wilce of the Depot Staff marched to the front of the dais carrying the Regimental Brooch and the Colonel of the Regiment offered an address to the Colonel-in-Chief. In it he spoke of the pride of the Regiment in having a Royal Colonel-in-Chief, of the obligations placed on it by such an honour and ended by presenting Her Royal Highness with the Regimental Brooch.

In her reply, the Princess Margaret thanked Brigadier Backhouse for the warm welcome she had received and also for the gift of the Regimental Brooch. She ended by saying how pleased she was to be appointed Colonel-in-Chief of the Regiment and expressed confidence that it would continue to fulfil its duty with distinction and renown.

The Parade then offered three cheers to Her Royal Highness, in which they were joined by the large crowd of spectators. There then followed a final Royal Salute and march past. A number of further presentations were made at the conclusion of the parade and the Princess then took luncheon with the Officers in the Officers' Mess. After luncheon Her Royal Highness was presented to the Depot Warrant Officers as she made her way to her car. Before leaving, past soldiers lining the route, she was presented with a bouquet of red and yellow roses by the Depot Commander's daughter.

After such an outstanding occasion, the remainder of 1954 passed by without any particularly significant happenings. A Company Recruit Passing Out Parades were taken by the Colonel of the Regiment and on one occasion by the Depot Commander.

The thirty-fifth annual dinner of the Sergeants' Dinner Club took place on 9 October when 120 members met under the chairmanship of Brigadier I.L. Wight, DSO, OBE. A message of loyal greetings was sent to the Colonel-in-Chief to mark the occasion and Her Royal Highness warmly responded.

At the beginning of 1955 senior appointments at the Depot were held as follows:

OC:	Major C.A. Boycott, MBE
Adjt:	Captain R.M. Holman
QM:	Major H.R. Cotton
RSM:	RSM Duffy
OC A Company:	Major P.B. Forrest, MC
CSM:	CSM Ramplin
OC B Company:	Captain C. Hopkins
	(Royal Norfolk Regiment)

The Depot Hockey Team had an extremely successful season in the winter of 1954/55, culminating in beating 11th Regiment, School of Military Engineering, to win the Eastern Command Minor Units Hockey Championships at Colchester on 19 April.

On 24 April Daffodil Sunday came round once more. The flowers were in full bloom and Spring was in the air as 2,000 or so visitors entered Gibraltar Barracks gates to enjoy the occasion. The Mayor of Bury St Edmunds was among the guests. The Band of the 4th Battalion gave a concert on the square during the afternoon and the Regimental Museum was a great attraction.

The Depot Rifle Meeting was held at Thetford Ranges on 28 and 29 April. Sergeant Rinder of A Company was Champion Rifle Shot.

On 7 May a well known figure at the Depot retired. Mr T. Last had been gardener in Gibraltar Barracks for seventeen years and was solely responsible for the beauty of the gardens and grounds. On his last day of work the Colonel of the Regiment, on behalf of the Regiment, presented Mr Last with a clock as a token of esteem and he was ceremonially escorted out of the Barracks by the permanent staff pushing him in a gardener's wheelbarrow.

The Passing Out Parade of recruits on 15 May was taken by Colonel R.B. Senior, who had just taken over as East Anglian Brigade Colonel from Colonel Osborne-Smith.

At the Passing Out Parade on 3 June the salute was taken by His Worship the Mayor of Bury St Edmunds.

Major H.R. Cotton, the Depot Quartermaster, had been awarded the MBE in The Queen's Birthday Honours List, and on this Passing Out Parade he was presented with the Meritorious Service Medal which he had been awarded earlier in April. A well-deserved double distinction was thus achieved by Major Cotton in the space of three months, in his fortieth year of service in the Regiment.

The Queen's Birthday was celebrated at a parade on the square of Gibraltar Barracks on 9 June. The Colours of the 3rd Battalion were on parade, carried by Lieutenant A.K. Catchpole and 2nd Lieutenant N. St G. Watkins.

20 June saw a further reorganization of the Depot. B Company was disbanded, leaving A Company with additional staff to carry out the holding function of the defunct B Company. As part of the reorganization, all Depot staff in Blenheim Camp were relocated in Gibraltar Barracks. It was something of a tight squeeze, necessitated by the fact that a battalion of infantry, the 1st Battalion, the King's (Liverpool) Regiment, was to move into Blenheim Camp at the end of the month.

On 28 June a small athletics team went to Colchester to compete in the East Anglian District Meeting. The competition was somewhat severe and the team finished fourth out of five teams entered.

The Annual Sergeants' Mess Rifle Meeting took place in July, with the RSM winning the Champion Shot's prize.

Also in July, the Depot provided a small Guard of Honour at the dedication of the War Memorial at the village of Haughley.

Brigadier R.H. Maxwell, CB took the salute at the Recruit Passing Out Parade of Gaza and Minden Platoons on 22 July and on the following day the Officers' Mess held a tennis tournament, the first since before the War. Fifteen pairs took part in a knock-out competition and afterwards were entertained to tea.

The Annual Old Comrades Minden Reunion was held on 24 July, on a day of glorious sunshine. Some 600 attended, fewer than usual, probably because of the supreme effort to be present at the 1954 reunion, when the Colonel-in-Chief made her first visit to a Regimental function.

The Drumhead Service was conducted by the Depot Chaplain, the Reverend K.W. Brassell. After lunch the Band of the 4th Battalion played a concert which was followed by a light-hearted entertainment provided by the Cambridge Highlights Concert Party. The Old Comrades also thoroughly enjoyed seeing the film made of the presentation of Colours to the 1st Battalion in Germany in May.

On 3 September the annual dinner of the Sergeants Past and Present was held in the Rock Theatre. Brigadier Maxwell took the chair and 125 members and guests attended, including the President of the Club, Brigadier Backhouse, Colonel of the Regiment, and two Vice-Presidents, Colonel Nicholson and Colonel Cutbill.

Colonel Senior, East Anglian Brigade Colonel, took the salute when Gibraltar and Malaya Platoons passed out on 16 September. Music for the parade was provided by the Royal Marine Band from HMS *Ganges*.

The East Anglian District Rifle Meeting was held from 7 to 9 October. The Depot entered a strong team and were rewarded with a number of successes. The team won the Regular Army Team Match, the Minor Units LMG Pairs (Captain Holman and Sergeant Marjoram). The Falling Plate Team was beaten in the finals by the Depot of the Essex Regiment.

The seventy-first Annual Dinner of the Past and Present Officers of the Regiment took place on 20 October at the United Services Club in London. Seventy-five members attended.

A contingent of three officers and seventy men took part in the Remembrance Day Parade at Bury St Edmunds. The Colonel of the

Regiment laid a wreath on behalf of the Regiment and Major Boycott one on behalf of the Depot.

A Passing Out Parade of Gibraltar and Malaya Platoons on 9 December was inspected by Colonel J.H. Harrison, TC, MP, former Commanding Officer of the 4th Battalion. The Band of the 1st Battalion, the Royal Norfolk Regiment provided the music for the parade.

In December, 1955, also, the GOC East Anglian District, Major-General R.P. Harding, CB, DSO, visited the Depot to inspect recruit training.

The first recruit Passing Out Parade of the New Year took place on 20 January, 1956, when the Commanding Officer, the 1st Battalion, the King's Regiment, based in Blenheim Camp, inspected the parade of Minden and Gaza Platoons. The Band of the Royal Marines from HMS *Ganges* at Shotley played for the parade.

Colonel Senior carried out the annual administrative inspection of the Depot on 7 February. He inspected every aspect of training and administration and took the salute at a parade of the Depot staff and recruits.

March and April saw two more recruit Passing Out Parades, taken in March by Lieutenant-Colonel Smitherman, CO of the 4th Battalion and in April by the Colonel of the Regiment.

In April Major Boycott relinquished command of the Depot on retiring from the Army and he was succeeded by Major W.J. Calder, who came from being Training Major of the 4th Battalion.

In April, also, Major Cotton, QM of the Depot, retired from the Army after over forty years' service with the Regiment. He enlisted as a Band Boy at the age of fourteen in August, 1914.

Daffodil Sunday was held on 22 April when nearly 4,000 visitors once more availed themselves of the opportunity to view the Depot in its spring colours. The sun shone and the Band of the 4th Battalion played a concert of music and the PT Staff put on an impressive gymnastic display.

The annual Rifle Meeting took place on 14 and 15 May and the Champion Rifle Shot was Private Kennington of the Royal Norfolk Regiment. The correspondent for the *Regimental Gazette* was clearly amazed that he should have won, 'thereby beating all the best Shots in the Depot'! However, RSM Duffy did win the Sten competition and the Quartermaster, Captain G.S. Jasper, the Pistol.

The Director of Infantry, Major-General C.L. Firbank, CB, CBE, DSO, visited the Depot on 16 May and, after inspecting training, addressed the officers on the subject of the reorganization of the Army.

The East Anglian District Rifle Meeting took place on 8 and 9 June and the Depot team came away with a number of trophies and individual successes. The team won the Falling Plate Competition, the Minor Units Competition, the Young Soldiers Competition and the Sten Machine Carbine Match.

The June Recruit Passing Out Parade of Gibraltar and Malaya Platoons was inspected by Colonel Sir Robert Gooch, Bart, DSO, DL, JP, Honorary Colonel of the 4th Battalion. The Band of the 1st Battalion, the King's Regiment provided the music for this parade for the last time. The Battalion left Blenheim Camp in July, bound for BAOR and was replaced by the 1st Battalion, the Argyll and Sutherland Highlanders.

Something over 500 Old Comrades and their families braved the atrocious weather to attend the Annual Reunion on 29 July. Gale-force winds and continuous driving rain forced the implementation of the wet weather programme and the display by the Band and Drums of the 1st Battalion and the Drumhead Service took place under cover in the Rock Theatre.

Virtually the complete permanent staff of the Depot, together with all recruits, journeyed to Colchester on 1 August, Minden Day, to take part in the visit to the 1st Battalion of the Colonel-in-Chief.

The following day the CO of the 1st Battalion, Lieutenant-Colonel W.S. Bevan, took the salute at the Passing Out Parade of Minden and Gaza Platoons.

In September the Passing Out Parade of Gibraltar and Malaya Platoons was inspected by the GOC East Anglian District, Major-General Harding, and in October Gaza and Minden Platoons were inspected by His Worship the Mayor of Bury St Edmunds.

The annual dinner of the Sergeants Past and Present Dinner Club took place on 13 October, under the chairmanship of Brigadier Backhouse. 124 members and guests attended the Dinner.

The December Passing Out Parade of Gibraltar and Malaya Platoons was taken by the Commanding Officer the 1st Battalion, the Cambridgeshire Regiment, Lieutenant-Colonel W.F. Page, MC, TD.

As 1956 drew to a close, the six-weekly intakes of recruits, mostly National Servicemen, were fewer in number and the size of the Recruit Platoons diminished in consequence. 1957 was to witness a welcome increase in numbers of which most were soldiers on regular engagements. With National Service coming to an end, the National Service element continued to wither away.

The annual administrative inspection by Colonel Senior, East

Anglian Brigade Colonel, took place on 12 March, 1957, and on 29 March the Passing Out Parade of Gibraltar and Malaya Platoons was taken by the Commanding Officer of the 1st Battalion, the Argyll and Sutherland Highlanders.

The earliest Daffodil Sunday on record, 31 March, saw some 3,000 visitors to the Depot where the flowers made an impressive sight. The Mayor and Corporation of Bury St Edmunds were entertained to tea in the Officers' Mess.

The Annual Rifle Meeting was held at Thetford Ranges on 13 and 14 May. Colonel Senior won the Individual Rifle Competition and two young soldiers with only nine weeks' service won the LMG Pairs.

Brigadier Backhouse took the salute at the Passing Out Parade of Gaza and Minden Platoons on 17 May. It was his last opportunity to do so as Colonel of the Regiment, as on 10 June he completed his ten years' tenure of duty as Colonel.

Brigadier Backhouse had given a lifetime's loyal and devoted service to the Regiment, culminating in the last ten years of his Colonelcy during which it faced many challenges. He was, as the Editor of the *Regimental Gazette* said of him in the summer of 1957, 'essentially a modest, unassuming man', and as such he was perhaps the personification of the Regiment.

He was succeeded by Brigadier Maxwell whose difficult task it would be to guide the Regiment into amalgamation within only a matter of a couple of years after his appointment. Indeed, Brigadier Maxwell's first official task as Colonel was formally to announce the proposed amalgamation of the Regiment with the Royal Norfolk Regiment, which he did in a letter to Commanding Officers on 24 July, 1957.

The Annual Old Comrades' Association Reunion took place four days after Brigadier Maxwell's announcement. Some 350 members and their families attended the occasion, which followed the usual format. The Colonel of the Regiment spoke briefly after the Drumhead Service and asked all old soldiers to give their support to the forthcoming changes.

The July Passing Out Parade was inspected by the Mayor of Bury St Edmunds, and that in August by Brigadier H.E. Collett-White, DSO.

The annual dinner of the Sergeants' Dinner Club took place in the Rock Theatre on 14 September, under the chairmanship of the new Colonel of the Regiment. 126 members and guests sat down to dinner.

The seventy-third annual dinner of the Officers' Dinner Club was held on 25 October at the Army and Navy Club, also under the chairmanship of Brigadier Maxwell. The Secretary of State for War, the Rt Hon J.H. Hare, OBE, MP, was Guest of Honour.

Colonel Senior, East Anglian Brigade Colonel, took his last Passing Out Parade on 21 November and handed over to Colonel W.A. Heal, OBE, in December, 1957.

Major Calder relinquished command of the Depot in December and handed over to Major G.T.O. Springfield.

The first Recruit Passing Out Parade of 1958, on 3 January, was taken by Colonel Heal.

The Depot Football Team reached the finals of the East Anglian District Minor Units Cup on 21 February, but were knocked out by a unit from Shoeburyness. In April RSM Duffy handed over his responsibilities at the Depot to RSM Gingell, who returned from the 1st Battalion in Cyprus. Duffy had been RSM at the Depot for four years.

In May a large group of foreign Military Attachés was entertained for a day. They observed training in progress and were allowed to fire the Sterling sub-machine gun on the twentyfive yards range.

The Old Comrades' Association Reunion took place on 6 July and followed the usual procedure. The Drumhead Service began the day and after lunch there were various entertainments, including a Band Concert, a PT display and, finally, the beating of retreat by the Band and Drums of the 4th Battalion.

Minden Day was celebrated with a ceremonial parade at which the salute was taken by Colonel Heal, East Anglian Brigade Colonel. The Colours of the 3rd Battalion were carried by Lieutenant J.D. Churchill and Lieutenant P.W. Morton.

Major Springfield handed over command of the Depot to Major R.M. Williams, MC, after only a brief tour in command, on 15 August. Major Williams had been at the Depot some time already, in command of A Company.

The Annual Sergeants' Dinner took place on 13 September under the chairmanship of Colonel Heal. 102 members and guests attended the function. During his speech, Colonel Heal announced that the Depot had been chosen as the Brigade Depot for the newly amalgamated Regiments of the East Anglian Brigade. Gibraltar Barracks would close, except for the Officers' Mess and the Depot would actually be formed in Blenheim Camp in the first instance, until Gibraltar Barracks had been refurbished.

The seventy-fourth Annual Dinner of the Officers Dinner Club took place at the Army and Navy Club, under the chairmanship of Brigadier Maxwell, on 9 October. Fifty-four members attended the function and Brigadier C.J. Wilkinson, DSO, Colonel of the Royal Norfolk Regiment, was present as a guest of the Club.

The number of recruits trained at the Depot increased during 1958, although many were bound for other Regiments and Corps. Over eighty passed out on 17 October, at a parade taken by the Commanding Officer of the 1st Battalion, Lieutenant-Colonel W.S. Bevan, OBE.

In the winter of 1958/1959 the Depot was issued with the new self-loading rifle to replace the No 4 rifle. The quality of the new weapon soon became evident on the range, but its use on the drill square caused some problems. To cope with this, RSM Gingell was dispatched to the Grenadier Guards in London to ascertain the latest thinking on the new arms drill. As a result, the first Recruit Passing Out Parade with the self-loading rifle, on 16 January, 1959, went without a hitch. The recruits, who had never seen the old rifle, mastered the new movements with ease, unlike their instructors who found it strange not to slope arms!

The Depot Sports Teams achieved considerable success throughout the winter, without actually winning a single competition! The Football Team were runners up in both the Major and Minor Units District Competitions and in the Bury St Edmunds and District Cup. The Hockey Team were runners up in the Major Units District Competition.

As the end of National Service drew nearer, it became necessary to pay attention to the problem of improving the recruitment of regular soldiers into the Regiment. Initially and temporarily, Major H.S.R. Case, MBE, was made into a Recruiting Officer, in between postings. But on 7 March, Captain A.B. Horrex, MC, arrived to take over from him and also to act as Amalgamation Administration Officer. Both jobs gave him a great deal of work, on which he seemed to thrive. Recruiting regular soldiers was an up-hill struggle in a society where jobs were not hard to come by. As amalgamation drew near, the amount of work connected with it grew, and most of it fell onto the shoulders of the Depot staff.

Daffodil Sunday took place on 12 April and it was decided to change the format of the day and to place the emphasis squarely on recruiting. The gymnasium was used to stage an exhibition of modern Army weapons and a replica of the latest type of soldiers' married quarter was constructed on the stage. There were displays featuring life in the regular and territorial armies and the museum was, of course, open as well. Throughout the day there was a continuous showing of Regimental films. The Mayor and Corporation of Bury St Edmunds were entertained to tea in the Officers' Mess and the day wound up with the beating of retreat by the Band and Drums of the 4th Battalion. It was a very successful occasion with nearly 3,000 visitors to the Barracks.

The normal training activities of the Depot continued throughout the summer of 1959, but inevitably the approaching amalgamation was in the foreground of everyones thoughts and actions. Amalgamation meetings were frequent and, with the arrival of the 1st Battalion home from Cyprus in May, events followed one another with lightning rapidity, until suddenly on 29 August, 1959, the Suffolk Regiment was no more, and Gibraltar Barracks became overnight the Depot of the 1st East Anglian Regiment.

CHAPTER IX

THE TERRITORIAL ARMY IN SUFFOLK

AND CAMBRIDGESHIRE: 1947–1961

'Continuing an honourable tradition of voluntary service'

Part I

The majority of the territorial soldiers of East Anglia suffered grievously in the Second World War, when they spent over three and a half years in Japanese prisoner-of-war camps, following the fall of Singapore.

Among them were the men of the 4th and 5th Battalions, the Suffolk Regiment and the 1st and 2nd Battalion, the Cambridgeshire Regiment, whose survivors only returned home to the United Kingdom in the latter months of 1945 and in early 1946.

One might have expected that such bitter experiences would have extinguished forever the voluntary spirit of the young men of Suffolk and Cambridgeshire. Yet, when the Territorial Army (TA) was reborn in early 1947, it was, in both counties, the officers and men who had returned from captivity in the Far East who formed the nucleus of the newly embodied units.

The years that followed were years of turbulence for the TA. Life was not easy and change was endemic. The explanation can be found, in part, in the changing situation in Europe and the development of the Cold War. At one moment it seemed the Territorials would be needed to reinforce BAOR if the crisis developed. Then, when the Soviet Union acquired nuclear weapons, and a short if ghastly war was envisaged, there rose a need for home defence and support for civil government in the aftermath of wholesale destruction, and the TA was tasked to provide this support.

But this was not all. British responsibilities abroad were forced to change as the economy failed to sustain erstwhile major commitments. Successive Governments sought to slash Government expenditure and inevitably some chose to make cuts in defence spending. The TA suffered as a result, and although the 4th Battalion, the Suffolk Regiment and the 1st Battalion, the Cambridgeshire Regiment survived the amalgamation of the regular Regiment in 1959, they were to do so for only a very short while.

Though its role was to change over the years, the 4th Battalion, the Suffolk Regiment retained its traditional infantry identity from 1947 to 1961. But it was quite a different story for the Cambridgeshires. The Regiment did reform in 1947 but not as infantry. To the initial consternation of those who had served in the Regiment before, it became an Artillery unit – 629 (The Cambridgeshire Regiment) Light Anti-Aircraft Regiment, RA, TA. A lengthy title was thus made longer by retaining the traditional name of the Regiment, but it was not to be countenanced that it should be omitted.

But this was not all. In 1954 Anti-Aircraft Command was disbanded and the Cambridgeshire Regiment came near to being disbanded with it. It was only by dint of forceful lobbying in high places, in which the Lord-Lieutenant of Cambridgeshire, Captain R.G. Briscoe, MC, played a major part, that the Regiment survived to live on as a unit of the 16th Airborne Division (TA).

Thus 629 (The Cambridgeshire Regiment) Parachute Light Regiment, RA, TA, was born and infanteers who had overnight become gunners, now found themselves required to learn to parachute! That large numbers of officers and men of the Regiment did volunteer for this new and arduous adventure says much for the spirit that remained within it.

This novel and exciting departure was to last, however, only for two years. With the disbanding of the 16th Airborne Division (TA) in 1956, the Unit reverted to being infantry and, once more, was known simply and proudly as the 1st Battalion, the Cambridgeshire Regiment.

It slipped easily back into this role. It had, throughout its Gunner and Airborne days, continued to wear the Regimental Badge and, to the dismay of its Royal Artillery Permanent Staff Instructors, to carry its Colours on every possible ceremonial occasion!

For the Suffolk Regiment, the return to the Regimental fold of the Cambridgeshire Regiment was a happy event, reaffirming, as it did, the long history of association of the two kindred Regiments.

For the 'Terriers' of Suffolk and Cambridgeshire these years witnessed many changes beyond those already considered. Both Regiments found it sometimes difficult to bring themselves up to their establishment figures. Life in Britain after 1945 offered, with increased affluence, so many other opportunities for leisure pursuits, and work, too, was easily found, so that men who might otherwise have joined were tempted away from the TA by other distractions.

The ranks were filled in the early fifties when National Servicemen were required to join for three years, following their full-time service, and many continued to serve on voluntarily afterwards.

In both Suffolk and Cambridgeshire the TA formed part of the social fabric of the Counties and received great encouragement from their respective Lords-Lieutenant and much support from County Council and local authorities generally. Scarcely a national or local occasion happened without the TA participating and many would not have taken place at all without the major contribution provided by the TA. Whenever and wherever in the two Counties they paraded, the two Battalions continued to draw large crowds.

The pattern of training followed much the same format as before the Second World War, with Company 'drill nights' once a week, a number of weekend exercises throughout the year and, finally, the highlight of the annual cycle, the fifteen-day camp.

The Annual Camp, whether it was close to home on Stanford Battle Area or further afield in some more or less exotic place, was the one time of the year that a battalion could get a sense of its real worth. Training always took first priority, but there was time as well for the multitude of regimental activities that continued as in previous generations, to foster the regimental esprit de corps.

Training was greatly helped by a small staff of regular officers, warrant officers and NCOs and it went ahead steadily over the years and a surprisingly high standard was achieved.

Early in the fifties, drill halls became Territorial Army Centres. But the change in nomenclature did little to affect what went on in these sometimes smart new buildings, sometimes rather ancient 'holes in the corner'. Almost every town in both Counties had one, and as often as not, its caretaker could lay claim to a lifetime of service to the volunteers.

Not only did these centres provide stores and offices, and accommodation for training on the weekly drill nights, but they also had a major social function as well. The main halls in Ipswich and Cambridge witnessed numerous Regimental occasions, ranging from officers' or sergeants' dinners to all ranks' dances, to bazaars and film shows. But each one had its canteen which welcomed not only serving members of the TA, but old Comrades as well. No matter how small a Detachment, there seemed always to be a Christmas Social or a children's party. Notes in the *Regimental Gazette* from both the 4th Battalion, the Suffolk Regiment and the 1st Battalion, the Cambridgeshire Regiment, demonstrated, quarter after quarter, the family spirit that flourished as the years went by.

In the period covered by this history, there were many high days. But perhaps the most exciting and important were the occasions when the Colonel-in-Chief of the Suffolk Regiment and thus of the Cambridgeshire Regiment too, Her Royal Highness The Princess Margaret, CI, GCVO, visited the Battalions.

The 4th Battalion, the Suffolk Regiment was honoured with their visit in 1958, when the Colonel-in-Chief came to meet the Battalion at Benacre Hall, the home of Colonel Sir Robert Gooch, the Honorary Colonel of the Battalion.

For the Cambridgeshires, their opportunity came the following year when The Princess Margaret joined them at Ely to share in the Dedication of their Roll of Honour to those who fell in the Second World War, when it was placed in the Regimental Chapel in Ely Cathedral.

When the Suffolk Regiment amalgamated with the Royal Norfolk Regiment in 1959, and the regular element of the Regiment became a part of the 1st East Anglian Regiment, it was hoped that the 4th Battalion would keep alive the Regimental story and proudly continue to wear the Suffolk Regiment Badge. But it was not to do so for very long.

Following yet more changes, the 4th Battalion, the Suffolk Regiment and the 1st Battalion, the Cambridgeshire Regiment were, in their turn required to amalgamate and form, on 1 April, 1961, the 1st Battalion, the Suffolk and Cambridgeshire Regiment.

Part II

SUFFOLK

The 4th Battalion, the Suffolk Regiment was formally re-embodied on 12 April, 1947. The Territorial Officer selected to command the Battalion was Lieutenant-Colonel J.H. Harrison. A regular Adjutant, Captain C.A. Boycott (recently Second-in-Command of the 1st Battalion) had been appointed in March and he was charged with responsibility for raising the unit. To assist him, he had a regular RSM (V.H. Reeve), a CSM and one Sergeant.

Battalion Headquarters was located at the Portman Road Drill Hall in Ipswich and Company Detachments were formed at drill halls at Bury St Edmunds, Stowmarket, Halesworth, Framlingham and Woodbridge.

Recruiting began on 1 May and was accompanied by considerable publicity in local newspapers. Initial results were none too promising, but by the end of the month seven officers had been granted commissions and forty soldiers had applied to join the Battalion.

On 24 July Major G.S. Cubitt was appointed Second-in-Command of the Battalion.

The first range day since formation took place at Bromeswell Range on 31 August. Apart from the permanent staff, five officers and nineteen men attended.

Captain Boycott handed over as Adjutant to Captain R.J. Hildesley on 1 September.

A nine-day camp was held with No 12 PTC at Gibraltar Barracks at Bury St Edmunds, from 19 to 28 September. Sixty percent of officers and men attended.

The winter of 1947–48 saw a slow trickle of recruits joining the Battalion. New detachments were constituted at Leiston, Hadleigh and Haverhill.

In May 1948, all Companies fired the Annual Weapon Training Course at Bromeswell Range.

On 5 June, the Freedom of the Borough of Ipswich was conferred on the Suffolk Regiment. Before the ceremony the Battalion Colours were handed back to it by the Vicar of St Mary-le-Tower Church, Ipswich, where they had been in safe custody since the outbreak of War in September, 1939. The Parade for the Freedom Ceremony, commanded by the Depot Commander, comprised sixty men from the East Anglian Brigade Training Centre in Colchester, under the command of a Suffolk Regiment Officer, Major O.K. Leach, a detachment of forty men from the Battalion under the Second-in-Command, Major Cubitt, twenty Army Cadets and 250 members of the Old Comrades' Association. The Colour Party consisted of Captain J.H. Oldham, Captain M.H. Vinden, Colour-Sergeant Russell, Sergeant Clarke and Sergeant McGregor.

The ceremony took place in Christchurch Park and was followed by a march through the town, where large crowds gathered, and the salute was taken by the Lord-Lieutenant, Commander The Earl of Stradbroke.

The 1948 Annual Camp was held with the other Battalions of the Brigade (161st Independent Infantry Brigade) at Landguard Fort,

Felixstowe. Officers' Study Days were held and Specialist Cadres on carriers, driving and support weapons were organized for the men. A total of sixteen officers and fifty-two men (about seventy-five percent of the Battalion's strength) attended Camp. The Honorary Colonel of the Battalion, Lieutenant-Colonel E.P. Clarke, DSO, TD, attended a Dinner Night in the Officers' Mess at Camp.

The Battalion Rifle Meeting was held at Bromeswell Range on 26 September. Sergeant Clarke of HQ Company was individual winner, with D Company Commander, Major R.H.K. Wickham, TD, runner up.

His Majesty The King held a review of the TA in Hyde Park, London, on 31 October. The Commanding Officer, Lieutenant-Colonel Harrison, led a contingent of eleven officers and men of the Battalion, at the review.

Senior appointments in the Battalion at the end of 1948 were held as follows:

CO:	Lieutenant-Colonel J.H. Harrison, TD
2ic:	Major G.S. Cubitt, TD
Adjt:	Captain R.J. Hildesley, (Regular Officer)
QM:	Major U. Dockerill
RSM:	RSM Reeve
OC A Company: (Bury St Edmunds)	Captain P.D.A. Clarke
OC B Company: (Woodbridge)	Major L.G.E. Pusey
OC C Company: (Leiston)	Captain L.E.A. Catchpole
OC D Company: (Stowmarket)	Major J.H. Oldham
OC HQ Company: (Ipswich)	Major R.H.K. Wickham, TD

On 9 January, 1949, there was a sad reminder of the losses incurred by the Battalion in the Far East during the Second World War. At B Company's drill hall in Woodbridge a tablet commemorating those of the Company who had been killed in action, or died in captivity, was unveiled by the Colonel of the Regiment, Brigadier Backhouse (he had commanded the Brigade in the Far East in which the Battalion served during the Second World War).

Her Royal Highness The Duchess of Kent made an official visit to Ipswich on 6 April. A Guard of Honour from the Battalion paraded for the occasion. The Adjutant was in command of the forty-eight strong Guard, and the Colour Party comprised Captain Vinden, Lieutenant C.R.W.A. Millen, Colour-Sergeant Kerr, Sergeant McGregor and Sergeant Clarke.

On 21 April Major R.M. Marsh, a Regular Officer, was posted to the Battalion as Second-in-Command.

Annual Camp took place at Roman Way Camp, Colchester, from 3 to 17 July, 1949. Fifteen officers and seventy-six men attended camp and the Colonel of the Regiment and the Honorary Colonel of the Battalion paid visits to watch training in progress. Cadres for specialists were organized and a comprehensive period of field training, including live firing of mortars and the PIAT, was conducted.

In October the Anti-Tank Platoon travelled to Lulworth in Dorset to carry out live firing with their 6-pounder guns. They drove down on the Friday, fired all day Saturday and drove home again on the Sunday! The shooting, under the direction of Lieutenant P.S. Hetherington, was of a high quality.

The Battalion Rifle Meeting took place at Bromeswell Range on 30 October. The winner of the Rifle Competition was Sergeant D. Gaught of A Company and A Company won the Inter-Company Shoot.

RSM Reeve left the Battalion in October and his place was taken by RSM E. Isaacson.

The annual administrative inspection was carried out by the Brigade Commander, Brigadier J.R.T. Aldous, CBE, MC, on 17 November, 1949.

Captain Hildesley handed over the appointment of Adjutant to Captain P.S.W. Dean on 28 February, 1950, on retiring from the Army.

Throughout the spring of 1950, preparations were made to receive the first batches of National Servicemen, required to complete three years with the TA after their full-time service. The first of them reported for duty on 25 April.

The Battalion was at this time authorized to form a Company in Cambridgeshire, and detachments were established at Wisbech, Whittlesey and Newmarket.

March and April witnessed a number of visits to Battalion TA Centres (the newly introduced term for Drill Halls) by the new Brigade Commander, Brigadier C.H. Gurney, OBE.

Annual Camp for 1950 took place from 11 to 25 June at Bodney Camp on the Stanford Battle Area. It was a Brigade Camp and was held under canvas. Visitors to the Battalion while there included the Colonel of the Regiment, the GOC-in-C Eastern Command, Lieutenant-General Sir Gerald Templer and the GOC East Anglian District.

By 1 July the Battalion was functioning at fourteen TA Centres in Suffolk and Cambridgeshire.

On the 28th July a campaign to recruit a Band for the Battalion was initiated and the first four members were enlisted.

The Battalion Rifle Meeting took place on 1 October at Bromeswell Range. A Company won the Inter-Company Shield and Sergeant Spalding of A Company won the Individual Rifle Competition.

The Officers' Mess held a Ball at Seckford Hall near Woodbridge on 20 October. Over 140 guests were present including the Lord-Lieutenant, Commander The Earl of Stradbroke, the Colonel of the Regiment, Brigadier Backhouse, the Honorary Colonel of the Battalion, Colonel Clarke, and the District Commander, Major-General Firth.

Remembrance Sunday at Ipswich on 12 November saw the newly formed Band, twenty-seven strong, perform for the first time, under the Band Master, Mr W. Hurley.

At the end of December 1950, senior appointments in the Battalion were held as follows:

CO:	Lieutenant-Colonel J.H. Harrison, TD
2ic:	Major R.M. Marsh (Regular)
Adjt:	Captain P.S.W. Dean (Regular)
QM:	Major H.R. Cotton (Regular)
RSM:	RSM Isaacson (Regular)
A Company: (Bury St Edmunds)	Captain P.D.A. Clarke
B Company: (Whittlesey)	Lieutenant P. Kent
C Company: (Leiston)	Major L.E.A. Catchpole
D Company: (Stowmarket)	Major M.H. Vinden
Sp Company: (Woodbridge)	Major L.G.E. Pusey
HQ Company: (Ipswich)	Captain C.R.W.A. Millen

Range weekends at Bromeswell, Barton Mills and Sizewell were organized in March and April, 1951, and the Battalion Rifle Meeting took place on 20 May at Bromeswell Range. Colour-Sergeant Goddard of C Company won the Individual Rifle Cup, and his Company took the Inter-Company Shield.

Annual Camp for 1951 ran from 10 to 24 June and was held at Swingate near Dover. With the National Servicemen now swelling the ranks, four companies were formed. The Band also attended camp for the first time.

Visitors included the Lord-Lieutenant and the Honorary Colonel of the Battalion, who, during their visit, was formerly appointed a Deputy Lieutenant for the County.

On 12 August, Captain C.C. Wells led a team of three from the Battalion in the East Anglian District Motor Cycle Trials. The team came fourth in the competition, open to both Regular and TA Units.

Lieutenant-Colonel Harrison, MP, relinquished Command of the Battalion on 1 September, and was granted the Brevet rank of Colonel. He had commanded the Battalion since it was reformed in April, 1947, having previously served with the 5th Battalion and been a prisoner-of-war of the Japanese with that Battalion in the Far East during the Second World War. He was succeeded in command by a Regular Officer, Lieutenant-Colonel K.J.K Pye.

On 4 December, 1951, Colonel Clarke handed over the Honorary Colonelcy of the Battalion to Colonel H.R. Hooper, OBE, MC, TD, DL, JP. Colonel Clarke joined the Volunteers (predecessors to the 4th Battalion) in 1901 and thus could claim fifty years distinguished voluntary service to the Battalion, the Regiment and the County.

Battalion Headquarters moved during December from the old Portman Road Drill Hall to a new TA Centre in Great Gipping Street.

At the end of 1951, the strength of the Battalion stood at 330.

1952 saw a marked upturn in the quality of training within the Battalion, largely because the increased numbers resulting from the National Service intake brought companies and platoons closer to a realistic strength for tactical exercises. The year was also to witness some very creditable shooting results both in the District and the Bisley Meeting.

On 24 March RSM Isaacson left the Army and his place was taken by RSM Jasper, who came from the Depot.

In June camp was held under canvas at Bodney, on the Stanford Battle Area. Over 300 attended this camp, and for the first time since reforming after the War, it was not necessary to form composite companies for training purposes. The emphasis also shifted away from the individual training of previous years to tactical training at company level, and one exercise, set by Brigade, was at battalion level.

The Adjutant, Captain Dean, handed over to Captain R.M. Williams, MC, on 15 July.

At Bisley, in August, Sergeant Spalding of A Company won the Secretary of State for War's Cup, open to both regular and territorial soldiers. He had also earlier won the Arthur Churchman Cup at the Suffolk County Rifle Association Meeting.

1953 was to prove to be a busy year for the Battalion. In April it was involved in helping to administer the parades by the 1st Battalion on its return from Malaya, and then in May preparations were made for the Coronation of Her Majesty Queen Elizabeth II on 2 June.

The whole Battalion was delighted to learn, on the eve of the Coronation, that Her Royal Highness The Princess Margaret, had been appointed Colonel-in-Chief of the Regiment. A telegram was despatched by the CO on behalf of all ranks, expressing the pride they felt at the high honour conferred on the Regiment.

A telegram was received from the Princess in reply, sending her sincere thanks and expressing the hope that she might visit the Battalion.

On 26 May a party of eighteen other-ranks, under Lieutenant Morris, departed for London for street-lining duties for the Coronation, and the next day Major Vinden, with CSM Bailey and three soldiers, also left for London to march in the Coronation procession.

The Battalion took part in the Coronation Parade at Ipswich on 2 June, for which the Band provided the music.

On 7 June the Battalion team came second in The Suffolk County Rifle Association Team Competition. This was an outstanding achievement. In previous years the Battalion team had always trailed behind all other teams in the competition by at least 100 points. The success was the first of a number to follow during the year.

At the East Anglian District Rifle Meeting at the end of June, Sergeant Spalding of A Company came second in the Open Rifle Competition and Sergeant Gaught, also of A Company, won the Veterans' Competition. The Battalion team won the TA Team event and also the Falling Plate Competition, and swept the board in the Brigade Competition, which ran concurrently with the District Meeting.

On 5 August the Honorary Colonel of the Battalion, Colonel Hooper, died, having sadly only held the appointment for some eighteen months.

Colonel Hooper had joined the 4th Battalion early in 1914 and had served in France throughout the First World War, winning the MC and twice being Mentioned in Despatches. He continued to serve between the Wars and commanded the Battalion from 1932 until 1936. He gave full time service throughout the Second World War, raising, it seemed almost single-handed, the 1st/6th and 2nd/6th Battalions of the Regiment, and then, as a Staff Officer at Suffolk and Cambridgeshire Sub-District HQ where much of his boundless energy was directed towards fostering Home Guard Units in the two Counties.

Warrant Officers and NCOs of the Battalion acted as pall bearers at the funeral and the Battalion also furnished a Firing Party and Buglers at the burial.

Later in the year it was announced that Colonel Sir Robert Gooch (late the Life Guards) would succeed Colonel Hooper as Honorary Colonel of the Battalion.

Annual Camp for 1953 was held from 13 to 27 September. It was a large-scale affair, with both the East Anglian TA Brigades participating. The 161st Independent Infantry Brigade consisting of the 4th Battalion, the Royal Norfolk Regiment, the 4th Battalion, the Suffolk Regiment and the 4th Battalion, the Essex Regiment were in Windmill Hill Camp and the 162nd Independent Infantry Brigade comprising the 1st Battalion, the Hertfordshire Regiment, the 5th Battalion, the Bedfordshire and Hertfordshire Regiment and the 4th Battalion, the Northamptonshire Regiment, were at Tilshead Lodge Camp, both on Salisbury Plain.

All the Battalions were able to produce a large number of officers and men and the fortnight's training was conducted at battalion and brigade level, and culminated in Exercise Golden Flash, which was a two-sided brigade exercise, set by the GOC East Anglian District and umpired by his staff.

At the end of 1953, senior appointments in the Battalion were as follows:

CO:	Lieutenant-Colonel K.J.K. Pye (Regular)
2ic:	Major J.S.H. Smitherman, ERD
Adjt:	Captain R.M. Williams, MC (Regular)
QM:	Major H.S.R. Case, MBE (Regular)
RSM:	RSM T.C. Warren (Regular)

OC A Company: (Bury St Edmunds)	Major E.J.K. Patten
OC B Company: (Wisbech)	Major C.C. Wells, TD
OC C Company: (Leiston)	Major R.A.F. Kemp
OC D Company: (Stowmarket)	Major M.H. Vinden, TD
OC Sp Company: (Woodbridge)	Major V.H.V. Rose

The New Year's Honours List for 1954 included the award of the BEM to CSM E.H. Bailey of C Company for outstanding services to the Territorial Army.

CSM Bailey joined the 4th Battalion in 1921 and served continuously with it until 1945. He was promoted to CSM in 1938 and went with the Battalion to the Far East, where with his fellows he suffered as a prisoner-of-war till the end of the War. When the TA was reformed in 1947, he volunteered for service but was rejected on medical grounds. He immediately wrote to appeal to Mr Shinwell, the Secretary of State for War, and was given special dispensation to re-enlist.

CSM Bailey's record of loyalty and service was truly remarkable.

On 1 January, 1954, Captain Williams handed over the duties of Adjutant to Captain A.H.V. Gilmore, MC.

From the beginning of the year, comprehensive weekend training went ahead without interruption, until the Battalion proceeded to camp in June. All Companies made maximum use of ranges and the Annual Weapon Training course had been completed by the end of April.

Camp was held from 13 to 26 June at Napier Barracks, Shorncliffe, with thirty-one officers and 777 men attending. In contrast to the previous year, training was concentrated at platoon and company level, with but one exercise in the second week at battalion level.

The Colonel of the Regiment, the Honorary Colonel of the Battalion and several other senior officers, paid visits to the Battalion to watch training and Brigadier Backhouse and Colonel Sir Robert Gooch attended a Guest Night in the Officers' Mess.

On 1 September Lieutenant-Colonel Pye handed over command of the Battalion to Lieutenant-Colonel Smitherman, and Major Calder was posted to the Battalion as the Regular Training Major.

The Battalion Rifle Meeting was held on 19 September. Sergeant

Spalding of A Company was the Champion Shot and C Company won the Inter-Company Competition. At the end of the year it was learnt that the Battalion had won four Territorial Army Rifle Association Decentralized Competitions, which had been fired at Bromeswell Range in September. The successes were in the Lord-Lieutenants' Shield, the High Sheriffs' Shield, the Imperial Tobacco Cup and the Young Soldiers' Match.

The GOC East Anglian District, Major-General R.H. Bower, CBE, visited the TA Centre at Ipswich on 31 January, 1955. On 28 February RSM Warren handed over to RSM Boast, on being appointed to a QM Commission and being posted to the 1st Battalion.

Weekend training went ahead throughout the Spring, concentrating on the Annual Weapon Training course and preparations for Camp, which was to be very early this year in May.

Advance Parties for camp set out on 11 and 13 May, and the Battalion assembled at East Wretham on the Stanford Training Area on the following Sunday, 15 May. The whole Brigade was once more at camp at the same time. Training consisted largely of field training at company level but there was one battalion exercise and one brigade exercise in the second week.

The Honorary Colonel of the Battalion, Colonel Sir Robert Gooch, visited Camp and presented Shooting Trophies won in the 1954–1955 season.

With the disbanding of AA Command, an AA sub-unit in Lowestoft was transferred to the Battalion. Its members attended Camp and received conversion training into the infantry. At the same time, B Company, which had been based in Wisbech and Whittlesey, in the Isle of Ely, was disbanded.

Senior appointments in the Battalion soon after Camp were as follows:

CO:	Lieutenant-Colonel J.S.H. Smitherman, ERD
2ic/Training Major:	Major W.J. Calder (Regular)
Adjt:	Captain A.H.V. Gillmore, MC (Regular)
QM:	Major H.S.R. Case, MBE (Regular)
RSM:	RSM Boast (Regular)
OC A Company: (Bury St Edmunds)	Major C.C. Wells, TD
OC B Company: (Lowestoft)	Major J.C. Lawrie, TD

OC C Company: Major R.A.F. Kemp, TD
(Leiston)
OC D Company: Major M.H. Vinden, TD
(Stowmarket)
OC Sp Company: Major D.S. Sach
(Woodbridge)
OC HQ Company: Captain G.L. Brown
(Ipswich)

The Annual Rifle Meeting took place at Bromeswell Range on 21 August. CSM Pollen of D Company won the Individual Championship and C Company the Inter-Company Shield once more. In September Captain Gillmore handed over the duties of Adjutant to Captain H.D. Sutor.

At the end of 1955 War Office policy concerning the terms of service of National Servicemen completing their three years with the TA was changed. In future they were only to be required to attend one camp in the whole of their three years. This was to have dramatic effects from 1956 onwards, with much reduced attendance at Camp each year.

In order to mitigate the effects of these changes the early months of 1956 were devoted to a major campaign to persuade National Servicemen to convert to voluntary service. Sadly, although some success was achieved, it was not sufficient to prevent the Battalion from dwindling severely in numbers.

Changes in the pattern of training were also introduced in 1956, consequent on a modification of the role of many TA Units and a concentration on questions of Home Defence in the age of nuclear weapons, and, in particular, aid to the Civil Defence authorities. This new departure meant working closely with the Police and other emergency services.

In April Major Calder left the Battalion to take over command of the Depot and Major C.J.V. Fisher-Hoch took over from him as Training Major, having come from the 1st Battalion.

The Battalion furnished a Guard of Honour at Ipswich on 1 May and at Lowestoft on 2 May, when His Royal Highness The Duke of Edinburgh visited the two towns. The Guards were sixty strong on each occasion and the Band was also on parade.

At Ipswich the Guard of Honour was commanded by OC Sp Company, Major D.S. Sach, with Lieutenant M.P. Casey and Lieutenant C.O. Goodford also on parade, the latter carrying The Queen's Colour.

At Lowestoft, OC B Company, Major J.C. Lawrie, TD, was in

command with Lieutenant R. Hammersley and Lieutenant Good-ford also on parade.

Annual Camp in 1956 was again held early in the year from 12 to 26 May. It took plâce at Penhale near Newquay, with over 400 officers and men present. The reduced numbers consequent on the changed National Service commitment inhibited training to a degree, but it was gratifying to know that half those present were volunteers. The Colonel of the Regiment, Brigadier Backhouse, and the Honorary Colonel of the Battalion visited camp.

In August the new organization of the TA nationally, in two divisions, meant that the Battalion found itself in the newly named 161st Infantry Brigade as part of the 54th (East Anglian) Division, T.A.

At the Battalion Rifle Meeting at Bromeswell Range, Colour-Sergeant Spalding of A Company won the Individual Championship and HQ Company took the Inter-Company Shield away from C Company who had held it since 1950. On 12 September RSM McColl arrived from the 1st Battalion to take over from RSM Boast.

Training in the winter months of 1956 and 1957 was curtailed by the introduction of severe petrol rationing consequent upon the crisis in the Middle East, following the nationalization of the Suez Canal. Training weekends continued, but soldiers had to travel to them by train. Attendances were high despite these restrictions.

In 1957 the compulsory service of National Servicemen in the TA finally ceased, and almost overnight the strength of the Battalion dropped to 210. Major recruiting drives throughout the County won some success, but the prospects for the future could not be but uncertain. The general gloom was increased by other major changes resulting from Duncan Sandys' Defence Review, announced in April, 1957, which included the prospect of amalgamation for the regular component of the Regiment.

The Battalion Rifle Meeting took place at Bromeswell Range on 4 and 5 May. C Company regained the Company Shield and the Champion Shot was Sergeant Brock of Sp Company. Annual Camp was at Fingringhoe Camp near Colchester from 18 May to 1 June. It was the first all-volunteer camp for many years, with 220 officers and men out of a total strength of 231 attending. The training at camp comprised a wide variety of specialist cadres, and, as it was once more a Brigade Camp, even the Company Commanders attended a Brigade Senior Officers' Cadre!

It had been hoped that the Colonel-in-Chief, Her Royal Highness the Princess Margaret, would visit the Battalion during camp and

39. The officers of the 1st Battalion with the new Colonel of the Regiment at Kykko Camp, Nicosia in February, 1959. The new cap badge is already in use.

41. The War Memorial Homes were opened by the Lord-Lieutenant of Suffolk on 3 May, 1953.

42. The Lord-Lieutenant, Commander the Earl of Stradbroke, meets Regimental veterans, first occupants of the War Memorial Homes.

43. On her visit to the Depot in 1954 the Colonel-in-Chief met Mr Percy Watts, Officers' Mess Steward since 1928.

44. The Colonel-in-Chief visited an Old Comrades Reunion at the Depot in 1954. Here she inspects the Depot contingent on parade under the command of Captain J.G. Starling, MC.

45. HRH the Duke of Edinburgh meets senior ranks of the 4th Battalion when on a visit to Ipswich.

46. The Depot Permanent Staff on Minden Day, 1958.

47. The Colonel-in-Chief inspects the 4th Battalion at Benacre Hall, home of the Honorary Colonel of the Battalion, on 8 June, 1958.

48. HRH the Princess Margaret, CI, GCVO, on a visit to Ely in June, 1959. She is accompanied by Lieutenant-Colonel W.F. Page, MC, Commanding Officer of the 1st Battalion, the Cambridgeshire Regiment.

49. Brigadier R.H. Maxwell, CB, the Colonel of the Regiment, inspects the 1st Battalion on Parade for Minden Day for the last time.

50. A Contingent of the 1st Battalion, the Suffolk Regiment marches through Sudbury for the last time before amalgamation in 1959.

preparations and rehearsals had been completed before the day. Sadly, Her Royal Highness was unable to come, prevented by illness, and the parade was inspected instead by Major-General Harding, GOC 54th (East Anglian) Infantry Division, TA.

On returning from Camp to Ipswich, on 1 June, the Battalion marched through the town with Drums beating, Bayonets fixed and Colours flying, and the salute was taken at the Town Hall by the Mayor of Ipswich accompanied by the Honorary Colonel of the Battalion.

The Brigade and District Rifle Meetings were held in June, with the Battalion acquitting itself well in both competitions.

An interesting and exciting exercise, Exercise Footslog, took place in October, when the Battalion with other TA Units was deployed in Norfolk to capture RAF and United States pilots who were practising evading an enemy consequent on their aircraft being forced down over 'alien' territory. Of the 280 pilots who were dropped from vehicles all over the County, over 150 were captured.

Camp in 1958 was held at Dibgate Camp in Shorncliffe from 3 to 17 May. The first week was devoted to individual, section and platoon training, and the second week culminated in a three-day escape and evasion exercise run by Brigade HQ. While at camp, the Adjutancy passed from Captain Sutor to Captain T.D. Dean.

Normally the few weeks after camp in a TA Unit are relatively quiet, but this was far from the case for the Battalion in 1958. 8 June saw a visit of the Colonel-in-Chief, Her Royal Highness The Princess Margaret, CI, GCVO, to the Battalion. The occasion took place at Benacre Hall near Lowestoft, the home of Colonel Sir Robert Gooch, Honorary Colonel of the Battalion.

The Princess arrived at 1300 and was greeted by the Lord-Lieutenant, The Earl of Stradbroke, accompanied by the Colonel of the Regiment, Brigadier Maxwell, the Honorary Colonel of the Battalion, Sir Robert Gooch, and the Commanding Officer, Lieutenant-Colonel Smitherman.

After lunch the Battalion paraded at 1500. A Guard of Honour, commanded by Major Lawrie, with the Queen's Colour carried by Lieutenant G.R. Durrant, was formed up with the Band and Drums, with the remainder of the Battalion under Major R.A.F. Kemp, TD, at the rear.

Following a Royal Salute, the Princess inspected the Battalion and then the Guard of Honour marched past to 'Speed the Plough'. There then followed an address by the Colonel-in-Chief, to which the Commanding Officer replied. Lieutenant-Colonel Smitherman then called for three cheers for the Colonel-in-Chief, following which the Battalion marched off parade.

A large number of presentations were then made as the Colonel-in-Chief moved among those who had taken part in the parade, or had watched as members of the Old Comrades' Association or the Army Cadet Force.

It was a memorable day for the Battalion, heartily enjoyed by all who were fortunate enough to be present.

At the Brigade Rifle Meeting which was held on the following weekend, the Battalion Shooting Team swept the board, winning the Yorke Cup, the LMG Cup, the China Cup, the LMG Pairs, the Young Soldiers' Cup and the SMG Competition.

Her Majesty the Queen held a Review in Hyde Park on 22 June to celebrate the 50th Anniversary of the formation of the Territorial Army. Major Kemp, OC C Company, commanded a detachment of two officers and seventeen men at this Review. The Colours were carried by Lieutenant C.N. Leaning and Lieutenant J.D.L. Wight.

At the end of June Major Fisher-Hoch completed his tour with the Battalion as Training Major and Major Case handed over the duties of QM to Captain T.C. Warren, who was no stranger to the Battalion.

The Battalion sent a team to Bisley in July and Colour-Sergeant Spalding of A Company came fifth in the TA Hundred and shot for the TA against the Regular Army. In July also, Captain W.G.G. Lewis took a team of seventeen men to Holland to take part in the Nijmegen Marches.

On 31 August CSM Smith of C Company won the Individual Championship at the Battalion Rifle Meeting at Bromeswell Range.

The next day Lieutenant-Colonel Smitherman handed over command of the Battalion to Lieutenant-Colonel G.T.O. Springfield.

Training suffered severely during the winter of 1958/59 owing to major cuts in the training budget for the Battalion.

One major exercise in October again involved the Battalion in tracking down RAF pilots in Norfolk, intent on avoiding capture.

Training in 1959 began at a low level because of the financial restrictions, but camp did go ahead and was held at Okehampton Camp, Dartmoor from 23 May until 6 June. Twenty-two officers and 226 men attended and the training was run at Company level, except for an exercise in the second week planned and run by Brigade HQ.

In July, for the second year, the Battalion sent a team under Captain G.L. Brown to the Nijmegen Marches.

RSM Hazelwood replaced RSM Cressey in December, 1959.

With no particular financial strictures, training got off to a good start in 1960. Attendance figures at weekend training were high and great efforts were made to boost recruiting throughout the County by organizing open days and various displays.

The Battalion Rifle Meeting was held on 26 and 27 March, and C Company won the Inter-Company Competition.

The Brigade Meeting followed in April and the Battalion won the Unit Championship and also the Yorke Match and the SMC Cup.

The Shooting Team followed these successes on 1 May by jointly winning the Divisional Championships, tying with the 5th Battalion, the Northamptonshire Regiment.

The 1960 Annual Camp was held at Otterburn Camp in Northumberland, from 21 May to 4 June. Training started at company level and culminated in the last week with a three-day exercise devised by Brigade HQ.

At the end of June the Battalion provided a Guard together with the 4th Battalion, the Royal Norfolk Regiment at a parade granting the Freedom of Lowestoft to the 1st East Anglian Regiment (Royal Norfolk and Suffolk). The Parade was commanded by the Commanding Officer, Lieutenant-Colonel Springfield and the Battalion Guard by OC Sp Company, Major Lawrie. RSM Hazelwood was the parade RSM.

On 14 November Captain R.G. Wilson took over the duties of the Adjutant from Captain Dean.

Early in 1961 came the news that, consequent upon further reductions in the size of the TA, the Battalion would on 1 April, 1961, be amalgamated with the 1st Battalion, the Cambridgeshire Regiment, to form the 1st Battalion, the Suffolk and Cambridgeshire Regiment.

The 4th Battalion, the Suffolk Regiment thus ceased to exist as a Battalion after fifty-three years loyal and devoted voluntary service to The Crown.

CAMBRIDGESHIRE

In the previous volume of the Regimental History, the chapter devoted to the Cambridgeshire Regiment ended with a description of two memorable events which occurred in 1946. In February of that year a 'Cambridgeshire Weekend' was organized in Cambridge and Wisbech which culminated in a Service of Thanksgiving and Remembrance at the Cathedral in Ely. Then, on 29 September, the

Honorary Freedom of the Borough of Cambridge was conferred on the Regiment.

On both those occasions doubts and anxieties were expressed by many with regard to the future of the Regiment. The War Office was about to announce its plans for the organization of the newly-formed post-War Territorial Army, and it was far from clear what lay ahead.

Doubts were removed, though anxieties were scarcely allayed, at least initially, when it was announced that from 1 January, 1947, the Cambridgeshire Regiment would be reformed as a light anti-aircraft regiment of the Royal Artillery, to be known as 629 Light Anti-Aircraft Regiment, Royal Artillery (the Cambridgeshire Regiment) TA. Thus, for the first time since its creation in 1860, the Cambridgeshire Regiment would not be an infantry regiment, nor would it be part of the corps of the Suffolk Regiment which had always provided its Permanent Staff Officers and Instructors.

The change was viewed with mixed feelings, but among many in the County the volunteer spirit remained strong, despite the ravages of the so recent bitter wartime experiences in the Far East, and there was a singular determination to succeed in the new role.

Early in 1947 Major-General R.M. Luckock, CB, CMG, DSO, resigned the Honorary Colonelcy of the Regiment after holding the appointment with distinction for seventeen years. Colonel M.C. Clayton, DSO, OBE, DL, was appointed in his stead on 27 May, 1947. Colonel Clayton had joined the Cambridgeshire Regiment as a subaltern in 1910 and earned great distinction during the First World War winning the DSO in 1917 and being Mentioned in Despatches no less than five times. Closely identified with the fortunes of the Regiment for thirty-seven years, Colonel Clayton was the ideal man to lead it forward into the challenging times ahead.

Recruiting for the Regiment started actively early in 1947, and the first post-war regular Commanding Officer, Lieutenant-Colonel G. Colchester, DSO, RA, was appointed in the early summer.

Initially recruits came in slowly, but by August enough were assembled to participate in a weekend of training at Stiffkey Camp in North Norfolk. Most recruits were former Cambridgeshire infantry soldiers, so that their training was aimed at converting them to anti-aircraft gunners. This first weekend was counted a great success, with officers and men being initiated into the mysteries of gun drill.

A further weekend of training took place in October, 1947, and in the summer of 1948 the Regiment, though still few in numbers, went on its annual fifteen-day camp to Bude in Cornwall. There, for the first time, live firing of the 40mm light anti-aircraft guns was conducted and a high success rate was achieved firing at sleeve targets towed by aircraft.

By 1949 recruiting had increased sufficiently to establish Regimental Headquarters in Cambridge with P Battery also located in Cambridge, commanded by Major R. Grain, RA, Q Battery in Ely commanded by Major J.G.A. Beckett, RA, and R Battery in Wisbech commanded by Major J.D. Bunkall, RA.

Lieutenant-Colonel Colchester handed over command of the Regiment in 1949 to Lieutenant-Colonel J.D. Ritchie, DSO, RA, and Major W.F. Page, MC, RA, was his Second-in-Command.

On 22 July, 1949, Wisbech honoured the Regiment by granting it the Freedom of the Borough in a ceremony which took place in the park. It was an impressive occasion with some 1,500 members of the Regiment, Old Comrades and detachments from the Home Guard and the Army Cadet Force being present.

The Honorary Colonel of the Regiment received the casket containing the scroll authorizing the freedom, and then, on behalf of the Regiment, signed the Roll of Freemen. In her speech of welcome to the Regiment, the Mayor of Wisbech spoke of the close association which the Borough had always had with the Regiment, in which so many men of Wisbech and the surrounding district had served.

The Colours of the Cambridgeshire Regiment were on parade, carried by Captain P.D. Storie-Pugh, MBE, MC, RA, and Captain K. Scott, RA. They served as a reminder of the infantry origins of the Regiment and were still carried on ceremonial occasions, despite the conversion to a unit of Royal Artillery. The Cambridgeshire badge and buttons were also still worn by officers and men of the Regiment.

In 1950 Major Beckett took over from Major Page as 2ic. Consequent on this appointment Major K. Scott, RA, OC P (Cambridge) Battery, moved to take over Q (Ely and Chatteris) Battery from Major Beckett and Major Storie-Pugh took over P Battery from Major Scott.

The difficulties of building up the strength of the Regiment, shared by all TA units at the time, continued until the Government's decision, prompted by the deteriorating international situation and finally the outbreak of the Korean War, that National Service soldiers would be required to serve a three-year engagement in the TA, following their period of full-time service.

Former wartime soldiers still on the Z Reserve were also required at this time to undergo two weeks training a year and, as a result, in the early fifties the strength of the Regiment at last built up sufficiently to allow it to function effectively in its light anti-aircraft role.

360 men attended camp at Stiffkey in 1951 and in the following year over 600 were present when the annual camp took place at Towyn in Wales.

In November, 1952, Major Beckett assumed command of the Regiment from Lieutenant-Colonel Ritchie and thus became the first Territorial Officer to command since reforming after the Second World War.

In November also, the Regiment underwent a reorganization, changing from three batteries of three troops to four batteries of two troops. The fourth battery was found by splitting P (Cambridge) Battery into two. The new S Battery also had a troop in Newmarket and was commanded by Major W.L. Livermore, RA. In June, 1953, the War Office authorized the formation of a Band for the Regiment and recruiting went ahead straight away. Mr A.E. Tucker, former Band Master of the Regiment from 1922 to 1945, helped form the Band initially, but Mr J.D. Jacobs was appointed as the Band Master within a few weeks.

Annual Camp in 1953 took place from 1 to 15 August, once again at Bude in Cornwall. Training prior to camp had been concentrated on gun drill and once at Bude this paid dividends, with all four batteries achieving a high standard during live firing practices. P (Cambridge) Battery was awarded the Cup in the Inter-Battery Competition. During the second week a composite battery commanded by Major Scott completed a forty-eight-hour deployment exercise during which added realism was achieved as Spitfire aircraft carried out simulated attacks on the gun positions.

The Lord-Lieutenant of Cambridgeshire, Captain Briscoe, visited the Regiment during the second week of camp.

In September, 1953, RSM Bartlett who had been the Regular RSM of the Regiment since 1947, handed over to another Regular RSM, RSM Jackson.

In 1954 Annual Camp took place at Stiffkey in Norfolk, when the training highlight was once more the two-day deployment exercise. Some two hundred miles were covered during the exercise and the guns were frequently 'attacked' by US Sabre jet fighters.

Over 500 officers and men attended the camp and important visitors included the GOC-in-C AA Command, the AA Brigade Commander, Brigadier R. Chater, the Lord-Lieutenant and the Honorary Colonel of the Regiment. In August Band Master Jacobs retired and his place was taken by Band Master C.B. Mott.

Towards the end of the year the disbanding of AA Command renewed anxieties for the future of the Regiment. At first it seemed that it would simply be disbanded as well, but a campaign was immediately put into action to bring pressure on the War Office for this not to happen.

The campaign was led by the Lord-Lieutenant, who was always a tireless and enthusiastic supporter of the Regiment. He persuaded the MPs for Cambridgeshire and the Isle of Ely also to apply pressure, which they did, both on the War Office and in the House of Commons. As a result a reprieve was won for the Regiment, or perhaps something more, for it was from 1 April, 1955, allowed to serve on as a parachute gunner regiment. It was to be equipped with 4.2 in. mortars and its new title was 629 (The Cambridge Regiment) Parachute Light Regiment, RA, TA. As such it was the only regiment of its kind, unique in both the Regular and Territorial Armies.

Training for the new role began immediately. As a parachute regiment, it could only accept volunteers and although most members of the Regiment (including all the Officers) applied to join, some were too old or medically unfit to do so and it was thus necessary to initiate a major recruiting campaign.

It should be added that, although the Regimental HQ and two of the batteries were based in the County, a third battery was located in Sheffield.

The first instruction in the new tasks took place at Cambridge on 24 April, when instructors came down from the 16th Airborne Division (TA) to explain the workings of the new regiment.

In July Annual Camp was held at RAF Abingdon where 170 officers and men were taught to parachute. The course was a tough one and several injuries were incurred as the training progressed. The Lord-Lieutenant paid his usual visit to camp, arriving appropriately enough in a Vampire jet aircraft, which flew in from RAF Oakington.

By the end of camp 140 officers and men had survived the rigours of training, to complete the requisite number of jumps which included three from Hastings aircraft. They were awarded their parachutist's wings at a 'Wings Parade' by the GOC 16th Airborne Division, (TA), Major-General F.D. Rome, CBE, DSO.

The Honorary Colonel of the Regiment, Colonel Clayton, accompanied Major-General Rome at the saluting base, when the Regiment, led by the CO, Lieutenant-Colonel Beckett, marched past.

The enthusiasm displayed within the Regiment for the new parachuting role was typified by the Regular QM, Major J.H.

Sanders, RA, who at the age of fifty-two had obtained special permission to do the jumping training. He got his wings at the final parade, but was told by Major-General Rome that on no account was he to jump again.

While at camp, Captain M.F.D. Henry, RA, took over from Major F.H. Blake, RA, as Regular Adjutant of the Regiment.

In September a further period of camp training was carried out at Weybourne Camp on the North Norfolk coast when a barriage balloon provided the opportunity for more men of the Regiment to gain parachuting experience.

Later in the same month thirty men, led by Major Storie-Pugh, carried out a demonstration jump as part of the annual Battle of Britain flying display at RAF Duxford.

On 27 October Her Majesty The Queen, accompanied by His Royal Highness The Duke of Edinburgh, paid a visit to Cambridge. The Regiment provided a Guard of Honour for the occasion outside the Guild Hall.

The Guard of Honour was commanded by Major Storie-Pugh and the Commanding Officer escorted The Queen to and from the inspection, which Her Majesty insisted on completing, despite the incessant rain.

In May, 1956, the War Office announced the decision to disband the 16th Airborne Division (TA) and once more the Regiment's role was changed. Its post-War association with the Royal Regiment of Artillery was brought to an end and it was again reformed as an infantry unit and became the 1st Battalion, the Cambridgeshire Regiment, forming part of the 162nd Independent Infantry Brigade.

Throughout the summer the conversion went ahead with companies using weekend training sessions for this purpose. Farewells were said to the Royal Artillery members of the permanent staff, and in their place, as a result of the old links with the Suffolk Regiment being reformed, came Suffolk Regimental officers, warrant officers and NCOs.

Lieutenant-Colonel Beckett continued briefly as Commanding Officer, with Major Page as 2ic, and in mid-July Major P.S.W. Dean, the Suffolk Regiment, joined the Battalion as Regular Training Major.

On 31 July Lieutenant-Colonel Beckett handed over command of the Battalion to Lieutenant-Colonel Page. The former had joined the Regiment in April, 1939, and served with it throughout the War, spending three and a half years as a prisoner-of-war in Japanese hands. He took over command, the first TA Officer to do so since the

War, in November, 1952, and led the Regiment through the traumas of conversion from LAA to Parachute Light and then back to an Infantry role. As the Honorary Colonel of the Regiment said at the time, the Regiment owed him a deep debt of gratitude for carrying it forward so successfully through difficult and trying times.

Annual Camp for 1956 was held from 25 August to 8 September at Dibgate Camp in Shorncliffe. It was a tented camp and rather spartan when compared with the luxuries previously experienced in permanent gunner range camps.

The training at camp was concentrated on weapon training and firing in the first week and tactics at section and platoon level in the second. There was a last chance for those with parachutist wings to do their annual qualifying jumps on Sunday 2 September, when a balloon was brought down from RAF Cardington.

Visitors to camp included the Lord-Lieutenant, Captain Briscoe, the Honorary Colonel of the Regiment, Colonel Clayton, and the Colonel of the Suffolk Regiment, Brigadier Backhouse.

The Battalion Rifle Meeting was held on the Hythe Ranges during camp, and the Inter-Company Championship was won by B Company, with CSM Bryant of B Company the Individual Champion Shot.

Soon after camp RSM Jackson was awarded the MSM, which all members of the Regiment felt he very much deserved. At the end of September, after three years on the permanent staff, he left the Regiment and his place was taken by RSM Norman from the Suffolk Regiment.

Training weekends continued throughout the autumn and great strides were made, not only in acquiring the basic infantry skills, but also in the specialist jobs within Sp Company and the Signals Platoon.

At the end of 1956, despite strenuous recruiting drives, the Battalion remained small in numbers and not all companies had been formed. There were twenty-five officers and eighty-five men, and senior appointments in the Battalion were as follows:

CO:	Lieutenant-Colonel W.F. Page, MC, TD
2ic:	Major P.D. Storie-Pugh, MBE, MC, TD
Training Major:	Major P.S.W. Dean (Regular)
Adjutant:	Captain J.P. Macdonald (Regular)
QM:	Major J.S. Sanders (Regular)
RSM:	RSM Norman (Regular)

OC HQ Company: (Cambridge)	Major K. Scott
CSM:	CSM Travers
OC B Company: (Ely)	Captain R.B. Keatley
CSM:	CSM Bryant
OC C Company: (Wisbech)	Major A.H. Lee, TD
CSM:	CSM Chapman
OC Sp Company:	Captain C.A. Taylor

Early in 1957 a Corps of Drums was formed under Drum Major Graves. Several of the drummers had been members of Army Cadet Force Corps of Drums and thus brought considerable experience with them.

Weekend training in the first half of the year was organized at both battalion and company level. One particularly valuable and interesting signals exercise took place in April involving a simulated advance to contact on a route from Cambridge to Felixstowe.

Companies also made good use of ranges and had largely completed firing the annual range course before camp.

The Battalion went to camp from 15 to 29 June at Fingringhoe near Colchester. It was a Brigade camp with HQ 162nd Infantry Brigade and the 1st Battalion, the Hertfordshire Regiment and the 5th Battalion, the Northamptonshire Regiment also under canvas.

Training was conducted by Brigade HQ and a number of specialist cadres were run during the fortnight. Sports also played a prominent part in the Battalion's activities and it succeeded in winning the Brigade Sports Trophy for the best achievement in all games played.

Immediately following camp, the Battalion Rifle Meeting was held and Sergeant Emmerson of C Company was the Champion Shot and B Company won the Inter-Company Competition.

On 3 November the Honorary Colonel of the Regiment, Colonel Clayton, died. His unexpected death – he had attended the annual Officers' Dinner Dance the previous evening – brought to an abrupt end forty-eight years' singular and devoted service to the Regiment. He joined in 1910, commanded the 1st Battalion towards the end of the First World War and again between the Wars. During the Second World War he had raised a Battalion of Home Guard and in its aftermath commanded an Army Cadet Force Battalion and in 1948 became the Honorary Colonel of the Regiment.

Scarcely recovered from this loss, the Regiment suffered another blow in December, when the Lord-Lieutenant, Captain Briscoe, died early in the month. He had been a tower of strength to the Regiment in its various stages of growth since reformation after the War. He used his not inconsiderable influence in high places whenever he was asked and showed a constant and close interest in the Regiment and the men who served in it.

On 10 December, the QM, Major Sanders retired from the Army. He had been with the regiment since 1955 and had seen it change from LAA to Parachute Light duties and then to its infantry role. His place was taken by Lieutenant H.H. Norman, the Suffolk Regiment, who was commissioned on 18 February, 1958, having been RSM of the Battalion for the previous eighteen months.

RSM Lyon replaced RSM Norman early in 1958 and his particular skills in the realms of shooting were of great benefit to the Battalion.

Also in the New Year, D Company was raised in Newmarket.

All ranges were heavily used at weekends in February and March and by April most members of the Battalion had fired their annual range course.

On 18 March Brigadier Backhouse was appointed Honorary Colonel of the Regiment in place of Colonel Clayton. Brigadier Backhouse had always taken a keen interest in the Cambridgeshire Regiment and the Battalion was pleased, further, to cement its links with the Suffolk Regiment of which he had until 1957 held the Colonelcy.

27 April saw A Company win the Inter-Company Championship at the annual Rifle Meeting while Sergeant Gillett of B Company was Individual Champion Shot.

Early in the summer Major Dean and Captain Macdonald, the Regular Training Major and Adjutant, left the Battalion on completion of two years on the permanent staff.

The 50th Anniversary of the Territorial Army was celebrated in June. Her Majesty The Queen held a Review in Hyde Park on the 22nd, at which the Battalion was represented by a Colour Party, comprising Lieutenant A.G. Stephen, Lieutenant W.H. Keatley, Colour-Sergeant Williams, Colour-Sergeant Challis and Sergeant Beaumont.

Bad weather looked likely to mar the celebrations in Cambridge, but they went ahead despite less than pleasant conditions. The Battalion contingent joined with other units in a march through the town, followed by a Drumhead Service and a Military display in the grounds of Jesus College.

In August Major Howgego, the Suffolk Regiment, arrived to take over the appointment of Regular Training Major.

Annual Camp in 1958 took place in September at Dibgate Camp, Shorncliffe. The whole of the 162nd Infantry Brigade were in camp and training took the form of a number of specialist cadres, co-ordinated by Brigade HQ. The Battalion also ran its own recruit training cadre for some thirty new recruits, under the direction of the 2ic, Major Storie-Pugh. The cadre was organized as an adventure training exercise and provided an exciting introduction to Army life for the new recruits.

Camp was unhappily overshadowed by the death of one young Officer, Lieutenant R. Hall, who was struck by lightning during a ferocious thunderstorm which hit the camp.

Almost immediately on returning from Shorncliffe, the Battalion was transferred to the 161st Infantry Brigade, to join the 4th Battalion, the Royal Norfolk Regiment and the 4th Battalion, the Suffolk Regiment. The training cycle continued in the same pattern as the change in the order of battle did not mean a change in role.

Early in 1959 the Brigade Commander, Brigadier J.R.I. Doyle, OBE, accompanied by his Brigade Major, Major W.C. Deller, carried out a series of annual administrative inspections at Battalion HQ and each of the Company locations. The Battalion was reported on favourably.

Annual Camp in 1959 took place at Plaisterdown Camp on Dartmoor from 22 May to 6 June. Training this year concentrated on low-level tactics at section and platoon level. In the second week all Battalions of the Brigade took part in an exercise run by Brigade HQ.

A Brigade Drumhead Service took place at Okehampton on the middle Sunday of camp. The Bands and Drums of the three Battalions paraded together and provided a most impressive display.

The Honorary Colonel of the Regiment, Brigadier Backhouse, visited the Battalion while at camp and joined the Officers at a Guest Night.

Soon after returning from camp, preparations went ahead for a very important Regimental occasion. On 21 June the 1939–1945 War Roll of Honour of the Regiment was to be dedicated in the Regimental Chapel in Ely Cathedral in the presence of Her Royal Highness The Princess Margaret, CI, GCVO, Colonel-in-Chief of the Suffolk Regiment.

On arrival at Cambridge airport Her Royal Highness inspected the Guard of Honour, commanded by Major Storie-Pugh. The Band under Band Master D.E. Peters was also on parade.

From the airport the Colonel-in-Chief drove straight to St John's College where she was entertained to luncheon by the Officers of the Regiment, together with the Lord-Lieutenant and the Master of St John's.

After luncheon Her Royal Highness drove to Ely for the formal part of her visit. The Roll of Honour, on which were the names of twenty two Officers and 738 men who had fallen in the Second World War, was brought into the Regimental Chapel in the Cathedral and the Service of Dedication took place before a congregation of over 2,500, led by the Colonel-in-Chief. The solemn service was conducted by the Dean and the Bishop of Ely dedicated the book containing the Roll of Honour.

Following the service, many members of the Regiment were presented to Her Royal Highness and then she was escorted to a dais from where she took the salute at a march past.

The Band and Drums led the parade at the head of which marched the Battalion, under the CO, Lieutenant-Colonel Page. Then came a large contingent of the Old Comrades' Association under a former CO of the 2nd Battalion, Lieutenant-Colonel E.L.V. Mapey, OBE, TD.

The 3rd and 4th (Cadet) Battalions under Major Fernie and Major Hyde followed the Old Comrades and bringing up the rear came the Regimental Taxi, driven by the QM Lieutenant Norman!

The Colonel-in-Chief expressed delight at seeing the taxi, but declined the QM's offer of a lift and shortly afterwards said her goodbyes and left in her own car for RAF Waterbeach.

It had been a marvellous day, for those with longer memories one of sadness of course, but all the same an outstanding and memorable occasion for all who were there.

On 1 August Lieutenant-Colonel Page handed over command to Lieutenant-Colonel Storie-Pugh, thus bringing to an end a long period of loyal and devoted service in the Regiment, which began before the Second World War. He was awarded the MC during the War and had served throughout the turmoil and change which had characterized the fortunes of the Regiment in the post-war years.

On 19 and 20 September the MMG Platoon and the 3″ Mortar Platoon came first in Brigade competitions organized during a training weekend on Stanford Training Area. And the following weekend, at the 54th (East Anglian) Infantry Division, TA, Rifle Meeting at Fingringhoe Ranges, Private Brown of B Company won the Young Soldiers' Cup and the Battalion the Young Soldiers' Team Cup.

The Christmas Shoot, now established as an annual event, with side shows and entertainments as well as small-bore shooting, was held in Cambridge in December with other organizations invited to attend.

On 9 and 10 January, 1960, Brigadier Doyle, Commander 161st Infantry Brigade carried out the annual administrative inspection.

Annual camp was held from 21 May to 4 June at Otterburn Camp in Northumberland and in July Major Howgego handed over the duties of Training Major and Adjutant to Major E.H. Morgan, MBE, MC.

Soon after camp it was announced that the Regiment was to undergo yet another transformation (its fourth since the Second World War) in 1961.

Several changes in the TA nationally were made by the War Office and among them was the amalgamation of the 1st Battalion, the Cambridgeshire Regiment with the 4th Battalion, the Suffolk Regiment, to form the 1st Battalion, the Suffolk and Cambridgeshire Regiment.

Just prior to amalgamation senior appointments in the Battalion were held as follows:

CO:	Lieutenant-Colonel P.D. Storie-Pugh, MBE, MC, TD
Training Major and Adjutant:	Major E.H. Morgan, MBE, MC (Regular)
QM:	Lieutenant H.H. Norman (Regular)
RSM:	RSM Lyon (Regular)
OC A Company: (Wisbech)	Major J.A. Forsythe, TD
OC B Company: (Ely)	Major L.S.L. Brown
OC C Company: (March)	Major A.H. Lee, TD
OC D Company: (Newmarket)	Captain J.R. Baggaley
OC HQ Company: (Cambridge)	Major J.R.L. Brashaw

It was agreed, prior to amalgamation, that two companies of the new Battalion would be recruited in Cambridgeshire. A Company would be formed in March and Wisbech and B Company would draw its men from Cambridge, Ely and Newmarket.

The date for amalgamation was 1 April, 1961, and on Sunday, 9 April a ceremony took place at Gibraltar Barracks in Bury St Edmunds, at which the Regimental Flags were lowered for the last time and the new flag hoisted. The Commanding Officer of the Battalion, Lieutenant-Colonel Storie-Pugh, assumed command of the new Battalion. The occasion was also significant for both the Suffolk Regiment and the Cambridgeshire Regiment, as being the last day that the badges of the two Regiments would be worn by any unit.

CHAPTER X

AMALGAMATION: 1959

'The Regiment Departs'

The Suez operation in 1956 was a reminder, if any was needed, that Great Britain was hard put to sustain its worldwide and imperial responsibilities. It was not the Army that failed at Suez, indeed it was within sight of success when the ceasefire was called. But rather, it was quite simply the case that our national economic circumstances would no longer allow us to 'go it alone' in the international role which for so long, we had played.

This sudden realization was translated into concrete terms in the immediate aftermath of the Suez crisis, by the new Prime Minister, Mr Harold Macmillan. His decisions then were to lead inevitably to a dramatic shrinkage in the size of the Army which culminated in the amalgamation of the Regiment with the Royal Norfolk Regiment.

On taking Office, Mr Macmillan appointed a new Minister of Defence, Duncan Sandys, and straight away instructed him to carry out a sweeping review of Defence Policy with a view to formulating 'policies to secure substantial reductions in expenditure and manpower'.

In April, 1957, Sandys published his White Paper in which it had been decided to bring an end to calling up men for National Service by 1960; to reduce the size of BAOR and other garrisons and to compensate by building up a strategic reserve, capable of being deployed worldwide should the need arise.

For the Infantry this meant a cut from seventy seven to sixty battalions. It was this statement alone that presaged major changes in the Regiment as in the Infantry at large and caused rumour and speculation to run rife over the next months.

The first indication of anxiety within the Regiment manifested itself in the Depot notes for the *Regimental Gazette* in the summer 1957 issue: 'This last quarter has been one of many rumours. It is profoundly hoped that the Regimental Depot will be allowed to carry on'.

In the same issue of the *Gazette*, came the announcement of the change over in Colonels of the Regiment. Brigadier Backhouse handed over on completion of his ten-year tour of duty to Brigadier Maxwell on 10 June, 1957, and it was already by then clear that the latter had taken up his appointment at a moment of dramatic change.

Field-Marshal Sir Gerald Templer, the CIGS, summoned all Colonels of Regiments to the War Office during June and July, 1957, and told them of the changes which were about to be announced and on 24 July, John Hare, Secretary of State for War, made the decisions public in the House of Commons.

That same day the Commanding Officers of the 1st Battalion and the Depot were allowed to open sealed letters which spelt out what the Regiment's future was to be.

The Colonel of the Regiment also sent a message to the Battalion and the Depot which amplified the bald War Office announcement:

'Reorganization of the Infantry
A Message from The Colonel of The Regiment.

We now know of the decision to amalgamate the Regiment with the Royal Norfolk Regiment. In all, some thirty regiments of Infantry are to be amalgamated, and you will be sure, as I am, that such a step will only be taken most regretfully in the urgent interests of the Country. It hurts all of us and is, of its kind, the biggest test which the Regiment has had to face.

I well know what a blow it will be to all of you as it is to me. But it has never been our way in the Suffolk Regiment to sit back at such a time and nurse our disappointment. We are not being disbanded, but amalgamated with a sister Regiment, with whom we have much in common, at a time when our reputation is at its highest.

I am confident and I have the authority of our Colonel-in-Chief to speak for Her Royal Highness in this, that every one of us will strive in the time that is left to us, to bring to our new partnership everything that is loyal and best in our long, proud history of over 270 years.

There are a great many problems to be dealt with, including the personal future of those who will be affected and the preservation of our Regimental treasures and connections. It would be wrong to make hasty decisions concerning them and you may rest assured that all possible thought will be given to them.

So, as Minden Day approaches let us look to the past for inspiration and to the future in confidence, which I and the Colonel of the Royal Norfolk Regiment share, that when the time comes, the reorganized Regiment will have a fair start and a happy future. May good fortune go with all who serve in it.

24 July, 1957
                                        R.H. Maxwell, Brigadier
                                        Colonel of The Regiment'

In Cyprus, the CO of the 1st Battalion, Lieutenant-Colonel W.S. Bevan, assembled the whole Battalion and made the amalgamation announcement, reading extracts also from letters from the Commander-in-Chief Middle East Land Forces and the General Officer Commanding Cyprus District, as well as the whole of Brigadier Maxwell's message. The CO concluded his address with an exhortation that everyone should accept what had been done and make the best of it. There was little else he could say. In Bury St Edmunds the dispelling of the rumours left everyone at the Depot feeling despondent and deflated, though outwardly a somewhat flippant air prevailed, with talk of 'Brigade cap badges, redundancy terms, chicken farms and the location of the new Depot, should it be required to move'.

The two Regiments had been given until the end of 1959 to arrange the amalgamation, and action was taken immediately by Brigadier Maxwell and Brigadier C.J. Wilkinson, DSO, the Colonel of the Royal Norfolk Regiment, to start planning for the amalgamation.

The first questions to be decided centred on the title of the newly amalgamated Regiment and its new badge, and these problems were bound up with wider considerations. All the other Regiments of the East Anglian Brigade, loosely tied together when it was formed in 1948, were also to suffer amalgamation: the Bedfordshire and Herfordshire Regiment with the Essex Regiment and the Royal Lincolnshire Regiment with the Northamptonshire Regiment. There was to be one Depot and one cap badge for all.

The Council of Colonels of the amalgamating Regiments wanted to perpetuate in the titles something of the identity of their old Regiments, but all suggestions were vetoed for one reason or another by the War Office. The problem was urgent as the Bedfordshire and Hertfordshire Regiment and the Essex Regiment were due to amalgamate early in 1958, and it was somewhat reluctantly agreed to call the three new Regiments the 1st, the 2nd and the 3rd East Anglian Regiments, in accordance with the seniority of the existing Regiments, each being allowed a secondary title. The Royal Norfolk and Suffolk Regiments would thus amalgamate to become the 1st East Anglian Regiment (Royal Norfolk and Suffolk).

The Suffolk Regiment Depot was nominated as the new East Anglian Brigade Depot where all training for the three Regiments would be conducted, and a small Regimental Headquarters of three Retired Officers would be established in the counties of the three new Regiments.

It was agreed that the new cap badge would comprise the Castle and Key of Gibraltar above a scroll bearing the words East Anglia, all in gilt upon a silver Garter Star. The Castle and Key of Gibraltar were common to the Suffolk, the Essex and the Northamptonshire Regiments and the Garter Star was associated both with the Royal Lincolnshire and the Bedfordshire and Hertfordshire Regiments. Without representation in the badge it was agreed that the Britannia buttons of the Royal Norfolk Regiment should be the buttons common to all three new Regiments.

With these major decisions taken, Brigadier Maxwell and Brigadier Wilkinson agreed on the establishment of an Inter-Regimental Committee comprising:

OC the Depot the Royal Norfolk Regiment
OC the Depot the Suffolk Regiment
CO 1st Battalion, the Royal Norfolk Regiment (or his representative)
CO 1st Battalion, the Suffolk Regiment (or his representative)
The Retired Officer, Depot the Royal Norfolk Regiment
The Retired Officer, Depot the Suffolk Regiment
a Secretary

The task of the Committee which began its work in June, 1958, was to examine all aspects of amalgamation and to make suggestions as to courses of action. After each meeting (they were chaired alternately by the two Depot Commanders) recommendations were submitted to the two Colonels of the Regiments for their joint approval.

In this way an enormous agenda was covered. Some items were agreed instantly and some took several meetings to resolve and needed the gathering together of a great deal of background information. There were occasional delays as opinions were sought, for example from the Commanding Officers of the Battalions, both of which were serving overseas.

The subjects varied widely, from the creation of a Regimental Committee through Benevolent Funds, a Regimental Journal to the wording of a Regimental Collect. In other words, they covered every conceivable aspect of lives of the two existing Regiments and the Regiment of the future.

It was agreed that Amalgamation Day would be 29 August, 1959, with the new Regiment forming in Aldershot Barracks in Iserlohn, where the 1st Battalion, the Royal Norfolk Regiment was stationed in BAOR at that time. Meanwhile, the 1st Battalion remained on active service in Cyprus, too busy to think about such things as amalgamation, though being forcibly reminded of it as its strength dwindled as drafts of National Servicemen tailed away and, on such occasions as when, on 1 December, 1958, the new East Anglian Regiment Cap Badge was taken into use.

Preparations for the amalgamation moved into top gear when the 1st Battalion arrived back in England from Cyprus on board the *Dilwara* on 19 May, 1959. As the ship docked, the Battalion was met by the Colonel of the Regiment, Brigadier Maxwell, the East Anglian Brigade Colonel, Colonel Heal, and the Commanding Officer of the 4th Battalion, Lieutenant-Colonel Springfield. The Band of the 4th Battalion was on the quayside and gave a stirring rendering of 'Speed the Plough'.

The Battalion was very small in numbers on returning home, and now, apart from a number of important and nostalgic ceremonial occasions, it simply remained for it to post out a number of officers and senior ranks, and prepare those who would go to make up the new Battalion, for drafting to Germany to join the 1st Battalion, the Royal Norfolk Regiment.

Immediately on arrival in the United Kingdom, everyone went on disembarkation leave, after which they reassembled in Sir John Moore Barracks in Shorncliffe.

On 20 June, 1959, the last Officers' Regimental Ball of the Suffolk Regiment was held at the Athenaeum at Bury St Edmunds. A large number of guests from the County was invited and a host of serving and retired officers and their wives were present. It was a happy and memorable occasion, though needless to say, tinged with sadness.

The Boroughs of Bury St Edmunds, Ipswich and Sudbury had expressed a wish that the Battalion would exercise its right as Freemen to march through their streets for the last time and preparations were made in Shorncliffe to do so.

A representative detachment was drilled and rehearsed for these occasions. It was commanded by Major Fairholme and numbered

107 all ranks, including CSM R. Evans, MM, Colour Sergeant Nichols, Sergeant Pope, Sergeant Sainsbury, Sergeant Watson and Sergeant Kelly. The Regimental Colour was carried by Lieutenant W.J.B. Peat. The Band and Drums, fifty strong under Band Master G.A. Holben and Drum Major Hitchen, were also to take part.

The first parade was held at Bury St Edmunds on 11 July. The Detachment formed up in the Abbey Gardens and the Lord-Lieutenant, Commander The Earl of Stradbroke, accompanied by the Major of Bury St Edmunds, Mr F.G. Banks, was greeted with a Royal Salute. The Lord-Lieutenant and the Mayor carried out an inspection, accompanied by the Colonel of the Regiment and the Commanding Officer of the 1st Battalion, Lieutenant-Colonel K.M.J. Dewar, OBE.

Both the Lord-Lieutenant and the Mayor then addressed the parade and Brigadier Maxwell responded. The ceremonial ended with the Detachment, led by the Band and Drums, marching through the streets of Bury St Edmunds where the salute was taken on Angel Hill by the Lord Lieutenant.

In the evening, the Band and Drums Beat Retreat on Angel Hill before a large assembly, which was greatly moved, when at the conclusion the Regimental Flag was lowered from the staff high over the Abbey Gates for the last time.

A similar parade was staged in Sudbury on 15 July, when the Mayor of Sudbury, Colonel G.L.J. Tuck, CMG, DSO, a distinguished Officer of the Regiment, inspected the Detachment and made an address, which was responded to by the Colonel of the Regiment.

The Detachment marched through the streets of Sudbury after the Parade and in the evening the Band and Drums Beat Retreat on Market Hill.

Friday, 17 July saw the final parade at Ipswich. The Detachment formed up in Christchurch Park, where the Mayor, Mr R.J. Lewis, carried out an inspection. His address to the parade was responded to by the Colonel of the Regiment, and the celebrations closed with a march through the streets of Ipswich, where the Mayor took the salute from the steps of the Town Hall.

One last ceremonial occasion remained for the now much depleted Battalion. The Colonel of the Regiment took the salute at Sir John Moore Barracks in Shorncliffe at the last Minden Day Parade of the 1st Battalion, the Suffolk Regiment.

There were now left at Shorncliffe only those officers and men who were to go to Germany to join the 1st Battalion, the Royal Norfolk

Regiment, to form the new Regiment. They travelled to Harwich on 28 August and crossed to The Hook that night. The ship was seen off from Harwich by the Commanding Officer, Lieutenant-Colonel Dewar, the Adjutant, Captain P.D.L. Hopper, and a number of other officers. The party to form the new Battalion travelled under the command of Major P.B. Forrest, MC, who was to be 2ic of the new Battalion.

The party arrived in Iserlohn on 29 August, Amalgamation Day, and that evening a brief ceremony took place when the two halves of the new Battalion formed up and saluted, while the Regimental Flags of the Royal Norfolk Regiment and the Suffolk Regiment were lowered for the last time, and the flag of the 1st East Anglian Regiment hoisted to flutter at the masthead to usher in a new era and close the pages of 274 turbulent years of history, shared by both the old Regiments.

APPENDIX I

ROLL OF HONOUR

The following Officer, Non-Commissioned Officers and Men were killed in action or died on active service between 1946 and 1959.

Palestine 1946–1948	Craftsman Burke, REME attached
	AQMS J. Cole, REME attached
Malaya 1949–1953	Private B.V. Ansell
	Sergeant J.A. Ashdown
	Corporal S.J. Bailey
	Private J.O. Edwards
	Private L.G. Killick
	Private B. Larman
	Private F.L. Lewis
	Lance-Corporal F.T.C. Mallows
	Private R.A. Mills
	Private R. Moore
	Private D. Nobbs
	Private L.R. Payne
	Private W.G. Pearce
	Lance-Corporal H.R. Simmonds
	Bandsman M.S. Swann
	Lance-Corporal S.E. Thompsett
	Private H.C. Walker
	Sergeant D.B. Westin
	Private D. Wilson
Korea 1951	Captain N.A.M Balders (with the Royal Ulster Rifles)

APPENDIX II

HONOURS AND AWARDS

1947	MBE	RSM J. Chalk, MM
1948	CB	Brigadier R.H. Maxwell
	BEM	Sergeant A. Hendy
	MID	Lieutenant-Colonel G.H.M. Harper
		T/Lieutenant-Colonel I.L. Wight, OBE
		Major F.W. Garrard
		Captain P.B. Forrest, MC
		T/Captain W.C. Deller
		T/Captain W. Mayhew
		Lieutenant G.C. Howgego
		WOII K.T. Duffy
		WOII T.C. Warren
		WOII H.J. Gingell
		Corporal G.W. Wright
		A/Corporal B.R. Hambling
		A/Corporal F.B. Humpage
		Lance-Corporal B.R. Addis
		Private W.C. West
		Private E.L. Martin
1949	MID	Brigadier H.P. Sparks, CBE, MC
1950	DSO	Lieutenant-Colonel I.L. Wight, OBE
	MC	Captain A.F. Campbell
		2nd Lieutenant J.G. Starling
		2nd Lieutenant J.N. Kelly

	MM	Lance-Corporal D.E.R. Wicks
	MID	Lieutenant-Colonel I.L. Wight, DSO, OBE
		Major W.A. Heal, OBE
		Major J.C. Devey
		(The Northamptonshire Regiment)
		Lieutenant H.N. Moffitt (RAOC)
		2nd Lieutenant J.N. Kelly, MC
		A/Colour Sergeant H. Morling
		Sergeant J.A. Ashdown
		Sergeant R.H.H. Pratt
		Sergeant D.F.A. Vokins
		Private A.E. Race
1951	CBE	Brigadier E.M. Ransford
	DCM	A/Corporal W.J. Price
	MBE	Major C.A. Boycott
	MC	Lieutenant A.H.V. Gillmore
		2nd Lieutenant G.F.N. Charrington
		2nd Lieutenant F.A. Godfrey
	BEM	A/Colour Sergeant A.W. Calver
		Private E.G. Twigden
	MID	Major L. Field, MC
		Major A. Parkin
		Major C.J.V. Fisher-Hoch
		Captain G.C. Howgego
		Captain W.J. Calder
		Captain E.H. Morgan
		WOII S.C. Kingston
		Colour Sergeant B.T.W. Richardson
		Sergeant A.F. Cox
		Sergeant D.B. Westin
		A/Sergeant J.P. Dunne
		A/Sergeant H. Smith
		A/Sergeant R. Evans
		A/Sergeant C.A. Wilce
		Lance-Corporal L.G. Drew
1952	DSO	Lieutenant-Colonel P.A. Morcombe, OBE
	MBE	Major H.S.R. Case
	MC	Captain E.H. Morgan
		2nd Lieutenant A.B. Horrex
		2nd Lieutenant R.L. Hands
	MM	Sergeant R. Fowler

	MID	Lieutenant L.A. Palmer
		WOII F.G.W. Wilson
		WOII N McColl
		Sergeant A. Tracey
		A/Sergeant T. Archer
		Private R. Knight
1953	OBE	Major K.M.J. Dewar
	MBE	WOI C.A. Ainger
	MM	Sergeant R. Evans
	BEM	WOII E.H. Bailey
		Sergeant F.R. Rinder
	MID	Major W.S. Bevan
		Major E.T. Lummis
		T/Major F.J. Lockett
		2nd Lieutenant P.D.L Hopper
		A/Sergeant T.D. Kelly
		A/Sergeant C.R. Lawson
		A/Sergeant R.G. Smith
1954	CBE	Brigadier R.E. Goodwin, DSO
	MID	Major P.B. Forrest, MC
		Major C.L.D. Newell, MBE
		2nd Lieutenant P.B. Bird
1955	OBE	Major G.R. Heyland, MC
		Major W.J. Martin
	MBE	Major H.R. Cotton
	MSM	Major H.R. Cotton, MBE
	MID	Lieutenant-Colonel P.A. Morcombe, DSO, OBE
1956	OBE	Lieutenant-Colonel J.G.A. Beckett, TD (The Cambridgeshire Regiment)
1957	MSM	Sergeant V.G. Gilbert
	MID	A/Sergeant B. King
		A/Corporal H.K. Fowler
		Private S.J. Woods
1958	OBE	Lieutenant-Colonel W.S. Bevan
		Lieutenant-Colonel W.C. Smith
		Lieutenant-Colonel J.S.H. Smitherman, ERD
	BEM	Corporal J.L. Wiffen

	MID	Major M.G. Eliot
		Major G.T.O. Springfield
		Major F.D. Ingle
		Lieutenant J.G.M. North
		WOI H.J. Gingell
		Corporal A.F. Garrard
1959	CB	Major-General R.E. Goodwin, CBE, DSO
	OBE	Lieutenant-Colonel K.J.K. Pye
	MBE	Major E.H. Morgan, MC
	MC	Captain J.D. Churchill
	MID	Major P.D.F. Thursby
		Major A.L. Willdridge
		(The Northamptonshire Regiment)

APPENDIX III

THE APPOINTMENT OF COLONEL-IN-

CHIEF, THE SUFFOLK REGIMENT

Early in 1952, the Colonel of the Regiment, Brigadier E.H.W. Backhouse, D.L., after consultation with senior past and present Officers of the Regiment, decided that it would be proper for the Regiment to seek some recognition of its long and honourable service and in particular of the considerable distinction that the 1st Battalion was then achieving in Malaya.

He wrote the following letter to the War Office:

> From: Brigadier E.H.W. Backhouse, D.L.
> Colonel, The Suffolk Regiment
> Rowen House,
> Bury St Edmunds,
> Suffolk
> April 2nd 1952.

Sir,

COLONEL-IN-CHIEF – THE SUFFOLK REGIMENT

With reference to A.C.I. 209/46 regarding the appointment of Members of the Royal Family as Colonels-in-Chief, I have the honour, on behalf of the SUFFOLK Regiment, to make this humble application that Her Majesty the Queen may be graciously pleased to consider the loyal and earnest desire of every member of the Regiment, past and present, for Her to honour them by becoming their Colonel-in-Chief.

The Suffolk Regiment (formerly the XIIth Foot) was raised by the Duke of Norfolk in 1685 and is the twelfth oldest Regiment of Infantry of the Line. It has, however, not yet enjoyed the honour of having a Royal Colonel-in-Chief. The Regiment can claim that on one occasion it had a special

connection with a reigning Sovereign. The Battle of Dettingen on June 27th, 1743 was the last time that a King of England personally led his troops in an action. At one point in this battle, King George II placed himself at the head of the first line of British Infantry, in the centre of which was the XIIth Foot. The Suffolk Regiment commemorate this proud occasion on every Sovereign's Birthday Parade.

Since the end of the 1939–45 War, the 1st Battalion of the Regiment has been engaged almost continuously in active operations in aid of the Civil Power in Palestine and Malaya. In Malaya it has achieved the distinction of having the best operational record of any British Infantry in that country since the present disturbances started, and this fact has recently been publicly recognized in the Press in this country. During these difficult and arduous operations members of the Battalion have received the following awards:-

Distinguished Service Order	– 1
Military Cross	– 5
Distinguished Conduct Medal	– 1
Military Medal	– 2
British Empire Medal	– 2
Mentions in Despatches	–23

In view of these circumstances, I trust that this application may receive Her Majesty's favourable consideration.

I have the honour to be,

Sir,

Your obedient servant,

E.H.W. Backhouse, Brigadier (Rtd)

Colonel, The Suffolk Regiment

To: The Under-Secretary of State,
The War Office,
Lansdowne House,
Berkeley Square,
S.W.I.

The letter was acknowledged, but it was not until over a year later that the following substantive reply was received:

The War Office,
London, S.W.1.
29 May, 1953.

PERSONAL & CONFIDENTIAL

Sir,

I am directed to inform you that Her Majesty the Queen has been graciously pleased to honour The Suffolk Regiment with the appointment of Her Royal Highness The Princess Margaret as Colonel-in-Chief.

Notification of the appointment will appear in the Coronation Honours List to be published on Monday 1st June and I am to ask you to keep the appointment strictly confidential until that date.

I am, Sir,

Your obedient Servant,
Director of Personal Services

Brigadier E.H.W. Backhouse, D.L.,
  Colonel The Suffolk Regiment,
    Rowen House,
      BURY ST EDMUNDS,
      Suffolk.

The first formal public announcement of the appointment came in the following statement by the Colonel of the Regiment, which appeared in the *Regimental Gazette* for the second quarter of 1953.

Royal Colonel-in-Chief
On June 1st 1953, Her Majesty the Queen was graciously pleased to appoint Her Royal Highness, The Princess Margaret as Colonel-in-Chief The Suffolk Regiment. On that day this number of our Regimental Gazette was in the hands of the printers. It is therefore, only possible for me as Colonel of The Regiment, to express very briefly how deeply we all appreciate the conferment of this high honour. I know that all ranks, both past and present, will be filled with pride that Her Majesty has seen fit to pay the XIIth of Foot this great compliment.

All of us will look forward eagerly to the day when Her Royal Highness finds it possible to visit The Regiment and so receive the great reception that I know will await Her.

3rd June 1953
E.H.W. Backhouse
Colonel, The Suffolk Regiment.

During the next six years, until amalgamation, the Colonel-in-Chief made the following visits to the Regiment:

15 July, 1954	Her Royal Highness met families of the 1st Battalion in Dusseldorf.
25 July, 1954	Her Royal Highness attended the Old Comrades Association Reunion at the Depot and was presented with the Regimental Brooch.
23 May, 1955	Her Royal Highness presented new Colours to the 1st Battalion in Wuppertal.

1 August, 1956 Her Royal Highness visited the 1st Battalion at Roman Way Camp in Colchester.

8 June, 1958 Her Royal Highness visited the 4th Battalion at Benacre Hall, the home of the Honorary Colonel of the Battalion.

21 June, 1959 Her Royal Highness attended a service at Ely Cathedral at which the Cambridgeshire Regiment Role of Honour 1939–45 was dedicated.

The visits by the Colonel-in-Chief always gave all members of the Regiment, past and present, immense pleasure, whether they were occasions of high ceremony or simply family gatherings. It was thus a great relief, as amalgamation drew near, to learn on 4 March 1958, that the Colonel-in-Chief had been appointed by Her Majesty the Queen to continue in that Office with the new Regiment.

APPENDIX IV

COLONELS OF THE REGIMENT,

HONORARY COLONELS OF BATTALIONS,

COMMANDING OFFICERS,

ADJUTANTS, QUARTERMASTERS AND

REGIMENTAL SERGEANT MAJORS

Colonels of The Regiment:

1939–1947	Colonel W.N. Nicholson, CMG, DSO
1947–1957	Brigadier E.H.W. Backhouse, DL
1957–1959	Brigadier R.H. Maxwell, CB

Honorary Colonels of The 4th Battalion:

1946–1951	Colonel E.P. Clarke, DSO, TD, DL
1951–1953	Colonel H.R. Hooper, OBE, MC, TD, DL, JP
1953–1961	Colonel Sir Robert Gooch, Bart., DSO, DL, JP

Honorary Colonels of The Cambridgeshire Regiment:

1930–1947	Major-General R.M. Luckock, CB, CMG, DSO
1947–1957	Colonel M.C. Clayton, DSO, OBE, TD, DL
1957–1961	Brigadier E.H.W. Backhouse, DL

Commanding Officers:

1st Battalion:

1945–1946	Lieutenant-Colonel F.A. Milnes
1946–1948	Lieutenant-Colonel G.H.M. Harper
1948–1950	Lieutenant-Colonel I.L. Wight, DSO, OBE
1950–1953	Lieutenant-Colonel P.A. Morcombe, DSO, OBE
1953–1956	Lieutenant-Colonel W.A. Heal, OBE
1956–1959	Lieutenant-Colonel W.S. Bevan, OBE
1959	Lieutenant-Colonel K.M.J. Dewar, OBE

2nd Battalion:

1945–1947	Lieutenant-Colonel H.W. Dean

4th Battalion:

1947–1951	Lieutenant-Colonel J.H. Harrison, TD, MP
1951–1954	Lieutenant-Colonel K.J.K. Pye
1954–1958	Lieutenant-Colonel J.S.H. Smitherman, OBE, ERD
1958–1961	Lieutenant-Colonel G.T.O. Springfield

The Depot:

1936–1948	Major F.V.C. Pereira
1948–1951	Major J.W. Josselyn
1951–1954	Major J.C.R. Eley
1954–1956	Major C.A. Boycott, MBE
1956–1957	Major W.J. Calder
1957–1958	Major G.T.O. Springfield
1958–1959	Major R.M. Williams, MC

629 LAA Regiment RA (The Cambridgeshire Regiment) TA:

1947–1949	Lieutenant-Colonel G. Colchester, DSO, RA
1949–1952	Lieutenant-Colonel J.D. Ritchie, DSO, RA
1952–1954	Lieutenant-Colonel J.G.A. Beckett, TD, RA, DL

629 (The Cambridgeshire Regiment) Parachute Light Regiment RA, TA:

1954–1956	Lieutenant-Colonel J.G.A. Beckett, OBE, TD, RA, DL

1st Battalion, The Cambridgeshire Regiment:

1956	Lieutenant-Colonel J.G.A. Beckett, OBE. TD, DL
1956–1959	Lieutenant-Colonel W.F. Page, MC, TD
1959–1961	Lieutenant-Colonel P.D. Storie-Pugh, MBE, MC, TD

Adjutants:

1st Battalion:

1946–1947	Captain R.M. Williams, MC
1947	Captain A.C.L. Sperling, MC
1947–1948	Captain H.E.W. Wiggington
1948	Captain F. Groom
1949–1951	Captain G.C. Howgego
1951–1952	Major C.J.V. Fisher-Hoch
1952–1954	Captain H.H. Moore, The Northamptonshire Regiment
1954–1956	Captain W.C. Deller
1956–1957	Major P.D.F. Thursby
1957–1958	Captain R.M. Holman
1958–1959	Captain P.D.L. Hopper

2nd Battalion:

1946–1947	Captain A.J. Boddington

4th Battalion:

1947	Captain C.A. Boycott

1947–1950	Captain R.J. Hildesley
1950–1952	Captain P.S.W. Dean
1952–1954	Captain R.M. Williams, MC
1954–1955	Captain A.H.V. Gillmore, MC
1955–1958	Captain H.D. Sutor
1958–1960	Captain T.D. Dean
1960–1961	Captain R.G. Wilson

The Depot:

1946–1950	Captain F.J. Lockett
1950	Captain N.A.M. Balders
1950–1951	Captain H.E.W. Wiggington
1951–1954	Captain H.J. Chisnall
1954–1955	Captain R.M. Holman
1955–1957	Captain R.G. Wilson
1957–1959	Captain J.G.M. North

629 LAA Regiment RA (The Cambridgeshire Regiment) TA:

1947–1950	Captain C.G. Leppard, RA
1950–1954	Major F.H. Blake, RA

629 (The Cambridgeshire Regiment) Parachute Light Regiment, RA, TA:

1954–1956	Captain M.F.D. Henry, RA

1st Battalion The Cambridgeshire Regiment:

1956–1958	Captain J.P. Macdonald
1958–1960	Major G.C. Howgego (Training Major and Adjutant)
1960–1961	Major E.H. Morgan, MBE, MC (Training Major and Adjutant)

Quartermasters:

1st Battalion:

1946–1947	Lieutenant F.H. Wyatt
1947–1948	Major F.W. Garrard
1948–1950	Captain J. Longstaff
1950–1952	Captain H.S.R. Case
1952–1955	Lieutenant G.S. Jasper
1955–1958	Captain T.C. Warren
1958	Major H.S.R. Case, MBE
1958–1959	Major L.B. Day (The Bedfordshire & Hertfordshire Regiment)

2nd Battalion:

1946–1947	Lieutenant H.W. Goodliff

4th Battalion:

1947–1950	Major U. Dockerill
1950–1951	Major H.R. Cotton
1951–1953	Major J. Longstaff

| 1953–1958 | Major H.S.R. Case, MBE |
| 1958–1961 | Captain T.C. Warren |

The Depot:

1946–1950	Captain H.R. Cotton
1950–1951	Major J. Longstaff
1951–1955	Major H.R. Cotton, MBE, MSM
1955–1959	Captain G.S. Jasper

629 LAA Regiment RA (The Cambridgeshire Regiment) TA:

| 1947–1954 | Major J.A. Hollingsworth, RA |

629 (The Cambridgeshire Regiment) Parachute Light Regiment, RA, TA:

| 1954–1955 | |
| 1955–1956 | Major J.H. Sanders, RA |

1st Battalion The Cambridgeshire Regiment:

| 1956–1957 | Major J.H. Sanders |
| 1958–1961 | Lieutenant H.H. Norman |

Regimental Sergeant Majors:

1st Battalion:

1946–1947	RSM Tridini
1947	A/RSM Ford
1947–1948	RSM E. Isaacson
1948	A/RSM S. Winter
1949–1951	RSM B.D. Windley (The Essex Regiment)
1951–1954	RSM K.T. Duffy
1954–1958	RSM H.J. Gingell
1958–1959	RSM E.J. Hazelwood

2nd Battalion:

| 1944–1947 | RSM G.S. Jasper |

4th Battalion:

1947–1949	RSM V.H. Reeve
1949–1951	RSM E. Isaacson
1951–1952	RSM G.S. Jasper
1953–1955	RSM T.C. Warren
1955–1956	RSM A.G. Boast
1956	RSM N. McColl
1956–1959	RSM Cressey
1959–1961	RSM E.J. Hazelwood

The Depot:

1939–1947	RSM J. Chalk, MBE, MM
1947–1951	RSM G.S. Jasper
1951–1954	RSM H.J. Gingell
1954–1958	RSM K.T. Duffy
1958–1959	RSM H.J. Gingell

629 LAA Regiment RA, (The Cambridgeshire Regiment) TA:
1947–1953   RSM A.E. Bartlett
1953–1954   RSM W. Jackson
629 (The Cambridgeshire Regiment) Parachute Light Regiment, RA, TA:
1954–1956   RSM W. Jackson
1st Battalion The Cambridgeshire Regiment:
1956–1958   RSM H.H. Norman
1958–1961   RSM V. Lyon

APPENDIX V

THE TWO HUNDREDTH ANNIVERSARY

OF THE BATTLE OF MINDEN

The Minden Dinner

The Battle of Minden was fought on 1 August, 1759, and that date has ever since been celebrated by the Regiments which were there as a day on which to remember the outstanding courage and tenacity of their forbears.

On 27 July, 1959, a Dinner was held at Guildhall in the City of London, to celebrate the bicentenary of the Battle.

The Dinner was held in the presence of Her Majesty Queen Elizabeth The Queen Mother, Colonel-in-Chief, The King's Own Yorkshire Light Infantry, Her Royal Highness The Princess Margaret, Colonel-in-Chief The Suffolk Regiment and Her Royal Highness The Duchess of Gloucester, Colonel-in-Chief, The King's Own Scottish Borderers. The Queen, herself Captain-General of The Royal Regiment of Artillery and Colonel-in-Chief The Royal Welsh Fusilliers, sent Her best wishes for this memorable occasion from Canada.

The following Officers of The Regiment were present:

Brigadier R.H. Maxwell, CB,
  Colonel of the Regiment
Colonel R.H. Andrew, CBE, MC
Lieutenant-Colonel S.H. Atkins
Brigadier E.H.W. Backhouse, DL
Lieutenant-Colonel N.M.
  Barnardiston
Lieutenant C.M.J. Barnes
Lieutenant J.L. Bazalgette
Major F.C. Berrill

Major C.A. Boycott, MBE
Major K.W. Brown, TD
Major E.G.W. Browne
Lieutenant-Colonel L.J. Baker,
  MC
Major W.J. Calder
Bt Lieutenant-Colonel A.F.
  Campbell, MC
Major-General J.A. Campbell,
  DSO

Lieutenant-Colonel W.M. Campbell, DSO, MC
Major P.R.W. Carthew, OBE
Lieutenant-Colonel H. Castle-Smith
2/Lieutenant P.F. Catchpole
Colonel E.P. Clarke, DSO, TD, DL
Major W.W. Cook
Major H.R. Cotton, MBE
Lieutenant G.P.V. Creagh
Major G.S. Cubitt, TD
Colonel A.M. Cutbill, MC
Lieutenant-Colonel E.R. Daglish
Lieutenant-Colonel H.W. Dean
Major P.S.W. Dean
Major W.C. Deller
Lieutenant-Colonel K.M.J. Dewar, OBE
Major W.D.G. Fairholme
Major C.J.V. Fisher-Hoch
Major F.E. Fernie
Captain P.C. Ford
Major P.B. Forrest, MC
Lieutenant-Colonel D.U. Fraser, MBE
Colonel R.B. Freeland
Major C.M. Fyson
Brigadier H.P. Gardham, CBE
Colonel Sir Robert Gooch, Bart., DSO, DL, JP
Major-General R.E. Goodwin, CB, CBE, DSO,
Lieutenant-Colonel G.T.E. Grey
Colonel J.H. Harrison, TD, MP
Colonel W.A. Heal, OBE
Colonel A.D.R. Heyland
Captain P.D.L. Hopper
Captain A.B. Horrex, MC
Major G.C. Howgego
Captain T. Hume
Brigadier R.H. Innes-Hopkins

2/Lieutenant I.W. Jefferson
Lieutenant-Colonel A.A. Johnson, MC
Captain A.J.A. Lacy
Major D.G. Lawrence
Major H.W. Lawrence
Captain R. Le Mare
Lieutenant N.J. Lewis
Major F.J. Lockett
Major E.T. Lummis
Canon W.M. Lummis, MC
Lieutenant M.J.R. Lunn
Major R.Q. March
Major W. Mayhew
Lieutenant-Colonel K.C. Menneer
Colonel F.A. Milnes
Captain E.D.D. Money
Lieutenant-Colonel H.B. Monier-Williams, OBE, MC
Lieutenant P.W. Morton
Colonel W.N. Nicholson, CMG, DSO
Captain J.G.M. North
Colonel F.V. Oborne
Lieutenant-Colonel I.G. Owen
2/Lieutenant M.M. Orr
Lieutenant-Colonel W.F. Page, MC, TD, The Cambridgshire Regiment
Captain L.A. Palmer
Lieutenant-Colonel A. Parkin
Major R.J. Pizzey, TD
Lieutenant The Hon. T.A. Ponsonby
Major J.R.B. Prescott, MC
Major L.G.E. Pusey, TD
Brigadier E.M. Ransford, CBE
2/Lieutenant S.A.J. Rowsell
Captain A.G. Rumbelow, MBE
Brigadier V.C. Russell, DSO, MC
Lieutenant-Colonel H.F. Slade

Bt. Lieutenant-Colonel W.C.
  Smith, OBE
Colonel J.S.H. Smitherman, OBE,
  ERD, MA
Major-General H.P. Sparks, CBE,
  MC
Lieutenant-Colonel G.T.O.
  Springfield
Major J.G. Starling, MC
Captain P. Thain
Lieutenant-Colonel F.W.C.
  Thomas
Major P.D.F. Thursby

Lieutenant R.L. Trevethick
Colonel G.L.J. Tuck, CMG, DSO
Major J.W. Tyndale
Major M.H. Vinden, TD
Lieutenant-Colonel O.A. Watts
Brigadier I.L. Wight, DSO, OBE,
  DL
Major J.H. Wightwick
Major R.M. Williams, MC
Lieutenant-Colonel F.T.D. Wilson,
  OBE
Major P.G. Wilson, MC
Captain R.G. Wilson

APPENDIX VI

THE SUFFOLK REGIMENT

WAR MEMORIAL HOMES

On 1 June, 1946, a Regimental Committee under the Chairmanship of the Colonel of the Regiment, Colonel W.N. Nicholson, CMG, DSO, recommended that an appeal be launched within the Regiment and the County in order to raise funds for the creation of a war memorial in memory of those members of the Regiment who were killed in action or who died on active service during the Second World War.

It was proposed that the memorial should take two forms. Firstly, a second bronze casket containing the Roll of Honour would be added to The Cenotaph in St Mary's Church at Bury St Edmunds. And secondly, a block of flats would be built in or near Bury St Edmunds to house elderly past members of the Regiment.

Initially, the Regiment decided to aim for the target figure of £10,000. The appeal was actually launched on 21 February, 1947, with a letter to all past and present members of the Regiment and relatives of those who died. Much publicity for the appeal was given by newspapers and journals in the County.

The response was immediate and by 6 March over £4,200 had been donated. Contributions came, not only from within the Regiment, but largely from firms, organizations and individuals in the County.

Money continued to flood in throughout 1947, and by the end of the year over £6,600 had been received. The committee, now chaired by the new Colonel of the Regiment, Brigadier E.H.W. Backhouse, gave instructions for the bronze casket to be made and for the Roll of Honour to be prepared. Despite the difficulties of building in the immediate post-War years, plans were made for the construction of the War Memorial Homes.

In 1948 the Appeal Committee handed over responsibility for the War

Memorial to the Suffolk Regiment Association, within which a committee of management was established.

The Roll of Honour was dedicated at St Mary's Church on 31 July, 1949.

In January, 1950, The Marquis of Bristol made a generous gift of part of a field belonging to Vinefields Farm which overlooked The Abbey Gardens in Bury St Edmunds. It was a perfect site, facing south and close to amenities within the town. An architect was appointed and plans for the erection of a block of eight flats went ahead.

By the end of 1950, the plans had been approved, a builder had been chosen and work on the site had begun.

It was decided that the group of flats should be named Minden Close. There were to be six at ground floor level and two on the first floor and each would contain a living room, a bedroom, a kitchen and a bathroom.

Building progressed throughout 1951 and 1952 and the flats were ready for occupation on Minden Day, 1 August, 1952. Notices had gone out inviting former soldiers of the Regiment to apply for a flat and the first occupants were:

No 1: L. Cogman (Private) served from 1917 to 1922 in Gibraltar and Egypt.

No 2: E. Sillet (Corporal) served from 1900 to 1919 in South Africa, India and France.

No 3: E.H. Pike (Corporal) served from 1899 to 1912 in India and Aden.

No 4: S. Bushan (Sergeant) served from 1901 to 1925 in Malta, Egypt, India and Gibraltar.

No 5: O. Parkinson (RSM) served from 1898 to 1922 in South Africa, India, Aden and France.

No 6: E.G. Bumpstead (Corporal) served from 1904 to 1919 in France.

No 7: H. Stannard (Private) served from 1908 to 1930 in Malta, Egypt, France, Salonika, India, Gibraltar and China.

No 8: C. Crisell (Private) served from 1908 to 1930 in Malta and France.

The Homes were officially opened on Sunday, 3 May, 1953, by the Lord Lieutenant of Suffolk, Commander The Earl of Stradbroke, RN (retd). A Guard of Honour was provided by the 1st Battalion, recently returned from Malaya, and, headed by the Band and Drums of the 1st Battalion, it marched to the Homes from Gibraltar Barracks.

A General Salute was given on the arrival of the Lord Lieutenant, and after he completed the inspection, the Colonel of the Regiment made a short address in which he thanked all those who had made the War Memorial Homes possible.

The Lord Lieutenant then declared the homes open and there followed a Service of Dedication conducted by The Bishop of St Edmundsbury and Ipswich, the Right Reverend Doctor Richard Brook, DD.

Before departing, the Lord Lieutenant visited the flats and met two of the occupants, Mr E.H. Pike and Mr E.G. Bumpstead.

APPENDIX VII

BATTLE HONOURS OF THE

SUFFOLK REGIMENT

'DETTINGEN', 'MINDEN', 'SERINGAPATAM', 'INDIA', 'SOUTH AFRICA 1851–2–3', 'NEW ZEALAND', 'AFGHANISTAN 1878–80', 'SOUTH AFRICA 1899–1902'.

The Great War – 22 Battalions – 'Mons', 'LE CATEAU', 'Retreat from Mons', 'Marne 1914', 'Aisne 1914', 'La Bassée 1914', 'Givenchy 1914', 'NEUVE CHAPELLE', 'YPRES 1915, '17, '18', 'Gravenstafel', 'St Julien', 'Frezenberg', 'Bellewaarde', 'Aubers', 'Hooge 1915', 'Loos', 'SOMME 1916, '18', 'Albert 1916, '18', 'Bazentin', 'Delville Wood', 'Pozières', 'Flers-Courcelette', 'Morval', 'Thiepval', 'Le Transloy', 'Ancre Heights', 'Ancre 1916, '18', 'ARRAS 1917, '18', 'Scarpe 1917, '18', 'Arleux', 'Pilckem', 'Langemarck 1917', 'Menin Road', 'Polygon Wood', 'Poelcappelle', 'Passchendaele', 'CAMBRAI 1917, '18', 'St Quentin', 'Bapaume 1918', 'Lys', 'Estaires', 'Messines 1918', 'Hazebrouck', 'Bailleul', 'Kemmel', 'Bethune', 'Scherpenberg', 'Amiens', 'HINDENBURG LINE', 'Epèhy', 'Canal du Nord', 'Courtrai', 'Selle', 'Valenciennes', 'Sambre', 'France and Flanders 1914–18', 'Struma', 'Doiran, 1918', 'MACEDONIA 1915–18', 'Suvla', 'LANDING AT SUVLA', 'Scimitar Hill', 'Gallipoli 1915', 'Egypt 1915–17', 'GAZA', 'El Mughar', 'Nebl Samwil', 'Jerusalem', 'Jaffa', 'Tel 'Asur', 'Megiddo', 'Sharon', 'Palestine 1917–18'.

The Second World War – 'DUNKIRK 1940', 'NORMANDY LANDING', 'ODON', 'FALAISE', 'VENRAIJ', 'BRINKUM', 'North-West Europe 1940, '44–'45', 'SINGAPORE ISLAND', 'Malaya 1942', 'NORTH ARAKAN', 'IMPHAL', 'BURMA 1943–45'.

(Those honours in capital letters appeared on the Colours.)

APPENDIX VIII

BATTLE HONOURS OF THE

CAMBRIDGESHIRE REGIMENT

'SOUTH AFRICA, 1900–1901'

The Great War – 'YPRES, 1915, 1917', 'Gravenstafel', 'St Julien', 'Frezenberg', 'SOMME, 1916, 1918', 'Thiepval', 'ANCRE HEIGHTS', 'Ancre, 1916', 'PILCKEM', 'Menin Road', 'Polygon Wood', 'Broodseinde', 'Poelcappelle', 'PASSCHENDAELE', 'St Quentin', 'Rosieres', 'Lys', 'KEMMEL', 'Scherpenberg', 'AMIENS', 'Albert, 1918', 'Bapaume, 1918', 'HINDENBURG LINE', 'Epèhy', 'St Quentin Canal', 'PURSUIT TO MONS', 'FRANCE AND FLANDERS, 1915–18'.

The Second World War – 'JOHORE', 'BATU PAHAT', 'SINGAPORE ISLAND', 'MALAYA 1942'.

APPENDIX IX

THE PRESENTATION OF COLOURS TO

THE 1ST BATTALION BY HER ROYAL

HIGHNESS THE PRINCESS MARGARET,

CI, GCVO, COLONEL-IN-CHIEF THE

SUFFOLK REGIMENT ON 23 MAY, 1955

(From an article in *The Regimental Journal*)

It was not until late in April that the date for the presentation of new Colours was announced, leaving but little time for the preparations necessary for such a great event. However, much had already been done in anticipation and in a short time the barracks began to take on a new look. The Garrison Engineer and his men became much in evidence. Attractive new gates were erected, improving the entrance and replacing the old red and white barrier for so long a daily target for the MT. Perhaps less attractive to some was the new guard room, built in a few days after a year of patient waiting.

In dry intervals the gardeners prepared the beds for the appropriate red and yellow flowers and laid out a floral castle near the entrance. At the same time preliminary parades were held to select the guards, and the Band and Drums worked hard to prepare the programme of music. These preparations were not without difficulties. The exercises in the over-crowded training programme went on, and in the middle of all it was decided to resurface the square so that parades had to be held in the barracks of our neighbours, the Durham Light Infantry, themselves preparing for their farewell parade.

For the first week of preparation the weather smiled and then, up to the very day, was depressingly dull, wet, and cold with interesting variations in the form of a gale which took off the tops of the newly erected spectators' stands, and a storm of icy sleet which all but ruined the flowers put in a few hours previously.

The weather was, as usual in Wuppertal, the main worry since there could be no question of a wet weather programme – the parade had to go on whatever the day, but at least everything possible was done to keep guests dry.

By the weekend before the parade practically all was ready. Stands to seat a thousand spectators had been erected. The gymnasium was wonderfully transformed into a red carpeted dining room and anteroom ready for the luncheon with Her Royal Highness. The complicated ceremonial for the Trooping of the old Colours and the presentation of the new Colours had been mastered and those on parade were full of confidence. Best of all, the weather forecast was encouraging.

On 19 May the Colonel of the Regiment and Mrs Backhouse arrived and during the following weekend the remainder of the welcome guests from England came. The party from the Depot included Major and Mrs Boycott, Major Cotton, RSM Duffy, RSM Newman, RQMS Chenery, C/Sgt Smith, Sgt Gilbert and Sgt R.G. Smith. With them came two old members of the Regiment from the Royal Hospital, Chelsea, Sgt Smith and Corporal Kemp. For Sgt Smith it was not his first visit to Germany as he had been with the occupation forces in Cologne after the 1914–18 War. From the 4th Battalion came Major Calder, Major Vinden, CSM McGregor and CQMS Walker. From other parts of Germany came Major and Mrs Titmarsh and Captain and Mrs Gilson Taylor. Major Thursby and Major Wiggington also came.

Monday, 23 May, dawned cool but dry and even a little sunshine appeared. Whilst last-minute arrangements were being made, Brigadier Backhouse, with Lt Wilson, ADC for the Princess and Lt Ford, went to the airfield at Wahn to welcome Her Royal Highness who then drove, with British and German Police escorts, to Wuppertal. After a short rest at the house of the Commanding Officer, where she accepted a bouquet from the people of Wuppertal, the Princess drove to the gymnasium to meet the Officers of the Regiment assembled in the ante-room.

Charming in light blue, and wearing her Regimental brooch, the Princess was greeted by the Commanding Officer who presented in turn each of the Officers, only a few of whom had previously met Her Royal Highness. The Officers then moved in to the dining room where the ladies were already waiting and the Princess took her place at the top table where also sat Brigadier and Mrs Backhouse, the Commanding Officer and Mrs Heal, Brigadier and Mrs Goodwin, Brigadier Wight and Captain Deller, the Adjutant. As a fitting background to the luncheon party the old Colours were displayed on the stage, flanked by drums and silver and banked with flowers. Red and yellow roses decorated the long tables. Grace was said by the Reverend R.J.F. Mayston, Assistant Chaplain General to the Forces in Germany.

After an excellent luncheon the Princess left again for the Commanding Officer's house accompanied by Mrs Heal. Crowds thronged at the gates of the barracks to catch a glimpse of her as she drove away, and at one time her car was slowed to a walking pace.

By this time the guests and spectators for the parade were arriving in force and the stands were almost full. Among those present were His Excellency, the British Ambassador, Sir Frederick Hoyer Millar, KCMG, with the Military Attache, and Major-General and Mrs C.B. Fairbanks. It was unfortunate that the day coincided with an exercise which prevented the attendance of the Commander-in-Chief, General Sir Richard Gale, the Corps Commander, Lt-General Sir Hugh Stockwell and the Divisional Commander, Major-General Wilsey, all of whom sent their regrets. German guests included Herr Dr Straeter, Herr Schmeissing, the Ober-burgermeister of Wuppertal and other State officials. Over two thousand spectators were present to watch the Battalion form up and the old Colours march on parade for the last time. The Escort for the Colours, No 1 Guard, was commanded by Major G.R. Heyland, OBE, MC.

Shortly after three o'clock the Royal cars entered barracks and drew up at the top of the steps to the square where a red carpet led down to the dais between boxes of scarlet geraniums. The Princess alighted and, escorted by the Colonel of the Regiment, walked slowly down to the dais to be received with a Royal salute. As the first bars of the National Anthem were played the Standard was broken at the central flagstaff between the Union Jack and the Regimental flag. The Commanding Officer reported the parade and, accompanied by Brigadier Backhouse, Captain Dawnay and the ADCs, Her Royal Highness inspected the ranks whilst the Band played the 'Eton Boating Song', 'Les Huguenots' and, to the great appreciation of the German guests, 'Gold and Silver'.

When Her Royal Highness had returned to the dais and taken her seat the ceremony of trooping the old Colours began. The Band, and the Drums carrying the bugles presented to the Battalion in 1953 by the people of Bury St Edmunds, Ipswich and Sudbury, moved to the Colours in slow time to 'Scipio' and returned in quick time to 'Sons of the Brave'.

The Escort for the Colours, then under Lt F.A. Godfrey, MC, moved forward, and to the Regimental Slow March the old Colours, carried by Lt J.P. Macdonald and 2/Lt J.G.M. North, were trooped and proudly marched off parade for the last time to 'Auld Lang Syne'. It was a most dignified, impressive and moving ceremony.

After a moment's pause the drummers marched forward to pile drums for the consecration service. The new Colours, made from silk woven in East Anglia, were brought forward by RQMS Calver, BEM, and CSM Lyon. The Assistant Chaplain General with the Reverend T.W. Metcalfe, Chaplain to the Battalion, and the assisting clergy, moved forward to the centre of the square and began the consecration service, to which had been added the Regimental Prayer. When the last words of the Blessing had been pronounced the Field Officers for the Colours, Major Heyland and Major Harvey, handed the Colours to Her Royal Highness who then handed them to the Colour Party Officers, Lt J.R. Heath and Lt J.D. Churchill. The Colours were received with a general salute and marched to the centre of the Battalion.

Her Royal Highness then addressed the Battalion and said:-
'Colonel Heal, Officers, Non-Commissioned Officers and Men of the 1st Battalion The Suffolk Regiment.

It gives me very real pleasure to be with you today, and to present to you these new Colours on behalf of the Queen.

A few moments ago we watched your old Colours, proudly carried for the last time, being marched off Parade. I feel that no one could have failed to be deeply moved at that moment. They were the oldest Colours still to be carried by a unit of the British Army; and the last Colours still in use which themselves had been borne into action at the head of their Regiment. Under them the 12th Regiment of Foot, who were then called the East Suffolk Regiment, won honour and renown far across the world, in Australasia, India and in Africa. More lately, on the coast of Normandy and in the jungles of Malaya, you have built a tradition of which England may be proud.

So in sadness we bid them farewell: those symbols of service which were honoured in their day by good men and true. They carried your battle honours – but a countless thousand honours are left untold: great courage and battles innumerable, always with that spirit of disciplined service, which is the very essence of the British Army.

Today, after 106 years, new Colours take their place. After so long a time it might be thought that this would mark a change or break, in your great traditions. But of course this will not be the case. The disaster of two great wars, and the power of destruction which the mind of man has now evolved, has not blinded us to a lasting truth. That is, I think, the importance of each individual soldier. In your hands, in your bearing towards your fellow men, be it whatever race, colour or creed, can depend the future of our civilized way of life.

I commend therefore to your keeping these new Colours. I know you will guard them as your fathers guarded them, not only with valour in battle, but with resolute and quiet service in times of peace. They have been dedicated, a few minutes ago, to the ideal of Christian duty; never to be unfurled save in a just cause. For they symbolize the three-fold loyalty of the soldier: the loyalty to your Queen, loyalty to your country and loyalty to your Regiment. True to these three, I am confident that in the years to come you will add new glory to your famous name.'

Replying to Her Royal Highness the Commanding Officer said:-

'Your Royal Highness,

On behalf of all ranks, of the 1st Battalion The Suffolk Regiment, of which you are Colonel-in-Chief, may I say how tremendously proud and honoured we are that you should have presented new Colours to us today on behalf of Her Majesty The Queen.

Those old Colours, which were just marched off parade, to many of us represented all or nearly all our service in the Regiment. We were tremendously proud of them and we were sad as they went off parade. Nevertheless, Your Royal Highness, I can assure you that this Regiment and the men now serving in it will honour the new Colours and will uphold the tradition of the Regiment as they have always done in the past, and will continue to serve in Her Majesty's Army as those of yore served in it, and that the 12th of Foot will retain its high reputation wherever it may go.

Thank you, Your Royal Highness.'

The Battalion then marched past to 'Speed the Plough', and having re-formed line, advanced in Review Order. After the Royal Salute three cheers were given for the Princess. The Princess then left the dais and, smiling at the excited children who surrounded her car, drove again to the Commanding Officer's house.

Soon afterwards Her Royal Highness returned to meet His Excellency the British Ambassador and other distinguished guests, both British and German, in the Officers' Mess. After these presentations the Princess signed her photographs and the Visitors' Book, and accompanied by the Colonel of the Regiment drove once more to the gymnasium where by this time some three hundred and fifty guests were assembled for tea. Champagne was served and, with a roll of drums, the Commanding Officer proposed a toast of the new Colours.

Her Royal Highness then visited the Sergeants' Mess where the Warrant Officers and Sergeants serving with the Battalion were presented. Group photographs were taken of the Officers and the Sergeants, with the Colonel-in-Chief and the Colonel of the Regiment.

At a quarter to six Her Royal Highness smilingly drove away amid the cheers of the troops lining the road from barracks. Brigadier Backhouse and the Commanding Officer also accompanied the Royal party to the airfield to bid farewell to the Princess.

So ended the first visit of our Colonel-in-Chief to the 1st Battalion, and the parade for the presentation of new Colours, described in the press with truth as 'A brilliant ceremonial' and a lasting credit to those who took part.

Later that evening at a happy celebration in the Officers' Mess, a silver salver was presented to the Commanding Officer, both in honour of the occasion and to mark the appreciation of his Officers.

To provide a proper end to such a day the Sergeants' Mess gave a Presentation of Colours Ball, inviting all the Officers and guests, with their ladies, as well as many friends from the Garrison. Many happy and convivial reunions took place and under the new Colours, set on the stage in the gymnasium, was a magnificent cake in the shape of a castle, with the Regimental badge, made specially for the day.

Again the Colours were toasted before being marched off at midnight to the Officers' Mess.

It was a great day for the Regiment, one which will live in the memories of those who were present.

APPENDIX X

MAJOR TROPHIES WON

BETWEEN 1946 AND 1959

1st Battalion:

1947	Palestine	2nd Infantry Brigade Rifle Championship
1950	Malaya	Far East Land Forces Inter-Unit Hockey Championship
1951	Malaya	Malaya Command Major Units Rifle Championship
1953	Trieste	BETFOR Rifle Championship
1954	Trieste	BETFOR Hockey Championship
1955	Trieste	BETFOR Athletics Championship
1955	BAOR	Rhine Army Shooting Championship Shield
1957	Cyprus	District Inter-Unit Rifle Championship

4th Battalion:

1952	Secretary of State for War's Cup for Individual Rifle: Bisley (Sergeant Spalding)
1953	East Anglian District TA Team Shooting Championship
1953	TARA Decentralized Competitions:
	Lord-Lieutenants' Shield
	High Sheriffs' Shield
	Imperial Tobacco Cup
	Young Soldiers' Match
1958	161st Infantry Brigade Shooting Championship
1959	161st Infantry Brigade Shooting Championship
1959	54th (East Anglian) Division Shooting Championship

The Depot:

1949	East Anglian District Minor Units Shooting Championship
1950	East Anglian District Minor Units Shooting Championship
1953	East Anglian District Athletics Championship
1954	East Anglian District Rifle Team Championship
1955	Eastern Command Minor Units Hockey Championship
1955	East Anglian District Rifle Team Championship
1956	East Anglian District Minor Units Shooting Championship

APPENDIX XI

REGIMENTAL AFFILIATIONS

The XIIth of Foot served for many years in the Nineteenth Century in Australia and New Zealand and built up a considerable reputation. It was probably from this that stemmed the affiliations early in the Twentieth Century with Regiments from both Australia and New Zealand.

In the period covered by this history, the connection long established with the 12th Battalion (The Launceston Regiment), Australian Infantry and the Auckland Regiment (The Countess of Ranfurly's Own) of New Zealand was maintained.

The link was always somewhat tenuous but nonetheless warm and it thrived largely out of the exchange of letters between the Colonels of the Regiments, further cemented by occasional visits and exchanges of greetings at Christmas or on Minden Day.

Colonel C.F. Seaward, DSO, MC, ED, Colonel of the Auckland Regiment, visited England in 1950 and spent some time at the Depot. He attended the Past and Present Officers' Dinner in London as the Guest of Honour and in the company of Brigadier Backhouse, visited the 4th Battalion at camp.

Following his visit, Colonel Seaward wrote a very interesting piece in the *Regimental Gazette*, published in 1951, providing as he said 'A brief review of prospects for members of the Regiment' contemplating emigrating to New Zealand at the end of their service. He must have been impressed by those of the Regiment he met for the tone of the article was extremely persuasive!

It seems clear that the Australian Army was going through a considerable reorganization in the post-War years. The name of the allied Regiment there changed on several occasions. In 1950 it altered from the 12th Battalion (The Launceston Regiment), Australian Infantry to the 12th/

40th Infantry Battalion (The Tasmania Regiment). Then in 1952 it was renamed simply the 12th Infantry Battalion (The Tasmania Regiment), and yet again later in that year it became the 12th Infantry Battalion (1st Battalion, The Tasmania Regiment). It finally settled down in 1953 as the 12th Infantry Battalion (The Launceston Regiment).

In 1953 a visit to New Zealand by Lieutenant-Colonel A.T. Edgar, MBE, a rubber planter in Selangor in Malaya and close friend of the 1st Battalion while on active service there, led to his publishing an article in the *Regimental Gazette* which described very effectively the current organization of the Auckland Regiment and clearly highlighted the close interest taken by that Regiment in the Suffolk Regiment.

In April, 1953, the Auckland Regiment received its Charter (the equivalent to the granting of the Freedom of a Borough or City in the United Kingdom) from the Mayor of Auckland and later in 1953 the Depot at Bury St Edmunds had the pleasure of entertaining Corporal Mackrill of the Auckland Regiment for a few days, he being in England as part of the New Zealand contingent at the Coronation celebrations.

In 1954 Her Majesty The Queen and His Royal Highness The Duke of Edinburgh made a tour of Australiasia and included a visit to Tasmania. The 12th Battalion (The Launceston Regiment) provided a Guard of Honour at Launceston airport for the Queen's departure and the occasion was described by the Commanding Officer of the Battalion, Lieutenant-Colonel M.L. Fotheringham, ED, in an article which he wrote for the *Regimental Gazette*.

The Officers of the Suffolk Regiment made gifts of a silver cup to both of the Allied Regiments in 1954. The cups were engraved with the Regimental Badges of the Regiments and a suitable inscription.

In 1956 Colonel Seaward, DSO, MC, ED, Colonel of the Auckland Regiment, retired after forty-two years service, almost all of it in one capacity or another with the Auckland Regiment. A congratulatory message was sent by Brigadier Backhouse on behalf of the Officers of the Suffolk Regiment.

Commanding Officers of the Launceston Regiment changed in 1956 with Lieutenant-Colonel Fotheringham ED, handing over to Lieutenant-Colonel B.H. Travers, OBE.

In 1958 an interesting ceremony took place at Port Arthur in Tasmania. In the years 1856–1860 when the XIIth of Foot was stationed there, it was a convict settlement and local history has it that on one occasion the Band of the XIIth of Foot played a concert to an audience largely composed of convicts! To commemorate this occasion The Band of the Royal Military College, Duntroon staged a Band Concert on the same site but with holiday-makers providing the audience. To maintain the link with the past, a detachment of all ranks of the 12th Battalion (The Launcestion Regiment) was also on parade. The Honorary Colonel of the Battalion, Colonel G.A.D. Youde, MC, and the Commanding Officer led the detachment.

It was learned in 1958, that Lieutenant-Colonel B.H. Travers, OBE, had handed over command of the Battalion to Lieutenant-Colonel L.J. Haydon and that in 1960, the centenary year of the Battalion, it was to be granted the Freedom of Launceston.

As amalgamation for the Suffolk Regiment drew near, it was pleasing to know that the affiliation with these two Regiments was to continue with the 1st East Anglian Regiment.

INDEX

Notes:
1. To avoid complicating the index the ranks of officers of the Suffolk Regiment and the Cambridgeshire Regiment and of other officers who served with those Regiments have been omitted.
2. In one or two cases where familiar names occur very frequently in the text I have deliberately omitted them from the index believing that their inclusion would serve no useful purpose. They can be located on the maps.

Aberdeen Camp, 146, 149, 151, 153
Abrahams, Sgt R., 32
Addis, LCpl B.R., 236
Adelphi Forest, 150, 158, 167
Ainger, WOI C.A., 238
Akaki, 164
Alamein Camp, 14, 17, 18, 21
Alamein, HMS, 158
Aldous, Brig J.R.T., 204
Alexandria, 9
Aliki Camp, 34, 35, 36, 37, 38, 39
Allan, L.W., 103, 108, 120, 125
Allen, R.M., 17
Amman, 16
Amies, Pte, 187
Amritsar, 26, 27, 29, 30, 31
Andrew, R.H., 249
Ansell, Pte B.V., 235
Anstee, Lt-Col G.A., 174, 177
Antenbring, CSM A., 31, 32
Apthorp, D.P., 17
Archer, Sgt T., 238
Ashdown, Sgt J.A., 60, 64, 235, 237
Aspinall, Sgt, 126
Athalassa Range, 155
Athens, 35, 37, 38, 39
Athroll, CSgt R., 32
Atkins, S.H., 249
Atkinson, Sgt, 104
Ayia Marina, 167
Ayia Varvara, 159

Backhouse, E.H.W., 33, 99, 111, 112, 142, 154, 175, 180, 181, 182, 183, 184, 185, 191, 193, 194, 203, 205, 209, 212, 221, 223, 224, 229, 240, 241, 242, 245, 249, 252, 258, 259, 266
Baggaley, J.R., 226

Bailey, CSM E.H., 207, 209, 238
Bailey, Cpl S.J., 81, 86, 235
Baker, Brig G.H., 146
Baker, L.J., 249
Balders, N.A.M., 179, 235, 246
Barbirolli, Sir John, 100
Barnardiston, N.M., 249
Barnes, C.M.J., 249
Barrett, Sgt, 178
Bartlett, RSM A.E., 218, 248
Bassovizza Ranges, 104, 105, 111
Batang Berjuntai, 84
Bates, CSM C., 126, 146, 158
Battle Royal, 117, 121
Batu Anam, 62
Batu Arang, 57, 58
Batu Caves, 78
Bazalel Street, Jerusalem, 18
Bazalgette, J.L., 132, 249
Beaumont, Sgt, 223
Beckett, J.G.A., 217, 218, 219, 220, 238, 245
Bedford-Roberts, J.G., 11
Bekok, 61, 62
Benn, M.J., 81
Bennington, Pte, 20
Berrill, F.C., 249
Bethlehem, 19, 20, 22
Bevan, W.S., 83, 94, 103, 108, 109, 133, 134, 143, 145, 157, 163, 165, 169, 193, 196, 230, 238, 244
Bird, P.B., 92, 238
Black, F., 67
Blake, F.H., 220, 246
Blaxland, Maj-Gen A.B., 27
Bliss, M.W., 32
Boast, CSM A.G., 9
RQMS, 86

RSM, 210, 212, 247
Boddington, A.J., 30, 31, 32, 245
Bonsor, Sgt N., 32
Borkenburg Training Area, 124, 127, 132
Borrodaile, Brig H.A., 105, 110
Boucher, Brig V., 103
Bourne, Lieut-Gen Sir Geoffrey, 155
Bower, Lieut-Gen Sir Roger, 157, 161, 169
Boycott, C.A., 8, 9, 12, 103, 109, 187, 188, 189, 192, 201, 237, 245, 249, 258
Bracey, Sgt J., 32
Bradshaw, Sgt, 56
Brashaw, J.R.L., 226
Brassell, Rev K.W., 188, 191
Briggs, Lieut-Gen Sir Harold, 58, 60
Brinkley, W.H., 100, 103, 105, 106, 109, 120, 145
Briscoe, Capt R.G., 199, 218, 221, 223
Bristol, The Marquis of, 253
Britten, C.E., 103, 120
Brock, Sgt, 212
Broga, 56, 59, 71, 80
Brown, C.A., 32
Brown, G.L., 211, 214
Brown, K.W., 249
Brown, L.S.L., 226
Brown, Pte, 225
Browne, E.G.W., 249
Bryant, CSM, 221, 222
Bukit Darah Estate, 67, 70, 71, 74, 76, 77
Bukit Prang Estate, 67, 70, 71, 76, 87
Bullen, CSM, 17
Bunbury, Brig F.R.St.P., 151, 167
Bunkall, J.D., 217
Burke, Cfmn, REME, 20, 235
Butler, Brig M.A.H., 148

Caesarea, 16
Cairo, 6, 8, 11, 12
Calder, W.J., 40, 158, 192, 195, 209, 210, 211, 237, 245, 249, 258
Calver, CSgt A.W., 237
  CSM, 103
  RQMS, 143, 149, 260
Camp 87E, 14, 17
Camp K, 154, 159, 160
Campbell, A.F., 36, 54, 162, 236, 249
Campbell, J.A., 249
Campbell, W.M., 250
Carey, QMSI, 187
Carpenter, Sgt, 187
Carthew, P.R.W., 250
Case, H.S.R., 63, 83, 84, 86, 196, 208, 210, 214, 237, 246, 247
Casey, M.P., 81, 211
'Cassandra', 81

Castle-Smith, H., 250
Catchpole, A.K., 87, 90, 93, 187, 190
Catchpole, L.E.A., 203, 205
Catchpole, P.F., 159, 161, 250
Cazenove, Brig A. de L., 31
Chalk, RSM J., 33, 236, 247
Challis, CSgt, 223
Chamberlain, D.A., 90
Chamberlain, Sgt P., 32
Champion, R.H., 129, 132, 133
Channon, K.A., 32
Chaplin, Pte, 148
Chapman, 2Lt, 167
Chapman, CSM, 222
Charrington, G.F.N., 62, 237
Chater, Brig R., 218
Chatten, Cpl, 130
Chenery, CSM, 103, 109
  RQMS, 258
Cheras Road Cemetery, 59, 67, 76, 93
Cheras, 93
Chisholm, Sgt R., 32
Chisnall, H.J., 125, 132, 135, 146, 149, 156, 157, 160, 183, 186, 246
Churchill, J.D., 126, 130, 195, 239, 260
Clarke, E.P., 203, 205, 206, 244, 250
Clarke, P.D.A., 203, 205
Clarke, Sgt, 202, 204
Clayton, M.C., 216, 219, 221, 222, 244
Clegg, CSgt J., 32
Clementi-Smith, P.S., 83
Coad, Maj-Gen B.A., 113
Cobbold, A.G.B., 94, 165
Colchester, G., 216, 217, 245
Cole, AQMS J., REME, 21, 235
Cole, Pte, 148
Collen, Brig K.H., 146
Collen, CSM, 63, 83, 94, 103, 109
Collet-White, Brig H.E., 194
Connolly, QMSI, 185
Cook, W.W., 36, 40, 54, 250
Cornish, Pte, 160
Cotton, H.R., 33, 176, 181, 183, 186, 189, 190, 192, 205, 238, 246, 247, 250, 258
Cox, Sgt A.F., 237
Crabtree, H., 9
Creagh, G.P.V., 250
Cressey, RSM, 215, 247
Crowe, 2 Lieut, 90
Cubitt, G.S., 202, 203, 250
Cunliffe, CSM, 31
Cunningham, Gen Sir Alan, 22
Cutbill, A.M., 184, 191, 250

Daglish, E.R., 250
Daily Mirror, 81
Dalhousie, 27

Damascus Gate, 22
Darling, Maj-Gen K.T., 164
Day, L.B., 165, 246
Dean, H.W., 27, 30, 31, 32, 179, 245, 250
Dean, P.S.W., 204, 205, 207, 220, 221, 223, 246, 250
Dean, T.D., 134, 213, 215, 246
Deller, W.C., 40, 103, 104, 106, 120, 125, 134, 224, 236, 245, 250, 258
Demetriou, Georghios, 152, 153
Dempsey, Gen Sir Miles, 12
Denning, Lieut-Gen Sir Reginald, 180
Devy, J.C., 40, 54, 63, 237
Dewar, K.M.J., 30, 31, 32, 72, 77, 83, 84, 86, 88, 92, 94, 103, 107, 108, 109, 157, 165, 169, 233, 234, 238, 244, 250
Dhavlos, 156, 157, 158
Dheftera, 162, 164
Dhenia, 159
Dighenis, 138
Dilwara, HMT, 35, 41, 54, 137, 144, 169, 232
Dina Camp, 29
Dingkil, 67, 90
Dockerill, U., 203, 246
Dorsten Training Area, 120
Doyle, Brig J.R.I., 224, 226
Drake, W., 32
Drakos, Markos, 140, 151
Drew, LCpl L.G., 237
  Sgt, 125
  CSM, 157
Duffy, CSM K.T., 17, 33
  RSM, 72, 76, 83, 93, 94, 102, 103, 110, 187, 189, 192, 195, 236, 247, 258
Dulton, Pte, 148
Dunne, Sgt J.P., 62, 83, 237
Durrant, G.R., 213

Edgar, Lieut-Col A.T., 266
Edis, CSM, 9
Edwards, Pte J.O., 235
Eliot, M.G., 144, 145, 155, 239
El Jira, 14
Elliott, Sgt G., 32
Ely, J.C.R., 181, 183, 186, 187, 245
Emmerson, Sgt, 222
Empire Parkeston, HMT, 102
Empire Test, HMT, 35, 39
Erskine, Lieut-Gen Sir George, 182
Evans, Sgt R., 90, 125, 237, 238
  CSgt, 133
  CSM, 146, 157, 165, 233
Eylenja, 162

Facey, Pte, 178
Fairholme, W.D.G., 113, 165, 183, 232, 250

Famagusta, 141, 154
Farmer, R.L., 91
Farrow, LCpl, 185
Fayid, 6, 7, 12, 13
Fenner, CSM, 102, 103, 109
Fernie, F.E., 225, 250
Ferozepore, 26, 28, 29, 30, 31, 32
Field, L., 63, 237
Firbank, Maj-Gen C.L., 132, 192
Fisher-Hoch, C.J.V., 63, 65, 83, 165, 166, 211, 214, 237, 245, 250
Foot, Sir Hugh, 156, 161, 163, 169
Ford, P.C., 250, 258
Ford, A/RSM, 247
Formations:
  Division, 1st Infantry, 14, 16, 36
  Division, 2nd Infantry, 115, 117, 121, 123, 124, 127, 128, 129
  Division, 3rd Infantry, 3, 8, 9, 12, 14, 130
  Division, 16th Airborne, 219, 220
  Division, 54th (East Anglian) Infantry, 212, 213
  Brigade, 1st Guards, 16, 163
  Brigade, 2nd Guards, 55, 57, 66
  Brigade, 2nd Infantry, 8, 14, 16, 17, 19, 36, 41
  Brigade, 4th Guards, 126, 129
  Brigade, 5th Infantry, 129
  Brigade, 6th Infantry, 115, 118, 121, 128, 129, 135, 136
  Brigade, 8th Infantry, 13, 14
  Brigade, 16th Independent Parachute, 148
  Brigade, 18th Infantry, 66, 76, 84, 87
  Brigade, 26th Gurkha Infantry, 61
  Brigade, 50th Independent, 146, 151, 164, 169
  Brigade, 161st Independent Infantry, 202, 208
  Brigade, 161st Infantry, 212, 224
  Brigade, 162nd Independent Infantry, 208, 220
  Brigade, 162nd Infantry, 222
  Brigade Group, 23rd British Independent, 29
  Brigade Group, 24th Independent, 103, 105, 110
Forrest, P.B., 165, 189, 234, 236, 238, 250
Forsythe, J.A., 226
Fotheringham, Lieut-Col M.L., 266
Fowler, Maj H., 180
Fowler, LCpl H.K., 150, 151
  A/Cpl, 238
Fowler, CSgt R., 125, 237
Franklin, P.H.A.L., 120
Fraser, D.U., 130, 135, 142, 143, 250
Fraser's Hill, 76

Freeland, R.B., 250
Freeman-Taylor, Col R.P., 180, 181, 184, 185, 187
French, CSgt R., 32
French, RQMS V., 32
Fyson, C.M., 250

Gale, Gen Sir Richard, 123
Garbett, Dr Cyril, Archbishop of York, 82
Gardham, H.P., 250
Garrard, Cpl A.F., 239
Garrard, F.W., 17, 236, 246
Garwood, Sgt, 184
Gaught, Sgt D., 204, 207
Gaza, 14
George Town, 53, 95, 96, 99
Georgie, HMT, 54
Gilbert, Sgt V.G., 143, 149, 156, 238, 258
Gillett, Sgt, 223
Gillmore, A.H.V., 69, 209, 210, 211, 237, 246
Gingell, CSM H.J., 17, 37, 54
    RSM, 110, 120, 123, 125, 134, 146, 157, 161, 183, 186, 195, 196, 236, 239, 247
Gleeson, Sgt, 102
Goddard, CSgt, 206
Godfrey, F.A., 89, 237, 259
Gooch, Sir Robert, 193, 201, 208, 209, 210, 213, 244, 250
Goodford, C.O., 211, 212
Goodliff, H.W., 30, 32, 246
Goodwin, R.E., 99, 121, 123, 125, 126, 128, 130, 131, 135, 136, 186, 238, 239, 250, 258
Gough Barracks, 26, 28, 29, 31
Grain, R., 217
Greenwood, Pte, 187
Grey, G.T.E., 251
Grivas, George, 138, 151, 152, 156
Groom, F., 245
Gurdan, J., 32
Gurney, Brig C.H., 204
Gurney, Sir Henry, 22, 76, 80
Gutteridge, Pte, 65

Hagana, 4
Haifa, 10, 15
Hales, S.N., 31
Hall, R., 224
Haltern Training Area, 127
Hambling, ACpl B.R., 236
Hammersley, R., 212
Hampden, Brig-Gen the Viscount, 174
Hands, L.R., 88, 237
Harding, Gen Sir John, 56
    Field-Marshal, 146, 155, 184
Harding, Maj-Gen R.P., 192, 193, 213

Harding Barracks, 99, 117, 118, 120, 123, 135
Hare, Rt Hon John, 151, 195, 229
Harper, G.H.M., 13, 15, 17, 36, 100, 236, 244
Harris, Sgt, 164
Harris, Cpl, 59
Harrison, J.H., 100, 192, 201, 203, 205, 206, 245, 250
Harvey, H.C., 109, 120, 125, 135, 260
Haydon, Lieut-Col L.J., 267
Hayes, Maj-Gen E.C., 180
Hazelwood, Sgt E.J., 185
    CSM, 135, 146
    RSM, 161, 165, 215, 247
Heal, W.A., 40, 54, 63, 97, 100, 102, 103, 109, 113, 120, 125, 128, 130, 133, 168, 195, 232, 237, 244, 250
Heath, J.R., 126, 260
Hebron, 23
Hedley, Maj-Gen R.C.O., 67, 74
Heining, Capt, 32
Hendy, Sgt A., 236
Henry, M.F.D., 220, 246
Hetherington, P.S., 204
Heyland, A.D.R., 250
Heyland, G.R., 125, 129, 134, 238, 259, 260
Hildesley, R.J., 30, 31, 32, 202, 203, 204, 246
Hill, J., 32
Hill, 2Lieut, 127
Hitchen, Drum Major, 159, 233
Hohne Ranges, 111
Holben, Band Master G.A., 133, 166, 233
Holdworthy, Brig A.W.W., 27
Hollingsworth, J.A., 247
Holman, R.M., 157, 165, 187, 189, 191, 245, 246
Hookham-Miller, D.E., 64, 65
Hooper, H.R., 206, 208, 244
Hopking, H.R., 179, 185
Hopkins, C., 189
Hopper, P.D.L., 86, 94, 165, 234, 238, 245, 250
Horrex, A.B., 81, 85, 94, 196, 237, 250
Hospice of Notre Dame de France, 22
Howell, C.J., 9
Howgego, G.C., 54, 63, 183, 185, 224, 226, 236, 237, 245, 246, 250
Hudson, V., 30
Hume, T., 250
Humpage, ACpl F.B., 236
Hurley, Band Master W., 205
Hutchings, CSM, 94
Hyde, Maj, 225

Ibans, 45, 68, 72, 77, 89, 91, 92, 93

Ingle, F.D., 134, 146, 155, 157, 239
Innes-Hopkins, R.H., 250
Irgun Zvei Leumi, 5, 16
Isaacson, RSM E., 17, 204, 205, 206, 247
Isdud, 14
Isherwood, 2Lieut, 149
Ismailia, 10

Jackson, Gen Sir Henry C., 174
Jackson, RSM W., 218, 221, 248
Jacobs, Band Master J.D., 218
Jaffa Gate, 22
Jasper, G.S., 27, 30, 32, 94, 103, 109, 120,
    176, 178, 179, 192, 206, 246, 247
Jenderam, 68, 83
Jepson, F.S., 32
Jerusalem, 5, 6, 8, 14, 17, 18, 19, 20, 21
Jhelum, 26, 29
Johnson, A.A., 250
Johnson, Pte, 82
Jones, Brig C.P., 19, 38, 41
Jones, CSM, 146, 149, 158, 165
Jones, Sgt, 163
Josselyn, J.W., 175, 176, 177, 179, 181, 245

Kachau, 58
Kakopetria, 145, 146, 147, 148, 149, 150,
    151, 152, 168
Kambia, 154, 165, 167, 168
Kambos, 167
Kampong Sungei Long, 56, 81
Katamon Quarter, 19
Keatley, W.H., 223
Keeble, CSM L., 9, 54, 63, 83, 94
Keeble, P.A.J., 32
Kefar Etsyon, 20
Keightley, Gen Sir Charles, 84, 95
Kelly, J.N., 40, 56, 58, 236, 237
Kelly, Cpl T.D., 187
    Sgt, 233, 238
Kemp, R.A.F., 209, 211, 213, 214
Kendrew, Maj-Gen D.A., 147, 154, 163
Kennington, Pte, 192
Kent, HRH the Duchess of, 203
Kent, P., 205
Kerr, CSgt, 204
Kerridge, CSM, 83, 94, 102, 103, 165
Khartoum, 12
Killick, Pte L.G., 71, 235
King, Cpl B., 150, 151
    A/Sgt 238
Kingston, CSM S.C., 17, 37, 237
Kinrara, 77
Klang, 76, 84, 86, 87, 90
Knight, Pte R., 238
Kong Har, 92
Kranji Military Cemetery, 95

Kuala Kubu Bahru, 56, 57, 77, 84, 85, 87
Kuala Selangor, 67
Kykko Camp, 140, 153, 154, 156, 158, 160,
    164, 167, 168, 169
Kykko Monastery, 162
Kyrenia, 138, 141, 154, 156
Kythrea, 162, 163, 164

Labis, 62
Lacey, A.J.A., 250
La-Frennais, CSM J., 32
Lahore, 24, 25, 27, 28, 29
Lake Timsah, 10, 11, 23
Lambert, Brig W.H., 84, 89
Larman, Pte B., 235
Laver, Cpl D., 91
Lawrence, D.G., 250
Lawrence, H.P., 30, 31
Lawrence, H.W., 250
Lawrence, Sgt, 143
Lawrie, J.C., 210, 211, 213, 215
Lawson, Sgt C.R., 238
Leach, O.K., 36, 39, 54, 63, 68, 202
Leaning, L.N., 214
Lee, A.H., 222, 226
Lefka, 139, 146, 149, 151
Le Mare, R., 250
Leppard, C.G., 246
Lewis, Pte F.L., 78, 235
Lewis, N.J., 250
Lewis, W.G.G., 214
Lieu Kon Kim, 52, 57, 69, 73, 80, 87, 88
Limassol, 145, 169
Ling, Sgt, 184
Lister, Brig D., 167
Lister, Sgt, 77
Livermore, W.L., 218
Lockett, F.J., 33, 84, 94, 105, 106, 124, 128,
    146, 176, 178, 179, 238, 246, 250
Longmore, Brig J.A., 174
Long Pin, 85
Longstaff, J., 37, 54, 179, 181, 246, 247
Loveday, CSM, 120, 165
Luckock, Maj-Gen R.M., 174, 216, 244
Lummis, E.T., 91, 93, 94, 104, 146, 149,
    157, 238, 250
Lummis, Reverend W.M., 181, 182, 188,
    250
Lunn, M.J.R., 250
Lyon, CSM V.G., 120, 132, 134, 157, 165
    RSM, 223, 226, 248, 260
Lythrodhonda, 162
Lyttelton, Rt Hon Oliver, 80

Macdonald, J.P., 107, 125, 130, 143, 221,
    223, 246, 259
Macdonald, SSI, 159

Mackrill, Cpl, 266
Macmillan, Lieut-Gen G.H.A., 19, 22
Mafraq, 16
Magpie, HMS, 108
Makarios, Archbishop, 138
Makhaeras Forest, 161, 162
Mallows, LCpl, F.T.C., 92, 235
Malyon, Pte, 122, 129
Mapey, E.L.V., 225
March, R.Q., 250
Marjoram, Sgt, 191
Marriott, B., 152, 153
Marsh, R.M., 15, 17, 204, 205
Martin, Pte E.L., 236
Martin, W.J., 77, 82, 83, 238
Maxwell, R.H., 154, 168, 191, 194, 196,
    213, 229, 230, 231, 232, 233, 236, 244,
    249
Mayes, E.E., 183
Mayhew, W., 236, 250
Mayhew, CSM, 109, 120
McColl, CSM N., 103, 109, 120, 125, 135,
    238
    RSM, 212, 247
McDowell, I.D., 17, 21
McGreggor, Sgt, 202, 204
    CSM, 258
McIlwaine, G.P., 31
McLellen, R.D., 31
McNally, Cpl, 65
Meacock, Cpl R., 72
Meade, Major W., 176
Meanee Barracks, 96, 100, 102
Measherim Quarter, 22
Meneer, K.C., 27, 250
Meniko, 159
Mermagen, R.P.H., 143, 147
Metaxa Square, 155
Metcalfe, Reverend T.W., 110, 112, 122,
    135, 149, 165, 166, 260
Meyer, J.S., 32
Miles, CSM, 83, 94
Millen, C.R.W.A., 204, 205
Miller, Drum Major, 40
Mills, B.G.H., 156, 157, 159
Mills, Pte R.A., 235
Milnes, F.A., 9, 12, 13, 33, 100, 175, 244,
    250
Mitchell, Sgt J., 32
Mitchenall, Band Master, A., 74, 182
Mitsero, 154, 160, 161, 164, 165, 167, 168
Moascar Garrison, 7, 10, 11, 13
Moffitt, H.N., 77, 237
Monchen-Gladbach, 111, 132
Money, E.D.D., 250
Monier-Williams, H.B., 177, 250

Montgomery, Field-Marshal Viscount, 13
Mooltan, SS, 32
Moore, H.H., 83, 94, 103, 106, 109, 245
Moore, Pte R., 76, 235
Moore, CSM, 75
Morcombe, P.A., 63, 83, 91, 94, 99, 102,
    237, 238, 244
Morgan, E.H., 69, 81, 83, 85, 94, 133, 226,
    237, 239, 246
Morgan, CSM, W., 9, 13
Morling, CSgt H., 237
Morphou, 139, 145, 146, 147, 148, 152
Morris, J.Y., 143
Morris, Lieut, 207
Morton, P.W., 195, 250
Mott, Band Master C.B., 218
Mount Kitsi, 37
Mount of Olives, 20
Mount Parnis, 35, 37
Mowle, Sgt D., 102, 126
Moyes, CSM, 165
Mullock, D., 127
Myhill, Cpl, 187

Napier Barracks, 24, 25, 26, 27, 29
Nathanya, 10, 14, 16, 19
Nazareth, 10
Nee Soon Transit Camp, 54
Nelson Lines, 7, 10, 11, 13
Neumarkt, 112, 113
Nevassa, HMT, 144
Neville, Brig C.A.R., 121
Newell, C.L.D., 238
Newett, Sgt, 133
Newman, CSM, 178
    RSM, 258
Nichols, Capt, 183
Nichols, CSgt, 233
Nicholson, W.N., 2, 33, 99, 174, 175, 181,
    191, 244, 250, 252
Nobbs, Pte D., 57, 235
Norman, H.H., 94, 120, 132, 135, 221, 223,
    225, 226, 247, 248
Norman, Sgt L., 32
North, J.G.M., 125, 150, 239, 246, 250, 259
Norton, Venerable H.R., 182, 188
Norwood, Pte, 82

Oborne, F.V., 250
Ogg, CSgt, 184
Oldham, J.H., 202, 203
O'Leary, CSgt J., 32
Olympus, 138
Operation Alka-Selza, 69
Operation Blackbird, 152
Operation Blast, 59

Operation Bullfinch, 152
Operation Churchman, 87, 89
Operation Dunmow, 61
Operation Jackpot, 59
Opertion Lemon, 56
Operation Matchbox, 161
Orange-Broomhead, F.M., 32
O'Reilly, M.D., 77, 81, 83, 94
Orounda, 162, 164
Orr, M.M., 158, 250
Osborne-Smith, Colonel R.E., 187, 190
Overloon, 130
Owen, I.G., 250

Page, W.F., 180, 193, 217, 220, 221, 225,
    245, 250
Palmer, L.A., 40, 184, 185, 238, 250
Pardess Hanna, 6, 14, 16, 17
Parkin, A., 54, 63, 83, 237, 250
Paton, Brig C.M., 180
Patten, E.J.K., 209
Payne, Pte L.R., 57, 234
Pearce, Pte W.G., 234
Peat, W.J.B., 167, 233
Peck, WOII, 178
Penny, CSM, 83
Pensotti, G., 149
Pensotti, M., 82
Perachorio, 164
Pereira, F.V.C., 33, 170, 174, 175, 176, 179,
    245
Peristerona, 162, 164, 167
Peters, Band Master D.E., 225
Pickering, CSgt J., 32
Piraeus, 34, 35, 36, 38
Pizzey, R.J., 250
Pollen, CSM, 211
Ponsonby, Maj-Gen Sir John, 182
Ponsonby, the Hon T.A., 62, 250
Pope, Sgt, 233
Port Dickson, 53, 81, 84
Porter, Sgt L., 32
Port Said, 23, 40, 54
Pratt, CSgt R.H.H., 149, 237
Prescott, J.R.B., 250
Price, LCpl W.J., 70, 71, 237
Pringle, CSM, 83
Punjab, 24, 27, 28, 30, 31
Pusey, L.G.E., 203, 205, 250
Putlos Ranges, 132
Pye, K.J.K., 16, 17, 18, 100, 184, 206, 208,
    209, 239, 245
Pye, Brig R.J.K., 66
Pyroi, 161, 164

Quassasin, 23
Qastina, 6, 14

Race, Pte A.E., 237
Ramplin, CSM J., 17, 37, 54, 63, 186, 189
Randall, CSM, 17, 38, 54, 63
Ransford, E.M., 237, 250
Rawang, 74, 78, 83, 84, 87
Rees, Sgt, 79
Reeve, RSM V.H., 201, 203, 204, 247
Rehoveth, 14
Rich, P.S., 31, 32
Richards, P.F.A., 31, 32
Richardson, CSgt B.T.W., 237
    CSM, 146, 155, 157
Ricketts, Maj-Gen A.H.G., 146
Ridout, Sgt, 105
Rinder, Sgt F.R., 187, 190, 238
Ritchie, J.D., 217, 218, 245
Roberts, P.D., 75
Robinson, Maj-Gen G.St.G., 180
Robinson, CSM, 120, 135, 143
Roman Way Camp, 137, 142, 144
Rome, Maj-Gen F.D., 219
Romema, 18
Rose, V.H.F., 209
Rossetti Barracks, 96, 99, 102
Rowsell, S.A.J., 250
Royal Norfolk Regiment, 2, 142, 194, 196,
    201, 229, 230, 231, 232, 234
Rumbelow, A.G., 250
Russell, V.C., 250
Russell, CSgt, 202

Sach, D.S., 211
Sainsbury, Sgt, 233
St Pauls, 22
Salonika, 35, 36, 38, 39, 40, 41, 54
Salt Lake Camp, 29
Samaria, SS, 23, 35
Sanders, J.H., 220, 221, 223, 247
Schmelz, 98, 99, 104, 112
Scott, A.J., 107
Scott, K., 217, 218, 222
Seaman, Sgt R., 32
Seaward, Col C.F., 178, 265, 266
Segamat, 51, 61, 62, 63
Semenyih, 65
Senior, Col R.B., 190, 192, 193, 195
Sennelager Training Area, 124, 126, 128,
    133, 134, 135
Sepang, 69, 74, 87, 90, 91, 92, 93
Serdang, 82
Shuna, 15, 16
Siggs, CSM L., 31, 32
Simmonds, LCpl H.R., 60, 235
Simpson, CSM G., 32
Sinai Desert, 9
Sitwell, Brig H.D.W., 178

Skitmore, M.V., 32
Slade, H.F., 250
Slim, Field Marshal Sir William, 39
Smith, Sgt H., 92, 237
Smith, Sgt R.G., 238
  CSgt, 258
Smith W.C., 109, 120, 125, 238, 251
Smith, CSM (Greece, 1948), 37
Smith, CSM (BAOR, 1955), 135
Smith, Sgt (D Company, Malaya, 1951), 73
Smitherman, J.S.H., 188, 192, 208, 209,
  210, 213, 214, 238, 245, 251
Sobraon Barracks, 35, 39
Solomon's Pools, 20, 23
Soltau Training Area, 126
Spalding, Sgt, 207, 210
  CSgt, 212, 214
Sparks, H.P., 236, 251
Spencer, Lieut-Col E.L., 32
Sperling, A.C.L., 9, 13, 245
Springfield, G.T.O., 135, 143, 146, 154,
  195, 214, 215, 232, 239, 245, 251
Starling, J.G., 40, 56, 57, 183, 185, 186,
  188, 236, 251
Stephen, A.G., 223
Stern Gang, 5
Stevenson, Pte, 86
Stockwell, Gen Sir Hugh, 94, 135
Stokoe, T.M., 9
Stone, Sgt G., 32
Storie-Pugh, P.D., 217, 220, 221, 224, 225,
  226, 227, 245
Strovolos, 163, 164
Stunnel, Band Master G., 40
Suez Canal, 9, 10
Sungei Besi, 51, 54, 55, 56, 57, 58, 61
Sungei Manggis, 76, 87, 90, 91
Susannah, SS, 14
Sutor, H.D., 113, 124, 211, 213, 246
Swann, Bandsman M.S., 235
Sweetwater Canal, 10

Tahag, 9, 11
Talbiah Quarter, 19
Taylor, C.A., 222
Taylor, H.G., 9, 258
Taylor, Sgt R.C.J., 121
Taylor, Cpl, 134
Tel Aviv, 10, 14
Telok Datoh, 92
Templer, Field-Marshal Sir Gerald, 53, 80,
  85, 89, 93, 94, 181, 205, 229
Tenang, 61
Thain, P., 40, 251
Theobald, W.A., 31
Thistle-Suffern, P.R.W., 86
Thomas, F.W.C., 251

Thomas, Sgt G., 59
Thompsett, LCpl S.E., 235
Thompson, Sgt A., 32
Thompson, Cpl, 71
Thorpe, Sgt R., 32
Thursby, P.D.F., 30, 31, 145, 157, 159, 239,
  245, 251, 258
Times, The, 81, 83, 95
Titmarsh, Maj, 258
Tobin, Pte, 65
Tracey, Sgt A., 238
Transjordan, 16
Travers, Lieut-Col B.H., 266, 267
Travers, CSM, 222
Trevethick, R.L., 251
Tridini, RSM G., 9, 247
Trollope, C.J.N., 127, 148
Troodos, 138, 139, 142, 145, 146, 148, 152,
  158, 162, 167
Tuck, G.L.J., 251
Tucker, Band Master A.E., 218
Twigden, Pte E.G., 237
Tyndale, J.W., 251

Ulu Caledonian Estate, 78
Units:
  4th Hussars, 59
  13th/18th Hussars, 69
  8th Royal Tank Regiment, 126, 128
  26th Field Regiment, RA, 58, 159
  54th Field Regiment, RA, 69
  43rd LAA Regiment, RA, 160
  93rd Battery, RA, 87
  3rd Bn, The Grenadier Guards, 55
  2nd Bn, The Coldstream Guards, 57, 58
  2nd Bn, The Scots Guards, 55, 56, 57,
    66, 126
  1st Bn, The Buffs, 128, 129, 134, 136
  1st Bn, The King's Regiment
    (Liverpool), 190, 192, 193
  1st Bn, The Royal Norfolk Regiment, 145
  4th Bn, The Royal Norfolk Regiment,
    208, 215, 224
  1st Bn, The Somerset Light Infantry, 94
  1st Bn, The Bedfordshire and
    Hertfordshire Regiment, 36, 38, 39, 40
  5th Bn, The Bedfordshire and
    Hertfordshire Regiment, 208
  1st Bn, The Hertfordshire Regiment,
    208, 222
  1st Bn, The Green Howards, 58, 61
  1st Bn, The Lancashire Fusiliers, 159,
    160, 167
  2nd Bn, The Lancashire Fusiliers, 105,
    111
  1st Bn, The Royal Welch Fusiliers, 167

1st Bn, The Cameronians, 81
1st Bn, The Worcestershire Regiment, 64, 92, 126
1st Bn, The East Surrey Regiment, 36, 38, 39
2nd Bn, The Duke of Cornwall's Light Infantry, 37
1st Bn, The Oxfordshire and Buckinghamshire Light Infantry, 41, 145
4th Bn, The Essex Regiment, 208
1st Bn, The Loyal Regiment (North Lancashire), 103, 112, 114
1st Bn, The Northamptonshire Regiment, 106
4th Bn, The Northamptonshire Regiment, 208
5th Bn, The Northamptonshire Regiment, 215, 222
1st Bn, The Royal Berkshire Regiment, 160
40th Commando, Royal Marines, 152
42nd Commando, Royal Marines, 83, 86
1st Bn, The Queen's Own Royal West Kent Regiment, 77, 84, 87
1st Bn, The King's Own Yorkshire Light Infantry, 65
1st Bn, The Manchester Regiment, 132
1st Bn, The Durham Light Infantry, 122
1st Bn, The Gordon Highlanders, 145
1st Bn, The Royal Ulster Rifles, 122, 126, 128, 136, 153
1st Bn, The Argyll and Sutherland Highlanders, 193, 194
2nd Bn, 2nd King Edward VII's Own Gurkha Rifles, 61
2nd Bn, 6th Gurkha Rifles, 61, 64
1st Bn, 7th Gurkha Rifles, 59, 60
2nd Bn, 7th Gurkha Rifles, 57
22nd Special Air Service Regiment, 87, 92
Urquhart, Maj-Gen R.E., 66, 84

Ville d'Oran, SS, 9
Vincent, Sgt W., 32
Vinden, M.H., 202, 204, 205, 207, 209, 211, 251, 258
Vokins, Sgt D.F.A., 237

Wain, A., 32
Wakefield, P., 186
Walker, Pte H.C., 83, 235
Walker, CQMS, 258
Wana Huts, 7
Wardieburn Camp, 52, 66, 70, 71, 73, 76, 77, 78, 80, 81, 84, 87

Warren, T.C., 17, 37, 134, 146, 157, 208, 210, 214, 236, 246, 247
Watkins, N.St.G., 190
Watson, Sgt, 233
Watts, O.A., 251
Watts, Mr Percy, 172, 188
Wells, C.C., 206, 209, 210
West, Pte W.C., 236
Westin, Sgt D.B., 70, 235, 237
Whistler, Gen Sir Lashmer, 130
White, Lieut-Col G.C., 146
White, Pte, 187
Wicker, CSgt E., 32
Wickham, R.H.K., 203
Wicks, CSM B., 32
Wicks, LCpl D.E.R., 58, 237
Wiffen, Cpl J.L., 153, 238
Wiggington, H.E.W., 17, 179, 245, 246, 258
Wiggington, R.W., 32
Wight, I.L., 18, 36, 54, 62, 100, 119, 189, 236, 237, 244, 251, 258
Wight, J.D.L., 214
Wightwick, J.H., 251
Wilce, Sgt C.A., 81, 188, 237
  CSgt, 143
Wilkinson, Brig C.J., 196, 230, 231
Willdridge, A.L., 120, 134, 148, 155, 157, 165, 239
Williams, R.M., 9, 15, 17, 195, 207, 208, 245, 246, 251
Williams, CSgt, 223
Wilsey, Maj-Gen J.H.O., 128
Wilson, Field Marshal Lord, 177
Wilson, Pte D., 81, 235
Wilson, WOII F.G.W., 238
Wilson, F.T.D., 251
Wilson, P.G., 251
Wilson, R.G., 106, 215, 246, 251, 258
Windley, RSM B.D., 54, 63, 72, 247
Winter, CSM S., 31, 32, 37, 54, 63, 247
Winterton, Maj-Gen Sir John, 103, 105, 112, 114
Woodall, Reverend H.G., 10
Woodhead, Sgt J., 32
Woods, Pte S.J., 150, 151, 238
Woodward, A.C., 9
Wright, Cpl G.W., 236
Wright, Sgt, 70
Wyatt, F.H., 9, 246

Xeros, 139, 140, 145, 146, 147, 148, 153

Youde, Lieut-Col G.A.D., 267

Zirbitz Kogel, 112